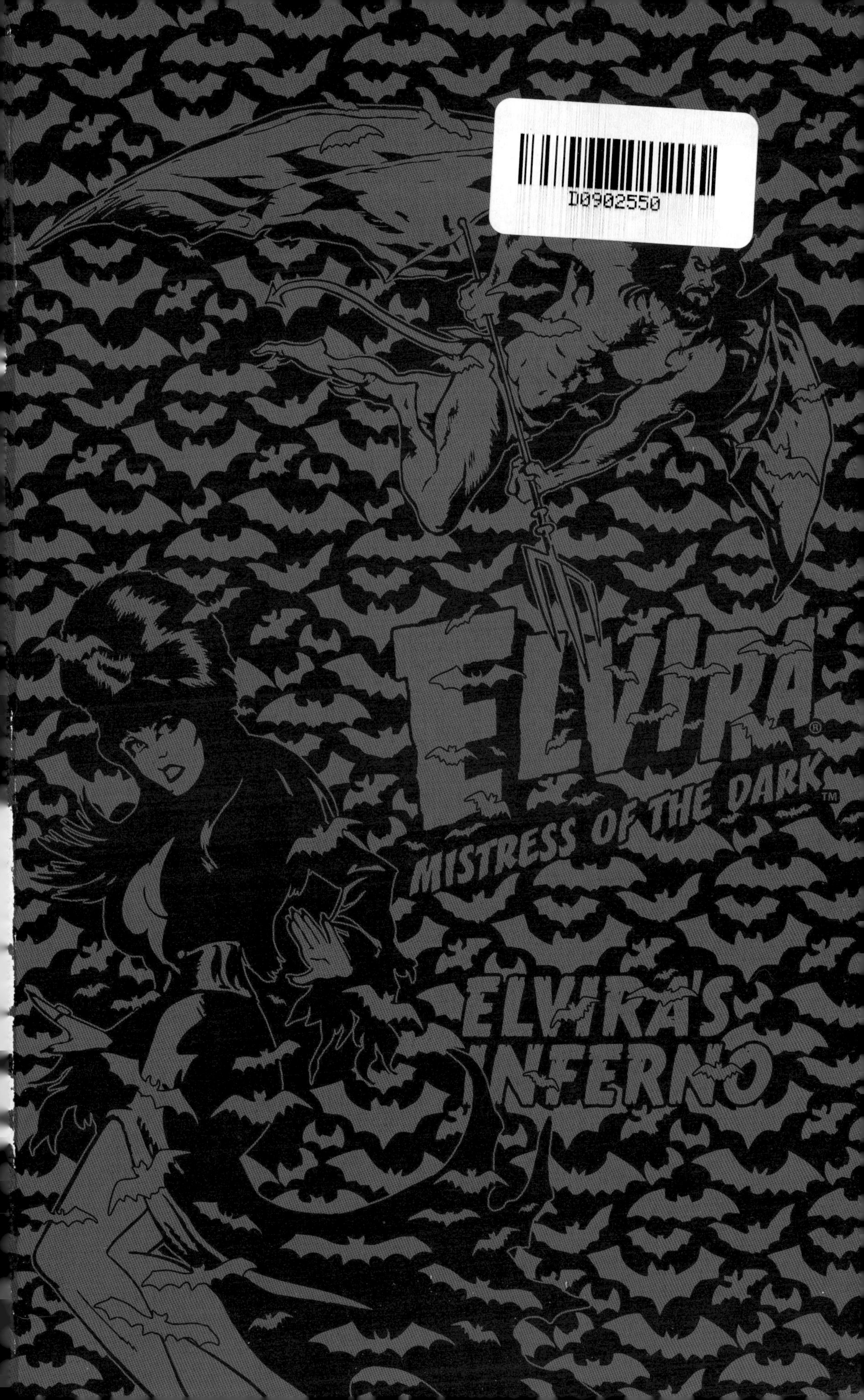
ELVIRA®
MISTRESS OF THE DARK™
ELVIRA'S
INFERNO

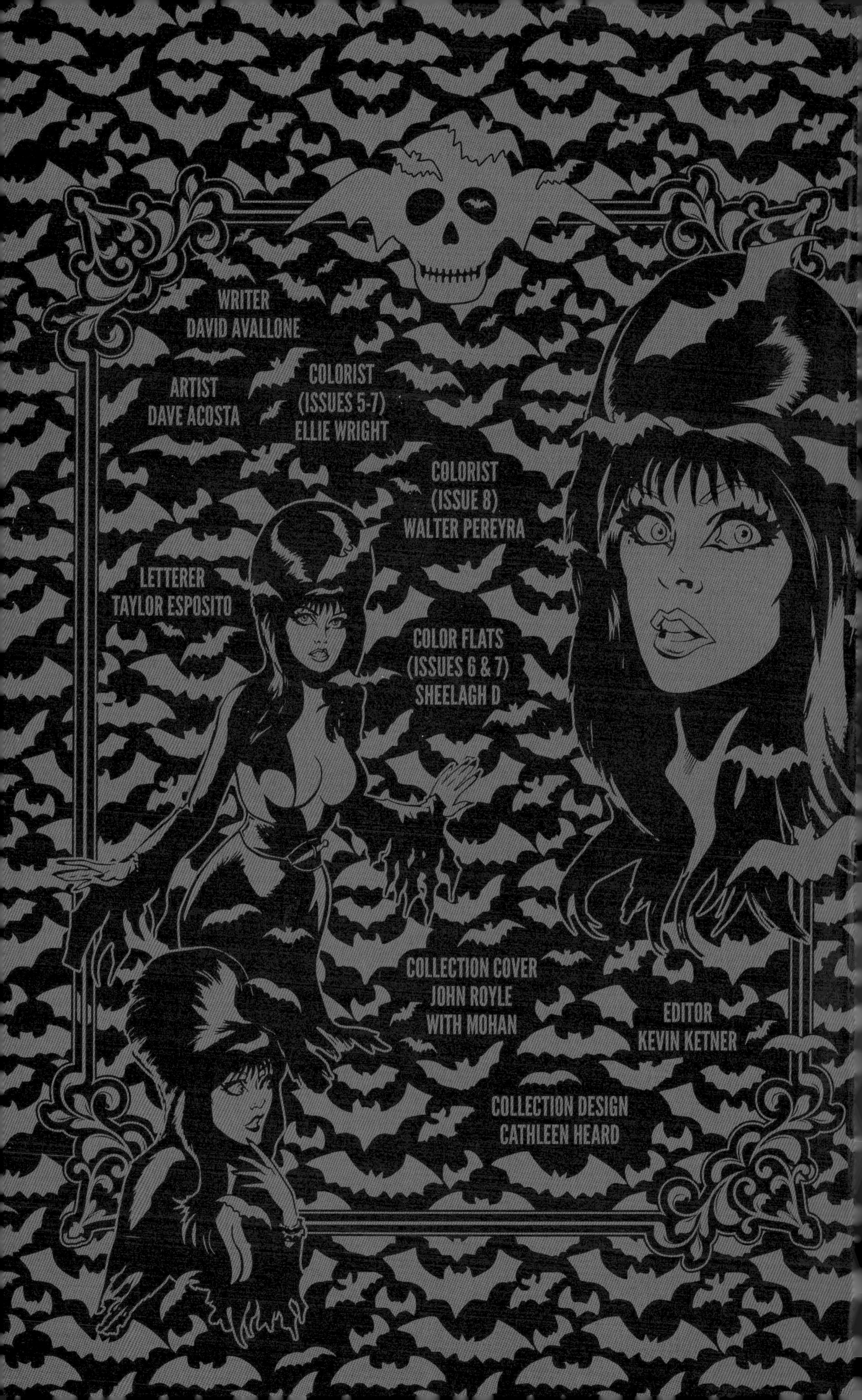

WRITER
DAVID AVALLONE

ARTIST
DAVE ACOSTA

COLORIST
(ISSUES 5-7)
ELLIE WRIGHT

COLORIST
(ISSUE 8)
WALTER PEREYRA

LETTERER
TAYLOR ESPOSITO

COLOR FLATS
(ISSUES 6 & 7)
SHEELAGH D

COLLECTION COVER
JOHN ROYLE
WITH MOHAN

EDITOR
KEVIN KETNER

COLLECTION DESIGN
CATHLEEN HEARD

DYNAMITE

Online at www.DYNAMITE.com
On Facebook /Dynamitecomics
On Instagram /Dynamitecomics
On Twitter @dynamitecomics

Nick Barrucci, CEO / Publisher
Juan Collado, President / COO
Brandon Dante Primavera, V.P. of IT and Operations

Joe Rybandt, Executive Editor
Matt Idelson, Senior Editor
Kevin Ketner, Editor

Cathleen Heard, Art Director
Rachel Kilbury, Digital Multimedia Associate
Alexis Persson, Graphic Designer
Katie Hidalgo, Graphic Designer

Alan Payne, V.P. of Sales and Marketing
Pat O'Connell, Sales Manager
Vincent Faust, Marketing Coordinator

Jay Spence, Director of Product Development
Mariano Nicieza, Director of Research & Development

Amy Jackson, Administrative Coordinator

5 COVER ART: JOSEPH MICHAEL LINSNER

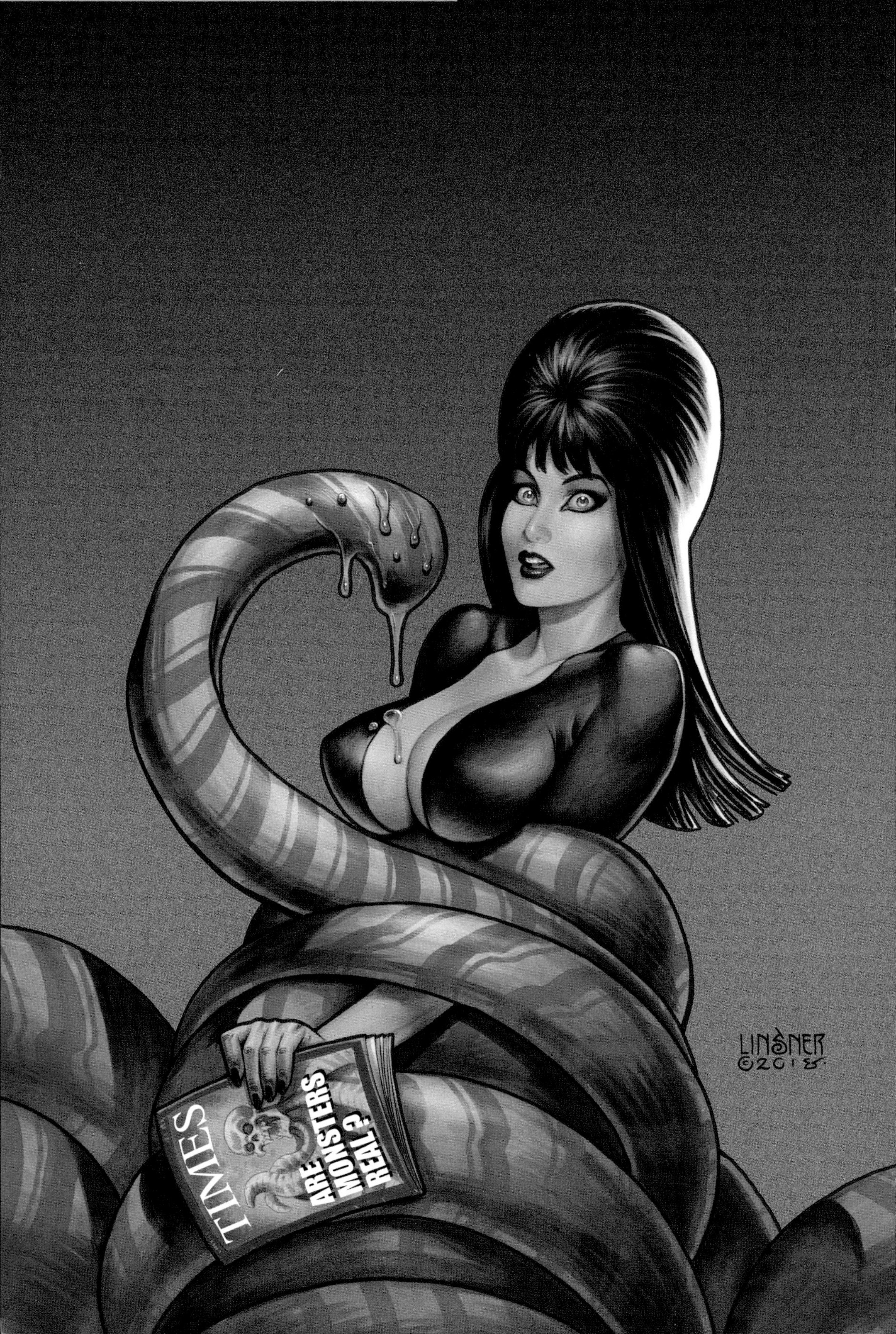

LINSNER
©2018
TIMES
ARE MONSTERS REAL?

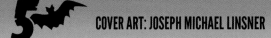

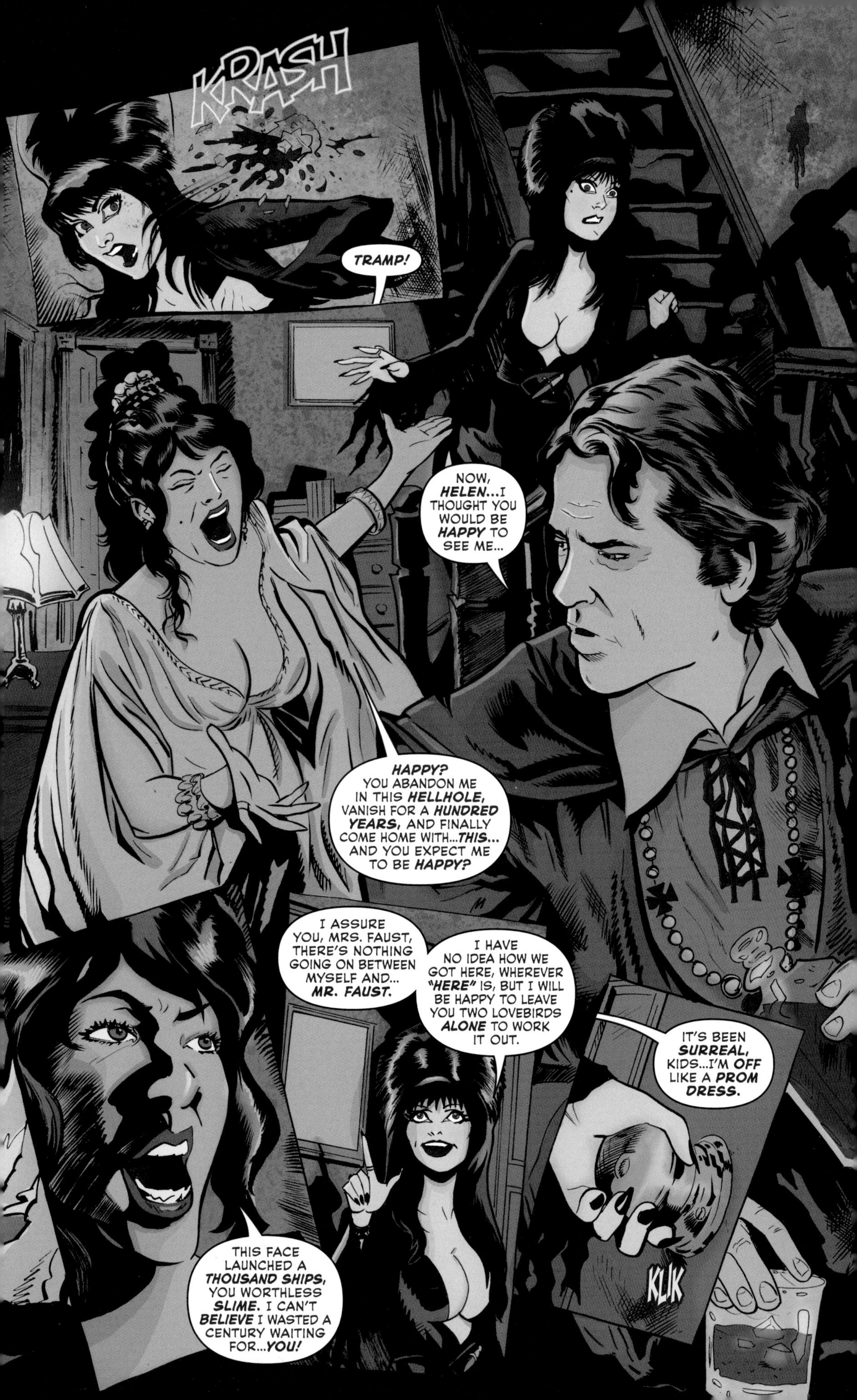
KRASH
TRAMP!
NOW, HELEN...I THOUGHT YOU WOULD BE HAPPY TO SEE ME...
HAPPY? YOU ABANDON ME IN THIS HELLHOLE, VANISH FOR A HUNDRED YEARS, AND FINALLY COME HOME WITH...THIS... AND YOU EXPECT ME TO BE HAPPY?
I ASSURE YOU, MRS. FAUST, THERE'S NOTHING GOING ON BETWEEN MYSELF AND... MR. FAUST.
I HAVE NO IDEA HOW WE GOT HERE, WHEREVER "HERE" IS, BUT I WILL BE HAPPY TO LEAVE YOU TWO LOVEBIRDS ALONE TO WORK IT OUT.
IT'S BEEN SURREAL, KIDS...I'M OFF LIKE A PROM DRESS.
THIS FACE LAUNCHED A THOUSAND SHIPS, YOU WORTHLESS SLIME. I CAN'T BELIEVE I WASTED A CENTURY WAITING FOR...YOU!
KLIK

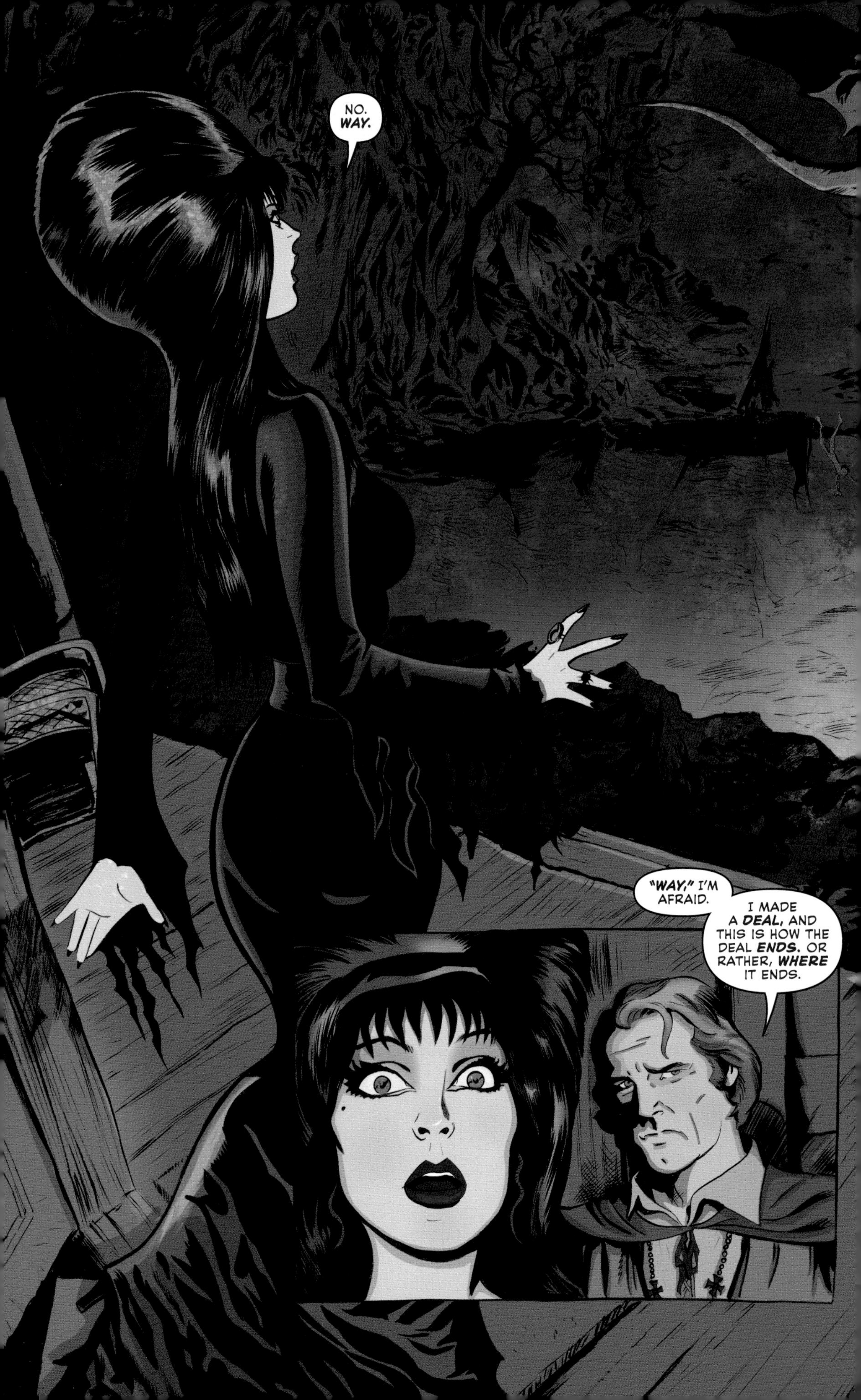
NO. WAY.
"WAY," I'M AFRAID.
I MADE A DEAL, AND THIS IS HOW THE DEAL ENDS. OR RATHER, WHERE IT ENDS.

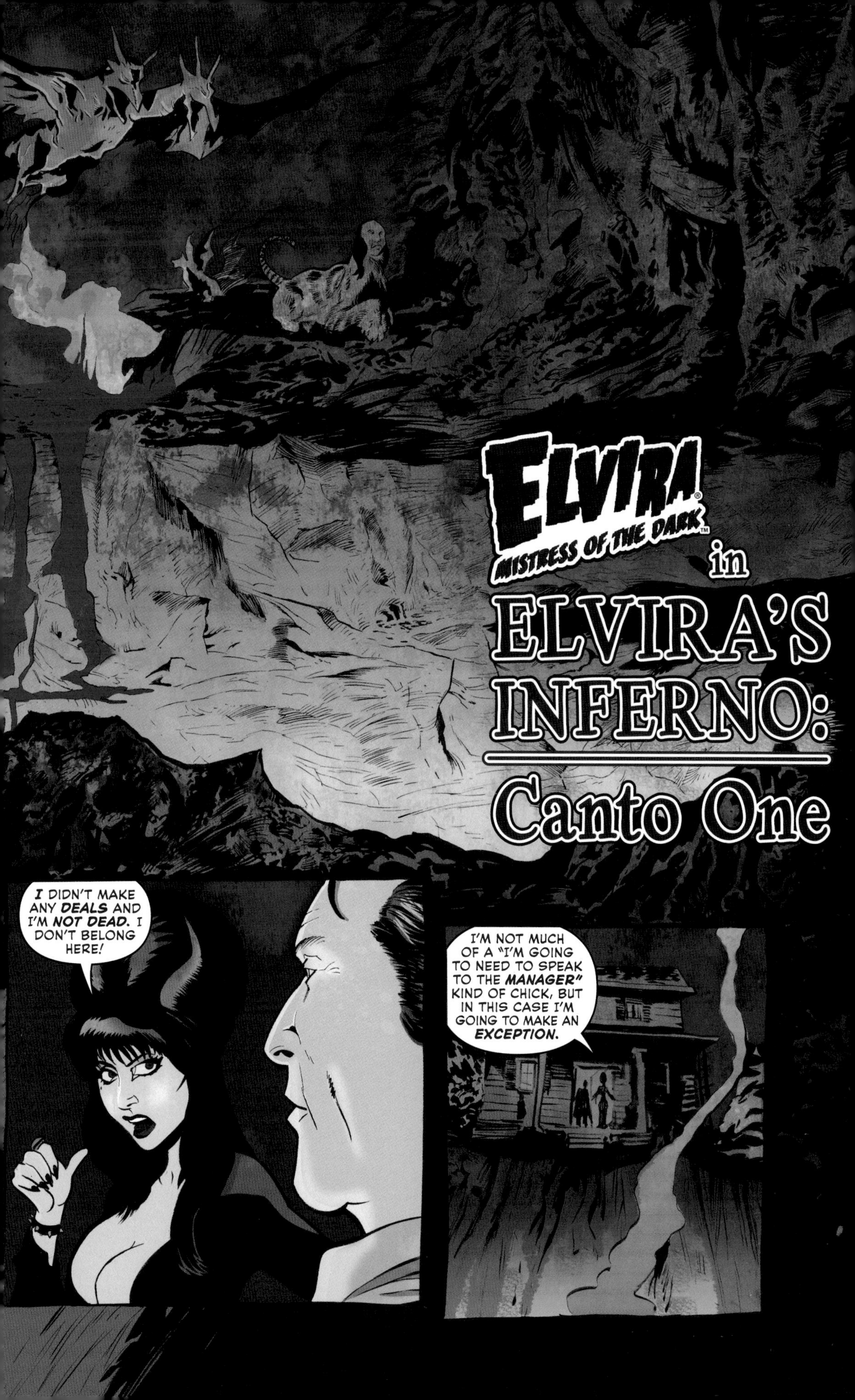
ELVIRA
MISTRESS OF THE DARK
in
ELVIRA'S INFERNO:
Canto One
I DIDN'T MAKE ANY DEALS AND I'M NOT DEAD. I DON'T BELONG HERE!
I'M NOT MUCH OF A "I'M GOING TO NEED TO SPEAK TO THE MANAGER" KIND OF CHICK, BUT IN THIS CASE I'M GOING TO MAKE AN EXCEPTION.

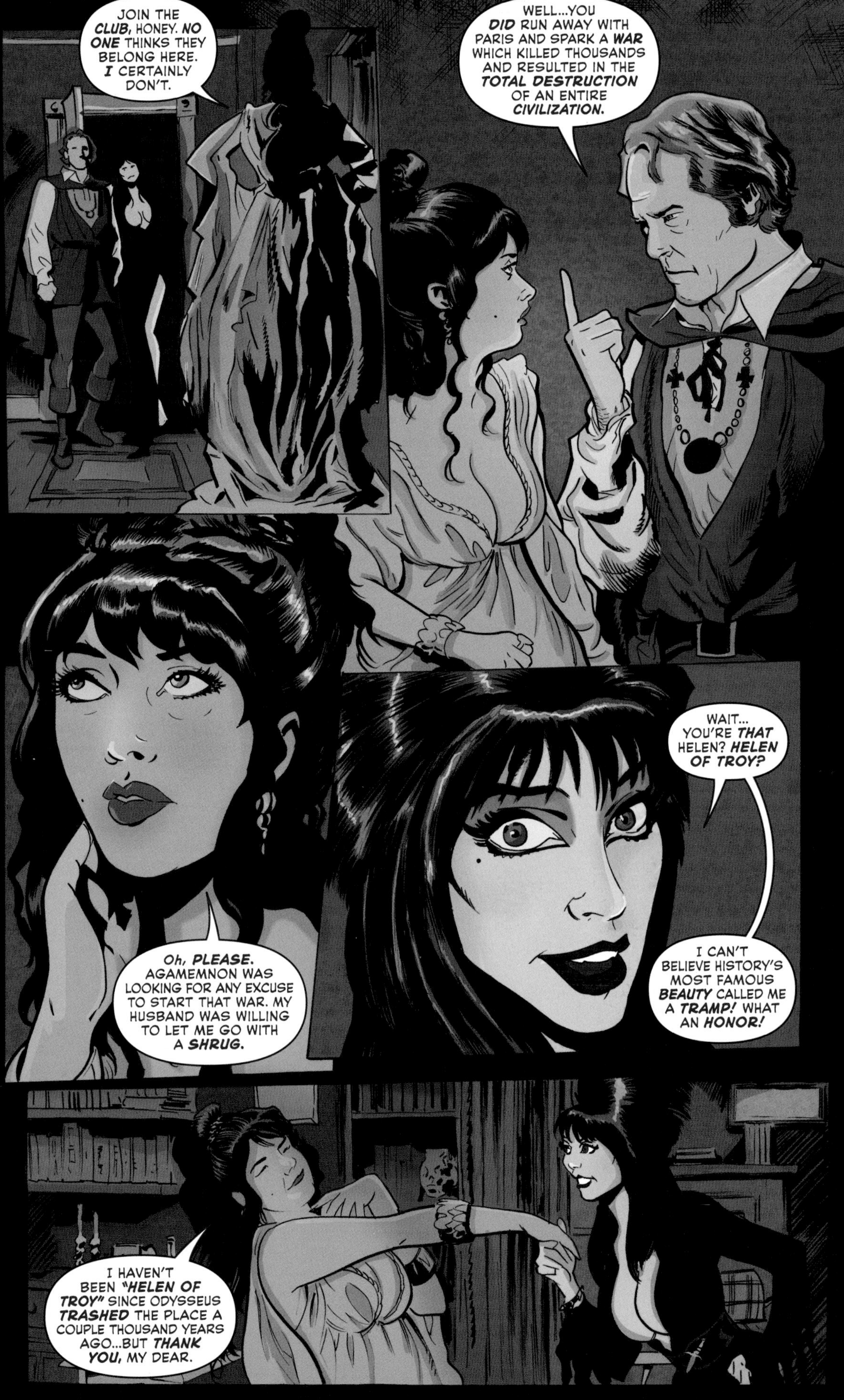
JOIN THE CLUB, HONEY. NO ONE THINKS THEY BELONG HERE. I CERTAINLY DON'T.
WELL...YOU DID RUN AWAY WITH PARIS AND SPARK A WAR WHICH KILLED THOUSANDS AND RESULTED IN THE TOTAL DESTRUCTION OF AN ENTIRE CIVILIZATION.
Oh, PLEASE. AGAMEMNON WAS LOOKING FOR ANY EXCUSE TO START THAT WAR. MY HUSBAND WAS WILLING TO LET ME GO WITH A SHRUG.
WAIT... YOU'RE THAT HELEN? HELEN OF TROY?
I CAN'T BELIEVE HISTORY'S MOST FAMOUS BEAUTY CALLED ME A TRAMP! WHAT AN HONOR!
I HAVEN'T BEEN "HELEN OF TROY" SINCE ODYSSEUS TRASHED THE PLACE A COUPLE THOUSAND YEARS AGO...BUT THANK YOU, MY DEAR.

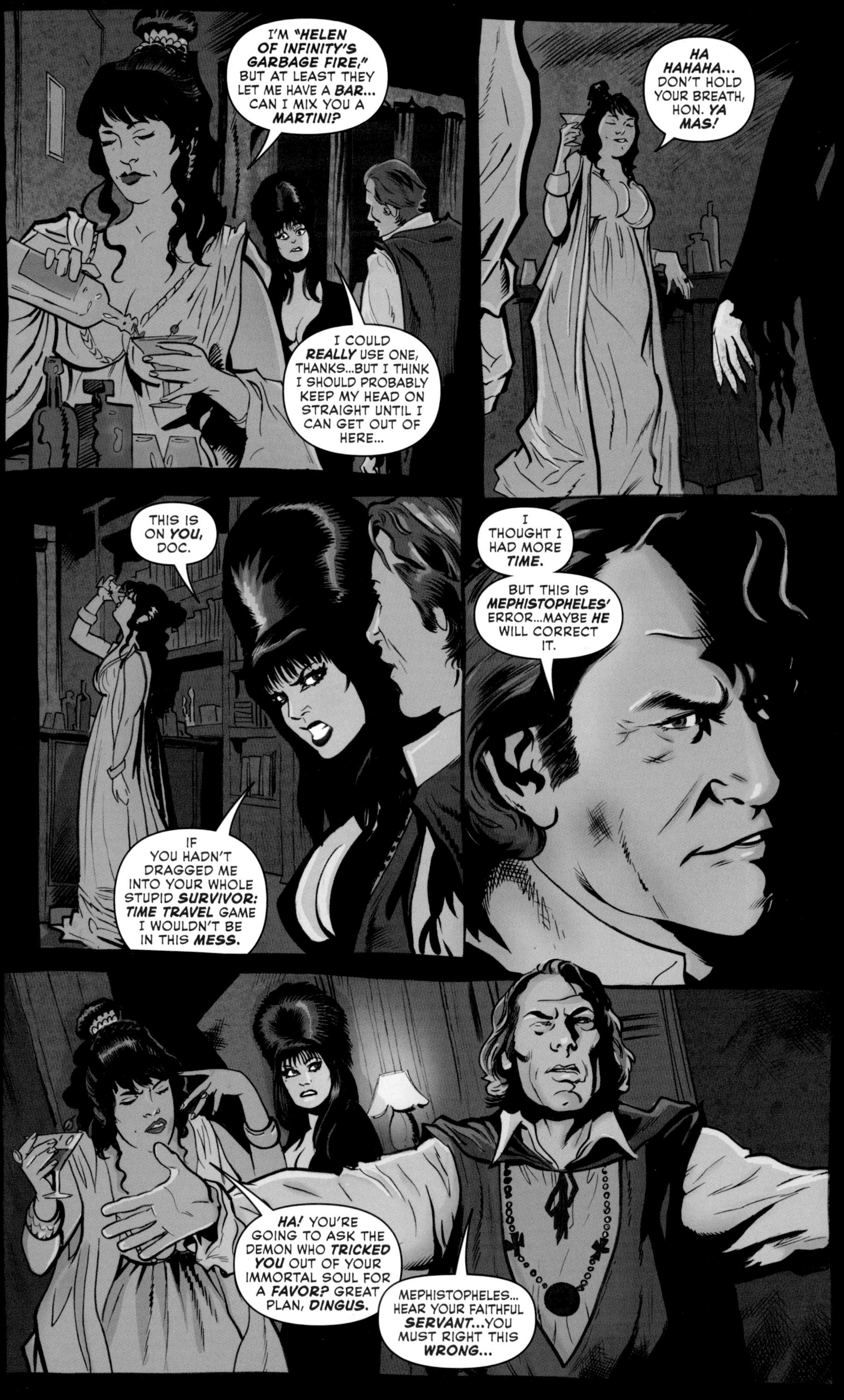
I'M "HELEN OF INFINITY'S GARBAGE FIRE," BUT AT LEAST THEY LET ME HAVE A BAR... CAN I MIX YOU A MARTINI?
I COULD REALLY USE ONE, THANKS...BUT I THINK I SHOULD PROBABLY KEEP MY HEAD ON STRAIGHT UNTIL I CAN GET OUT OF HERE...
HA HAHAHA... DON'T HOLD YOUR BREATH, HON. YA MAS!
THIS IS ON YOU, DOC.
IF YOU HADN'T DRAGGED ME INTO YOUR WHOLE STUPID SURVIVOR: TIME TRAVEL GAME I WOULDN'T BE IN THIS MESS.
I THOUGHT I HAD MORE TIME.
BUT THIS IS MEPHISTOPHELES' ERROR...MAYBE HE WILL CORRECT IT.
HA! YOU'RE GOING TO ASK THE DEMON WHO TRICKED YOU OUT OF YOUR IMMORTAL SOUL FOR A FAVOR? GREAT PLAN, DINGUS.
MEPHISTOPHELES... HEAR YOUR FAITHFUL SERVANT...YOU MUST RIGHT THIS WRONG...

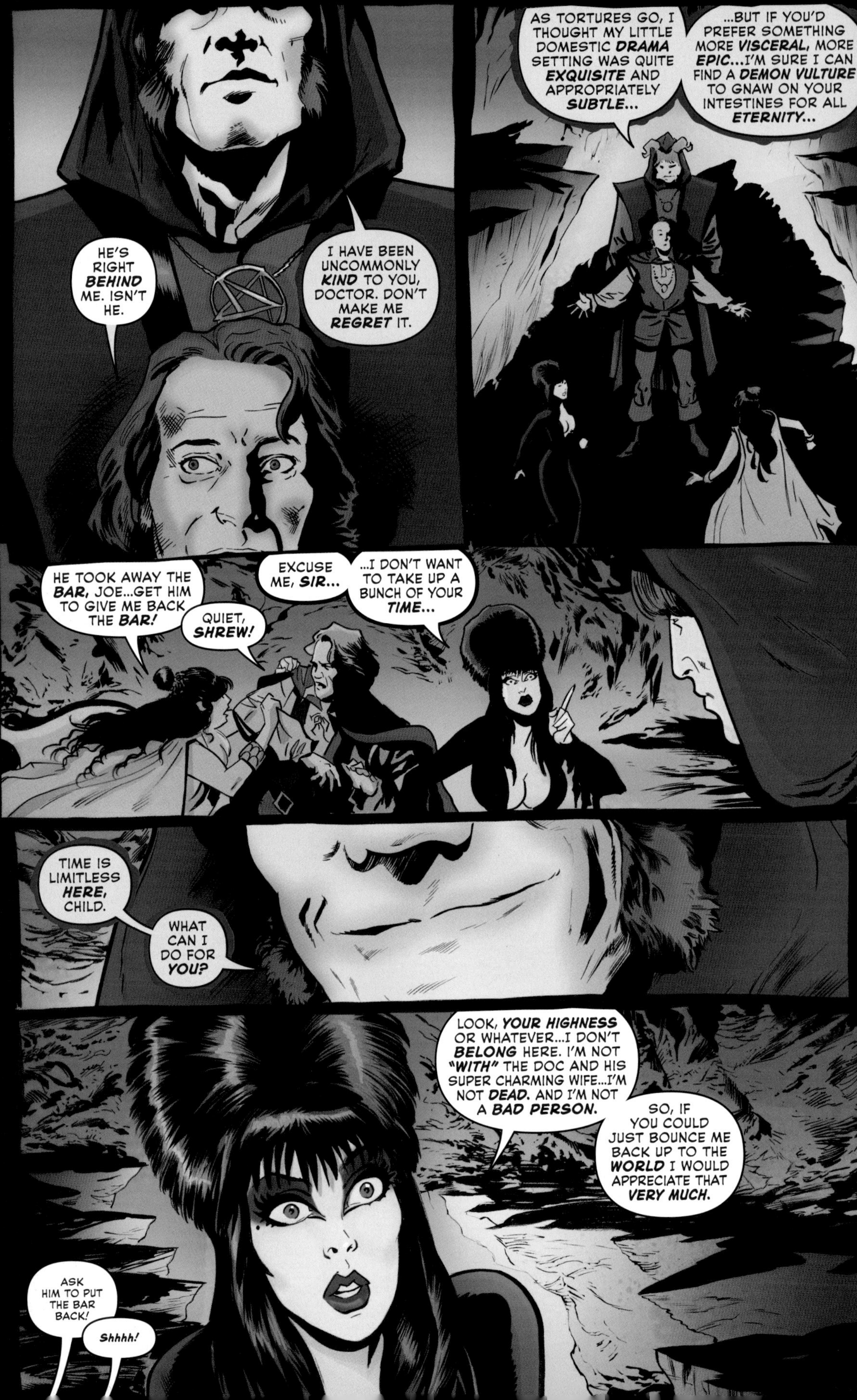
HE'S RIGHT BEHIND ME. ISN'T HE.
I HAVE BEEN UNCOMMONLY KIND TO YOU, DOCTOR. DON'T MAKE ME REGRET IT.
AS TORTURES GO, I THOUGHT MY LITTLE DOMESTIC DRAMA SETTING WAS QUITE EXQUISITE AND APPROPRIATELY SUBTLE...
...BUT IF YOU'D PREFER SOMETHING MORE VISCERAL, MORE EPIC...I'M SURE I CAN FIND A DEMON VULTURE TO GNAW ON YOUR INTESTINES FOR ALL ETERNITY...
HE TOOK AWAY THE BAR, JOE...GET HIM TO GIVE ME BACK THE BAR!
QUIET, SHREW!
EXCUSE ME, SIR...
...I DON'T WANT TO TAKE UP A BUNCH OF YOUR TIME...
TIME IS LIMITLESS HERE, CHILD.
WHAT CAN I DO FOR YOU?
LOOK, YOUR HIGHNESS OR WHATEVER...I DON'T BELONG HERE. I'M NOT "WITH" THE DOC AND HIS SUPER CHARMING WIFE...I'M NOT DEAD. AND I'M NOT A BAD PERSON.
SO, IF YOU COULD JUST BOUNCE ME BACK UP TO THE WORLD I WOULD APPRECIATE THAT VERY MUCH.
ASK HIM TO PUT THE BAR BACK!
Shhhh!

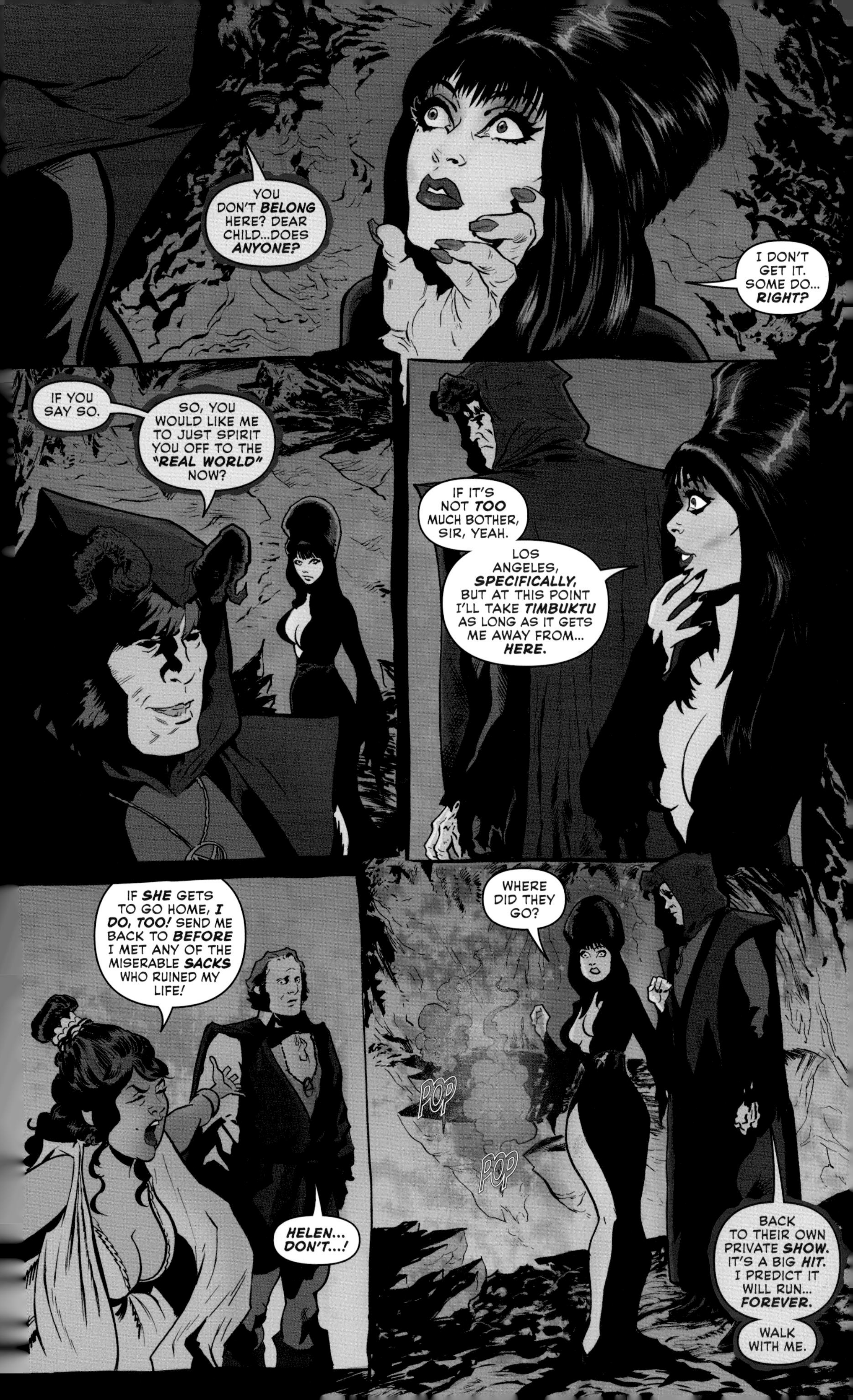
YOU DON'T BELONG HERE? DEAR CHILD...DOES ANYONE?
I DON'T GET IT. SOME DO... RIGHT?
IF YOU SAY SO.
SO, YOU WOULD LIKE ME TO JUST SPIRIT YOU OFF TO THE "REAL WORLD" NOW?
IF IT'S NOT TOO MUCH BOTHER, SIR, YEAH.
LOS ANGELES, SPECIFICALLY, BUT AT THIS POINT I'LL TAKE TIMBUKTU AS LONG AS IT GETS ME AWAY FROM... HERE.
IF SHE GETS TO GO HOME, I DO, TOO! SEND ME BACK TO BEFORE I MET ANY OF THE MISERABLE SACKS WHO RUINED MY LIFE!
HELEN... DON'T...!
WHERE DID THEY GO?
POP
POP
BACK TO THEIR OWN PRIVATE SHOW. IT'S A BIG HIT. I PREDICT IT WILL RUN... FOREVER.
WALK WITH ME.

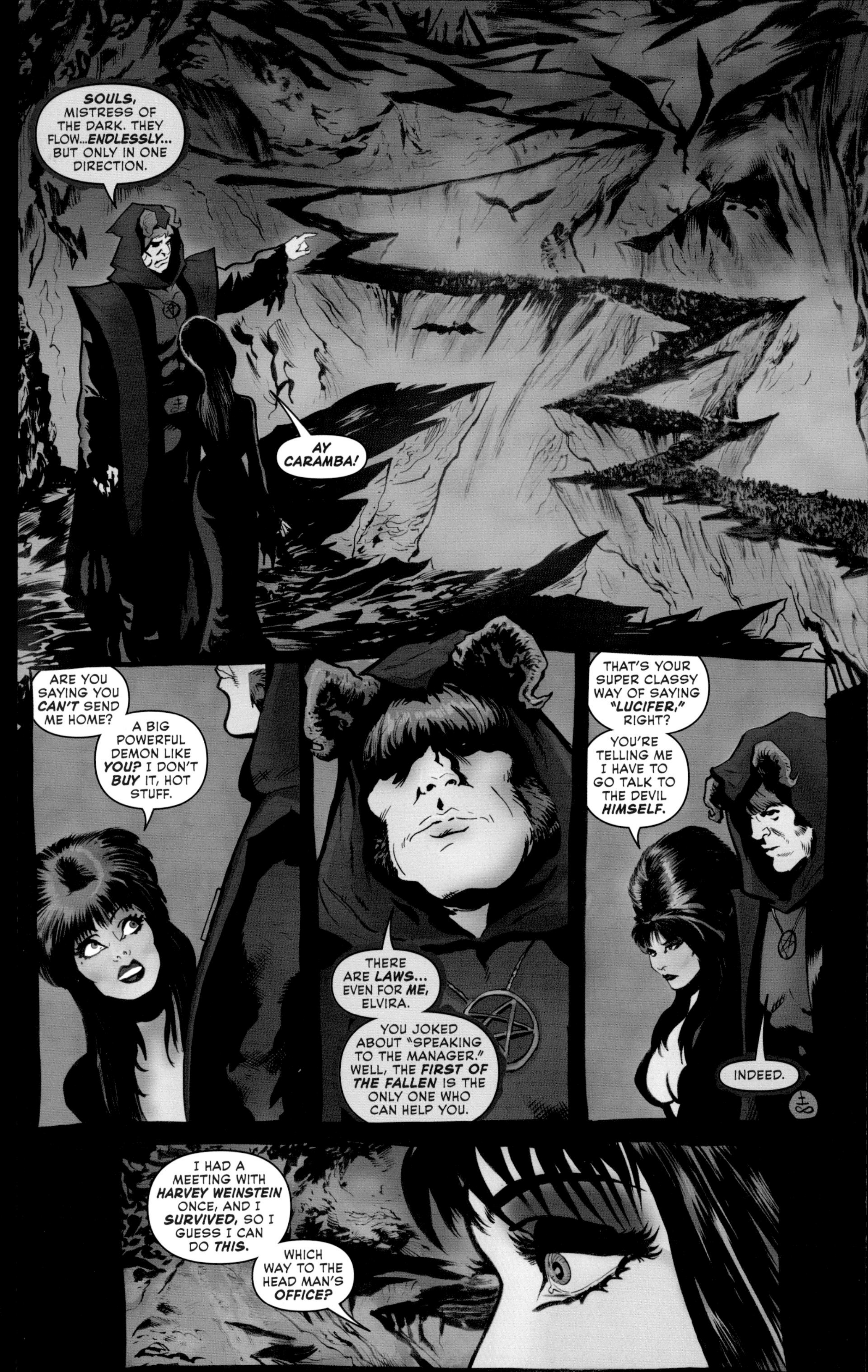
SOULS, MISTRESS OF THE DARK. THEY FLOW...ENDLESSLY... BUT ONLY IN ONE DIRECTION.
AY CARAMBA!
ARE YOU SAYING YOU CAN'T SEND ME HOME?
A BIG POWERFUL DEMON LIKE YOU? I DON'T BUY IT, HOT STUFF.
THERE ARE LAWS... EVEN FOR ME, ELVIRA.
YOU JOKED ABOUT "SPEAKING TO THE MANAGER." WELL, THE FIRST OF THE FALLEN IS THE ONLY ONE WHO CAN HELP YOU.
THAT'S YOUR SUPER CLASSY WAY OF SAYING "LUCIFER," RIGHT?
YOU'RE TELLING ME I HAVE TO GO TALK TO THE DEVIL HIMSELF.
INDEED.
I HAD A MEETING WITH HARVEY WEINSTEIN ONCE, AND I SURVIVED, SO I GUESS I CAN DO THIS.
WHICH WAY TO THE HEAD MAN'S OFFICE?

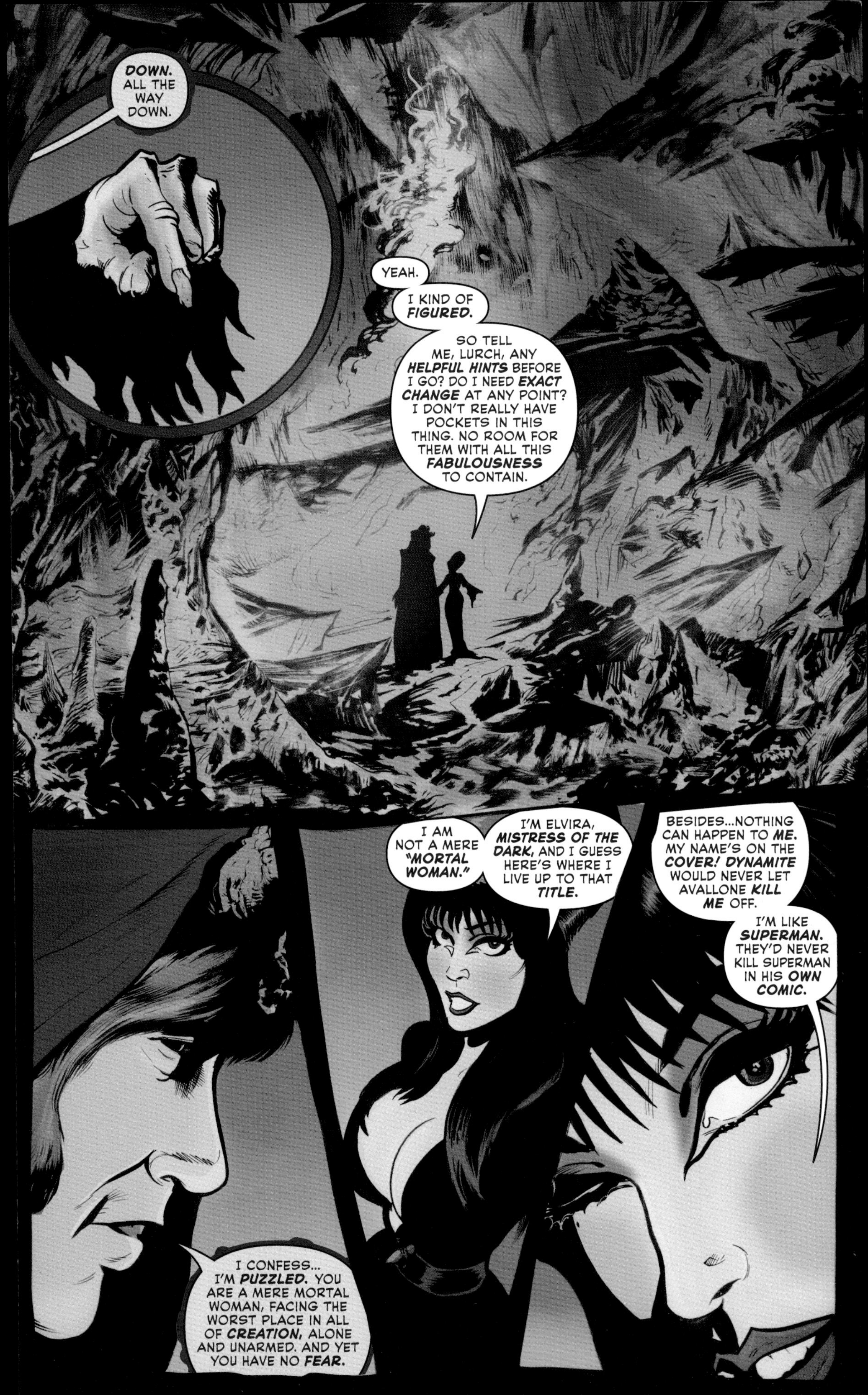
DOWN. ALL THE WAY DOWN.
YEAH.
I KIND OF FIGURED.
SO TELL ME, LURCH, ANY HELPFUL HINTS BEFORE I GO? DO I NEED EXACT CHANGE AT ANY POINT? I DON'T REALLY HAVE POCKETS IN THIS THING. NO ROOM FOR THEM WITH ALL THIS FABULOUSNESS TO CONTAIN.
I CONFESS... I'M PUZZLED. YOU ARE A MERE MORTAL WOMAN, FACING THE WORST PLACE IN ALL OF CREATION, ALONE AND UNARMED. AND YET YOU HAVE NO FEAR.
I AM NOT A MERE "MORTAL WOMAN."
I'M ELVIRA, MISTRESS OF THE DARK, AND I GUESS HERE'S WHERE I LIVE UP TO THAT TITLE.
BESIDES...NOTHING CAN HAPPEN TO ME. MY NAME'S ON THE COVER! DYNAMITE WOULD NEVER LET AVALLONE KILL ME OFF.
I'M LIKE SUPERMAN. THEY'D NEVER KILL SUPERMAN IN HIS OWN COMIC.

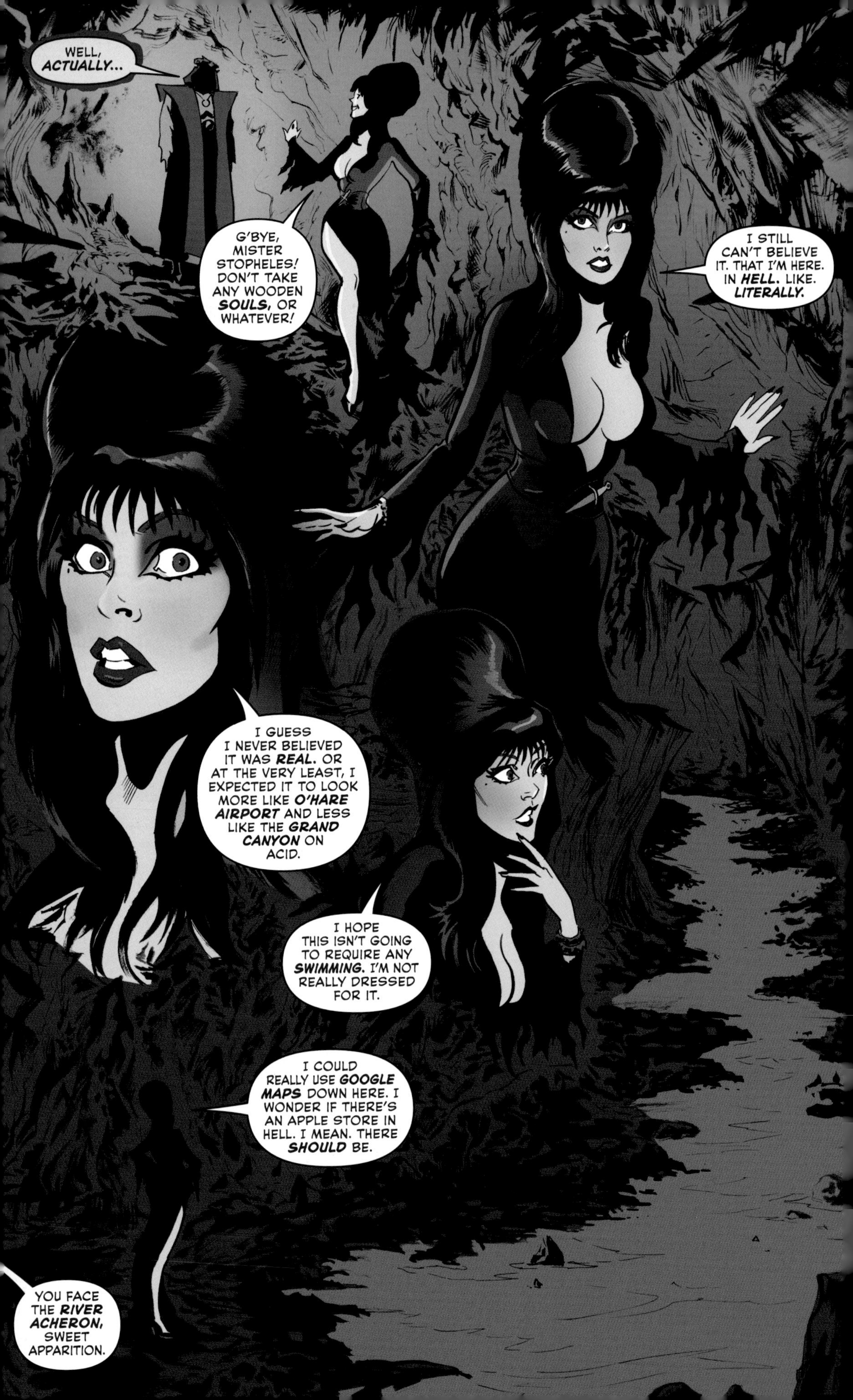

WELL, ACTUALLY...
G'BYE, MISTER STOPHELES! DON'T TAKE ANY WOODEN SOULS, OR WHATEVER!
I STILL CAN'T BELIEVE IT. THAT I'M HERE. IN HELL. LIKE. LITERALLY.
I GUESS I NEVER BELIEVED IT WAS REAL. OR AT THE VERY LEAST, I EXPECTED IT TO LOOK MORE LIKE O'HARE AIRPORT AND LESS LIKE THE GRAND CANYON ON ACID.
I HOPE THIS ISN'T GOING TO REQUIRE ANY SWIMMING. I'M NOT REALLY DRESSED FOR IT.
I COULD REALLY USE GOOGLE MAPS DOWN HERE. I WONDER IF THERE'S AN APPLE STORE IN HELL. I MEAN. THERE SHOULD BE.
YOU FACE THE RIVER ACHERON, SWEET APPARITION.

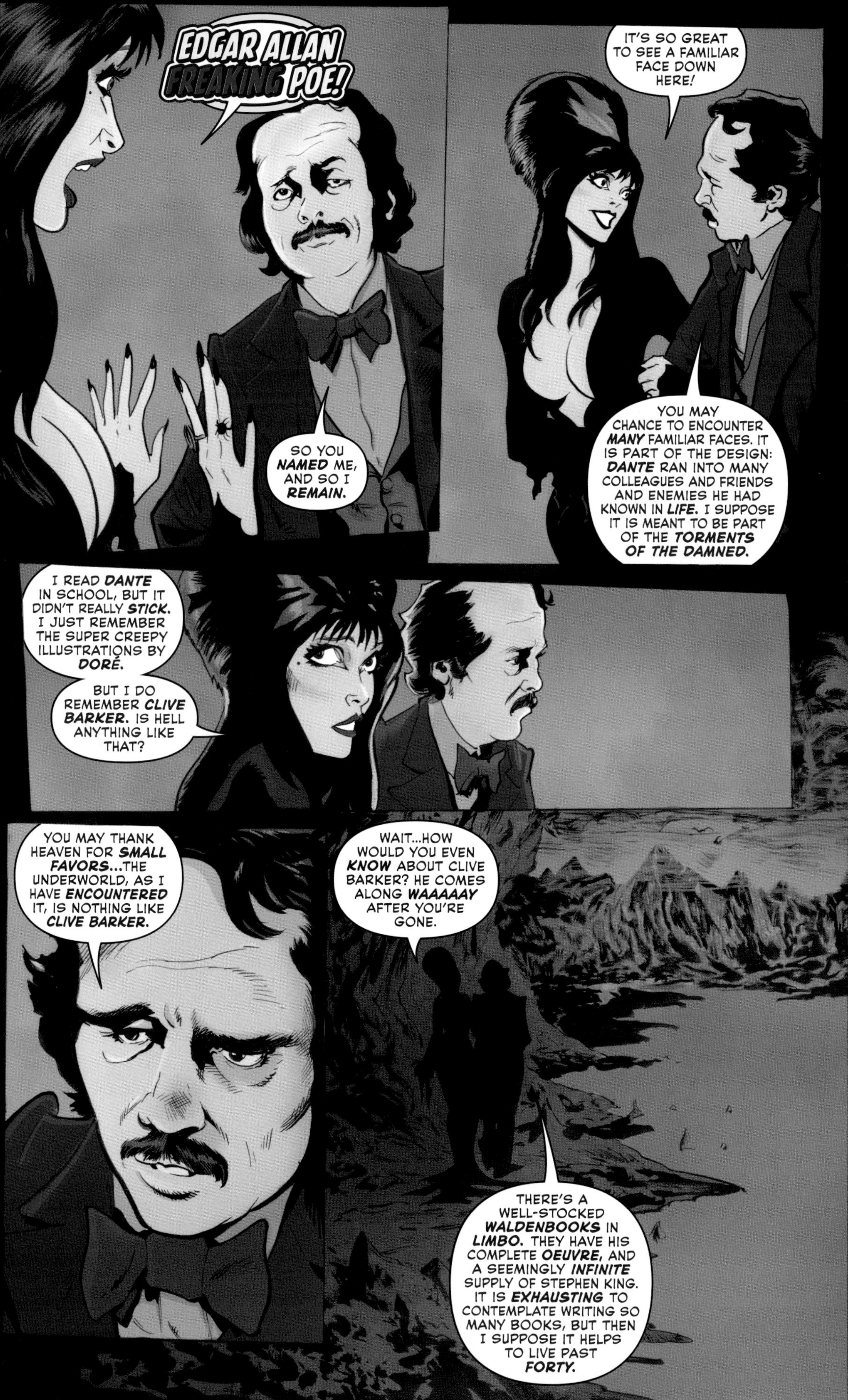
EDGAR ALLAN FREAKING POE!
SO YOU NAMED ME, AND SO I REMAIN.
IT'S SO GREAT TO SEE A FAMILIAR FACE DOWN HERE!
YOU MAY CHANCE TO ENCOUNTER MANY FAMILIAR FACES. IT IS PART OF THE DESIGN: DANTE RAN INTO MANY COLLEAGUES AND FRIENDS AND ENEMIES HE HAD KNOWN IN LIFE. I SUPPOSE IT IS MEANT TO BE PART OF THE TORMENTS OF THE DAMNED.
I READ DANTE IN SCHOOL, BUT IT DIDN'T REALLY STICK. I JUST REMEMBER THE SUPER CREEPY ILLUSTRATIONS BY DORÉ.
BUT I DO REMEMBER CLIVE BARKER. IS HELL ANYTHING LIKE THAT?
YOU MAY THANK HEAVEN FOR SMALL FAVORS...THE UNDERWORLD, AS I HAVE ENCOUNTERED IT, IS NOTHING LIKE CLIVE BARKER.
WAIT...HOW WOULD YOU EVEN KNOW ABOUT CLIVE BARKER? HE COMES ALONG WAAAAAY AFTER YOU'RE GONE.
THERE'S A WELL-STOCKED WALDENBOOKS IN LIMBO. THEY HAVE HIS COMPLETE OEUVRE, AND A SEEMINGLY INFINITE SUPPLY OF STEPHEN KING. IT IS EXHAUSTING TO CONTEMPLATE WRITING SO MANY BOOKS, BUT THEN I SUPPOSE IT HELPS TO LIVE PAST FORTY.

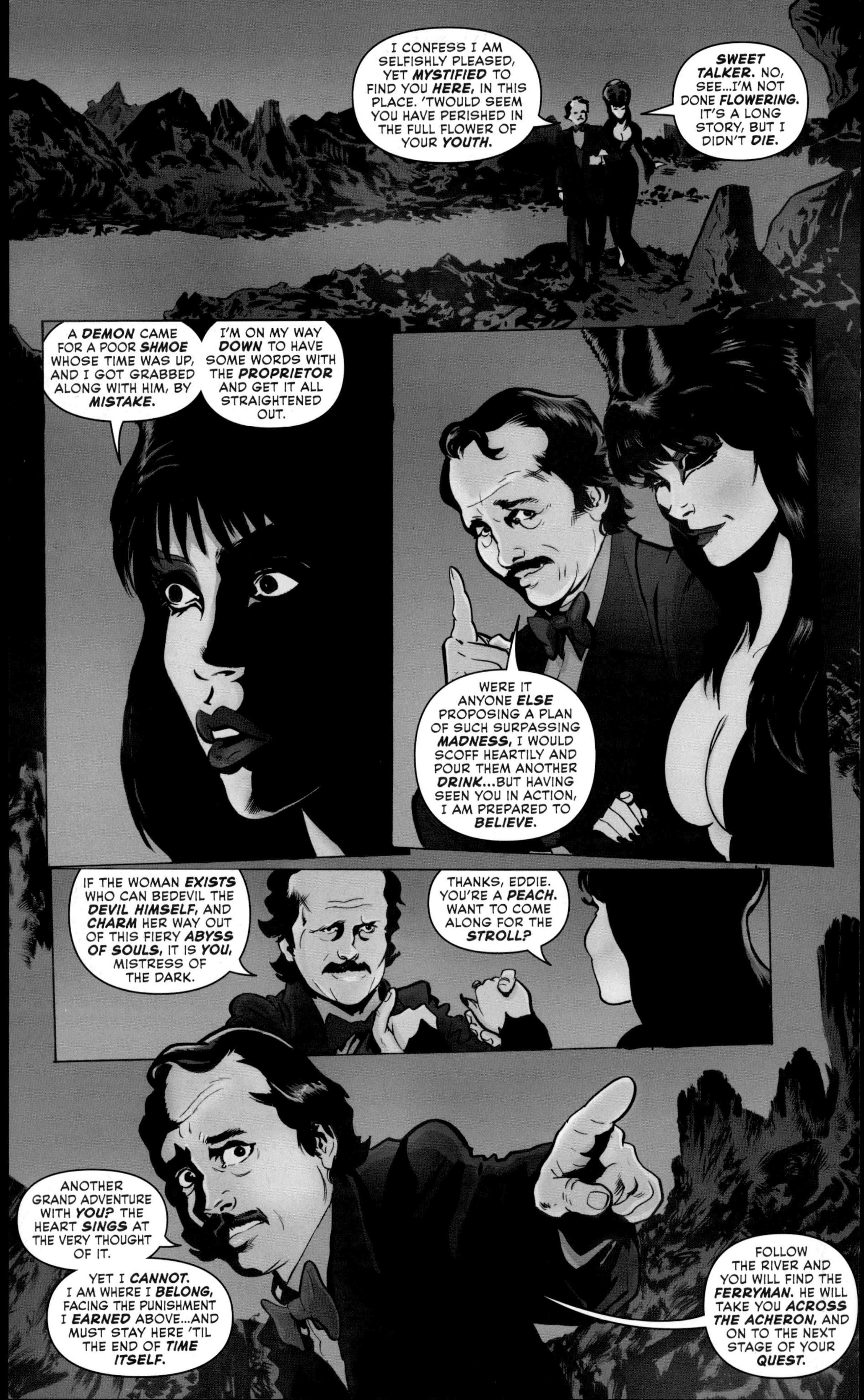
I CONFESS I AM SELFISHLY PLEASED, YET MYSTIFIED TO FIND YOU HERE, IN THIS PLACE. 'TWOULD SEEM YOU HAVE PERISHED IN THE FULL FLOWER OF YOUR YOUTH.
SWEET TALKER. NO, SEE...I'M NOT DONE FLOWERING. IT'S A LONG STORY, BUT I DIDN'T DIE.
A DEMON CAME FOR A POOR SHMOE WHOSE TIME WAS UP, AND I GOT GRABBED ALONG WITH HIM, BY MISTAKE.
I'M ON MY WAY DOWN TO HAVE SOME WORDS WITH THE PROPRIETOR AND GET IT ALL STRAIGHTENED OUT.
WERE IT ANYONE ELSE PROPOSING A PLAN OF SUCH SURPASSING MADNESS, I WOULD SCOFF HEARTILY AND POUR THEM ANOTHER DRINK...BUT HAVING SEEN YOU IN ACTION, I AM PREPARED TO BELIEVE.
IF THE WOMAN EXISTS WHO CAN BEDEVIL THE DEVIL HIMSELF, AND CHARM HER WAY OUT OF THIS FIERY ABYSS OF SOULS, IT IS YOU, MISTRESS OF THE DARK.
THANKS, EDDIE. YOU'RE A PEACH. WANT TO COME ALONG FOR THE STROLL?
ANOTHER GRAND ADVENTURE WITH YOU? THE HEART SINGS AT THE VERY THOUGHT OF IT.
YET I CANNOT. I AM WHERE I BELONG, FACING THE PUNISHMENT I EARNED ABOVE...AND MUST STAY HERE 'TIL THE END OF TIME ITSELF.
FOLLOW THE RIVER AND YOU WILL FIND THE FERRYMAN. HE WILL TAKE YOU ACROSS THE ACHERON, AND ON TO THE NEXT STAGE OF YOUR QUEST.

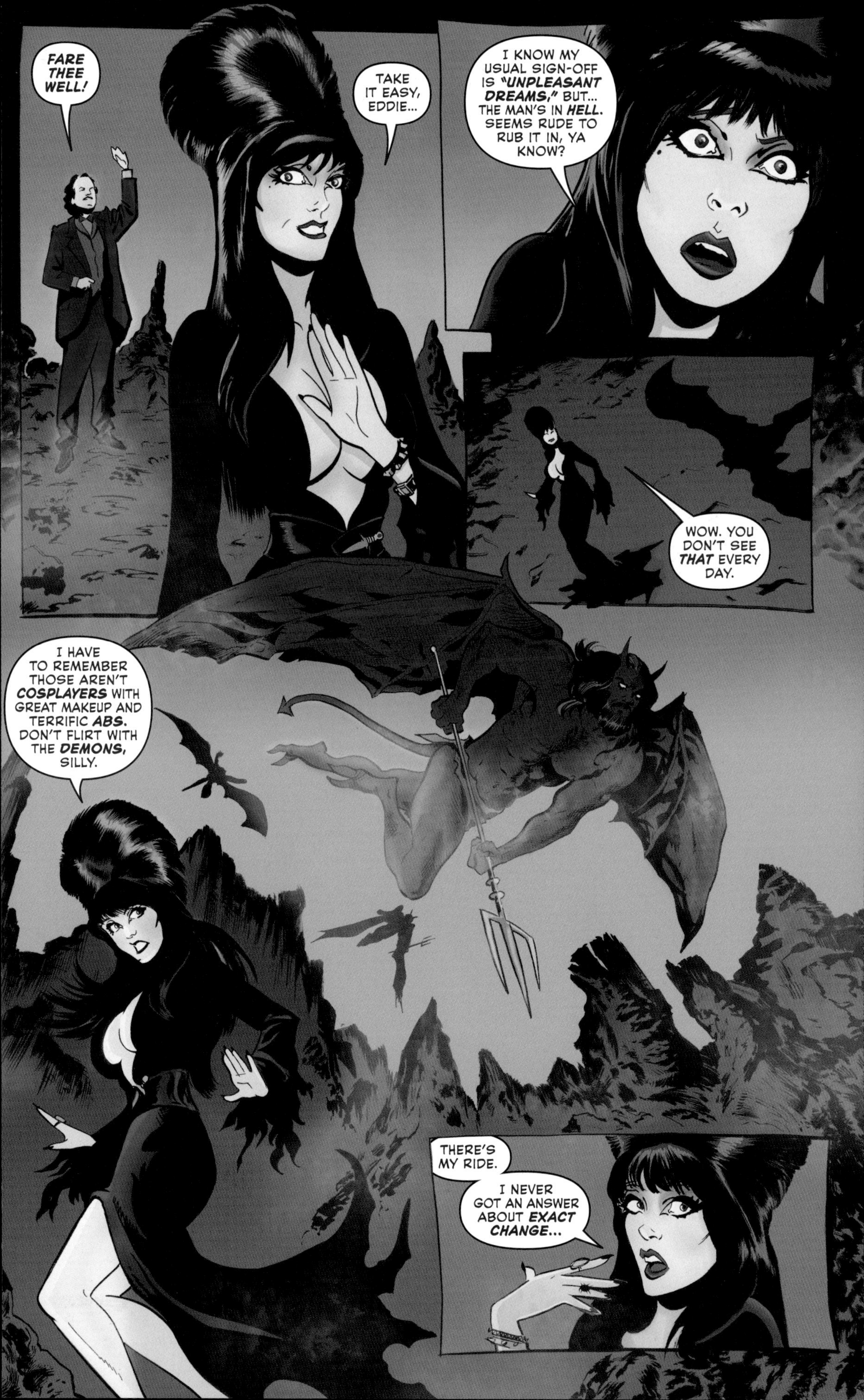
FARE THEE WELL!
TAKE IT EASY, EDDIE...
I KNOW MY USUAL SIGN-OFF IS "UNPLEASANT DREAMS," BUT... THE MAN'S IN HELL. SEEMS RUDE TO RUB IT IN, YA KNOW?
WOW. YOU DON'T SEE THAT EVERY DAY.
I HAVE TO REMEMBER THOSE AREN'T COSPLAYERS WITH GREAT MAKEUP AND TERRIFIC ABS. DON'T FLIRT WITH THE DEMONS, SILLY.
THERE'S MY RIDE.
I NEVER GOT AN ANSWER ABOUT EXACT CHANGE...

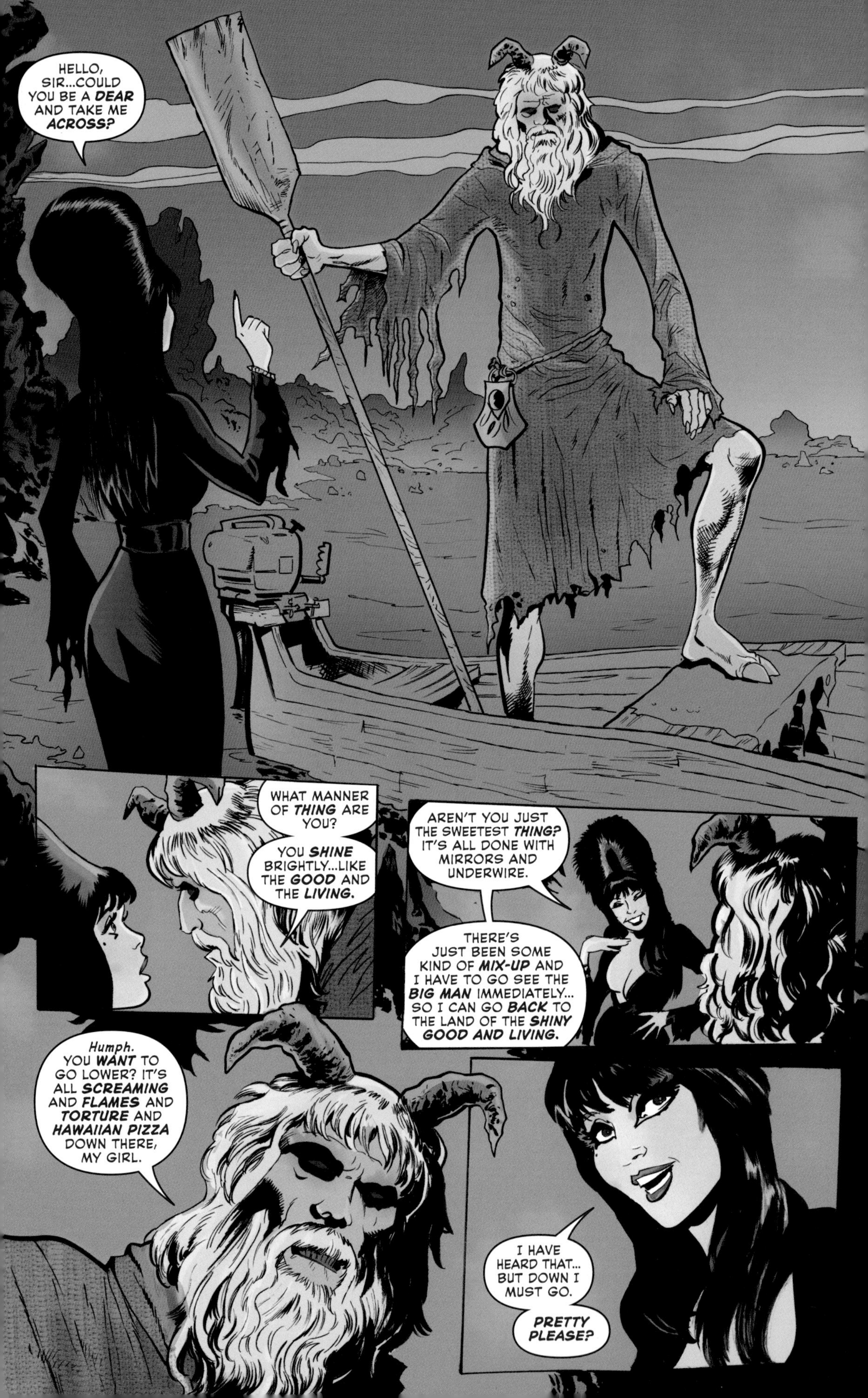
HELLO, SIR...COULD YOU BE A DEAR AND TAKE ME ACROSS?
WHAT MANNER OF THING ARE YOU?
YOU SHINE BRIGHTLY...LIKE THE GOOD AND THE LIVING.
AREN'T YOU JUST THE SWEETEST THING? IT'S ALL DONE WITH MIRRORS AND UNDERWIRE.
THERE'S JUST BEEN SOME KIND OF MIX-UP AND I HAVE TO GO SEE THE BIG MAN IMMEDIATELY... SO I CAN GO BACK TO THE LAND OF THE SHINY GOOD AND LIVING.
Humph. YOU WANT TO GO LOWER? IT'S ALL SCREAMING AND FLAMES AND TORTURE AND HAWAIIAN PIZZA DOWN THERE, MY GIRL.
I HAVE HEARD THAT... BUT DOWN I MUST GO.
PRETTY PLEASE?

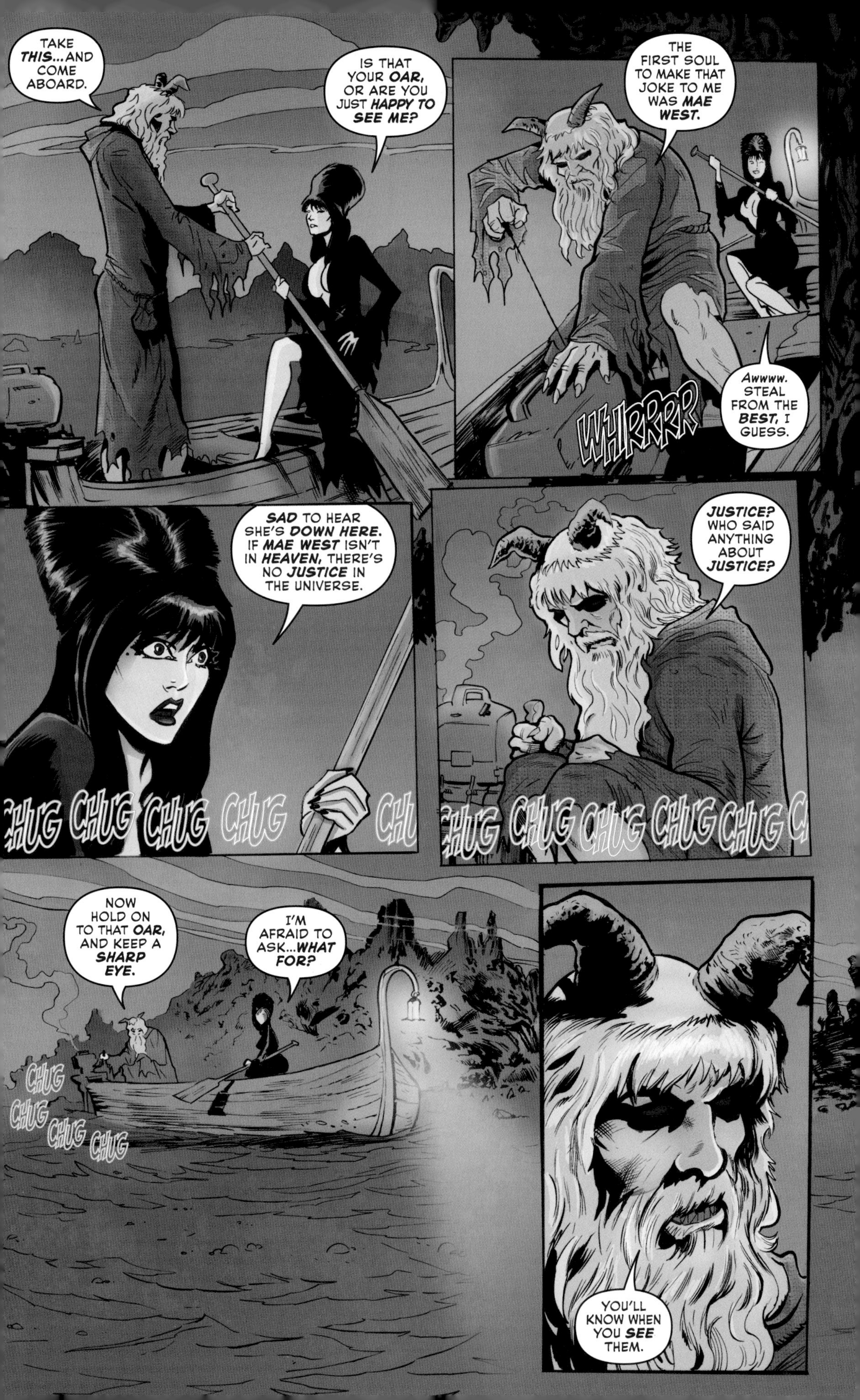
TAKE THIS...AND COME ABOARD.
IS THAT YOUR OAR, OR ARE YOU JUST HAPPY TO SEE ME?
THE FIRST SOUL TO MAKE THAT JOKE TO ME WAS MAE WEST.
WHIRRRR
Awwww. STEAL FROM THE BEST, I GUESS.
SAD TO HEAR SHE'S DOWN HERE. IF MAE WEST ISN'T IN HEAVEN, THERE'S NO JUSTICE IN THE UNIVERSE.
CHUG CHUG CHUG CHUG CHUG
JUSTICE? WHO SAID ANYTHING ABOUT JUSTICE?
CHUG CHUG CHUG CHUG CHUG
NOW HOLD ON TO THAT OAR, AND KEEP A SHARP EYE.
I'M AFRAID TO ASK...WHAT FOR?
CHUG CHUG CHUG CHUG
YOU'LL KNOW WHEN YOU SEE THEM.

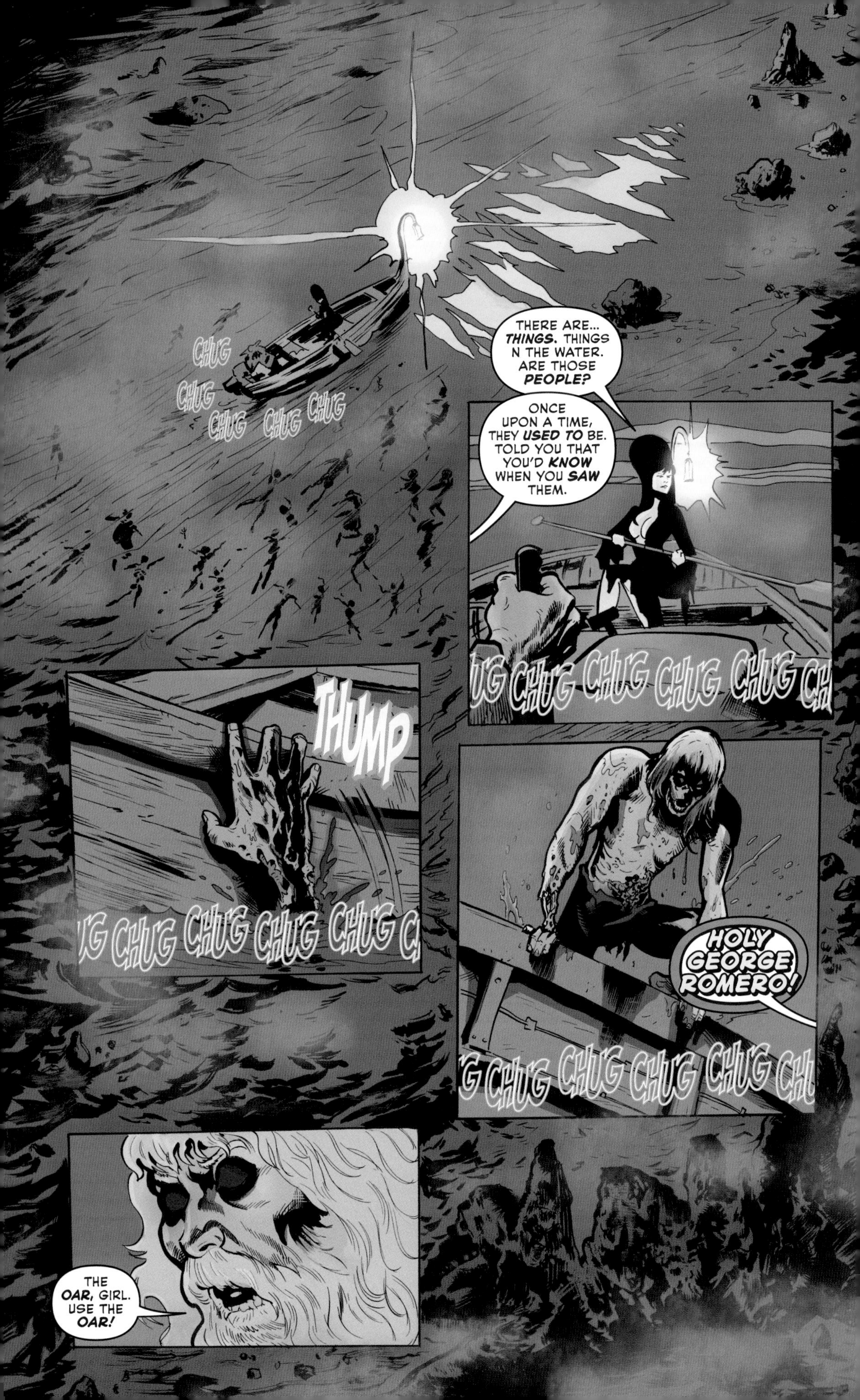
CHUG
CHUG
CHUG CHUG CHUG
THERE ARE... THINGS. THINGS N THE WATER. ARE THOSE PEOPLE?
ONCE UPON A TIME, THEY USED TO BE. TOLD YOU THAT YOU'D KNOW WHEN YOU SAW THEM.
CHUG CHUG CHUG CHUG
THUMP
CHUG CHUG CHUG
HOLY GEORGE ROMERO!
CHUG CHUG CHUG
THE OAR, GIRL. USE THE OAR!

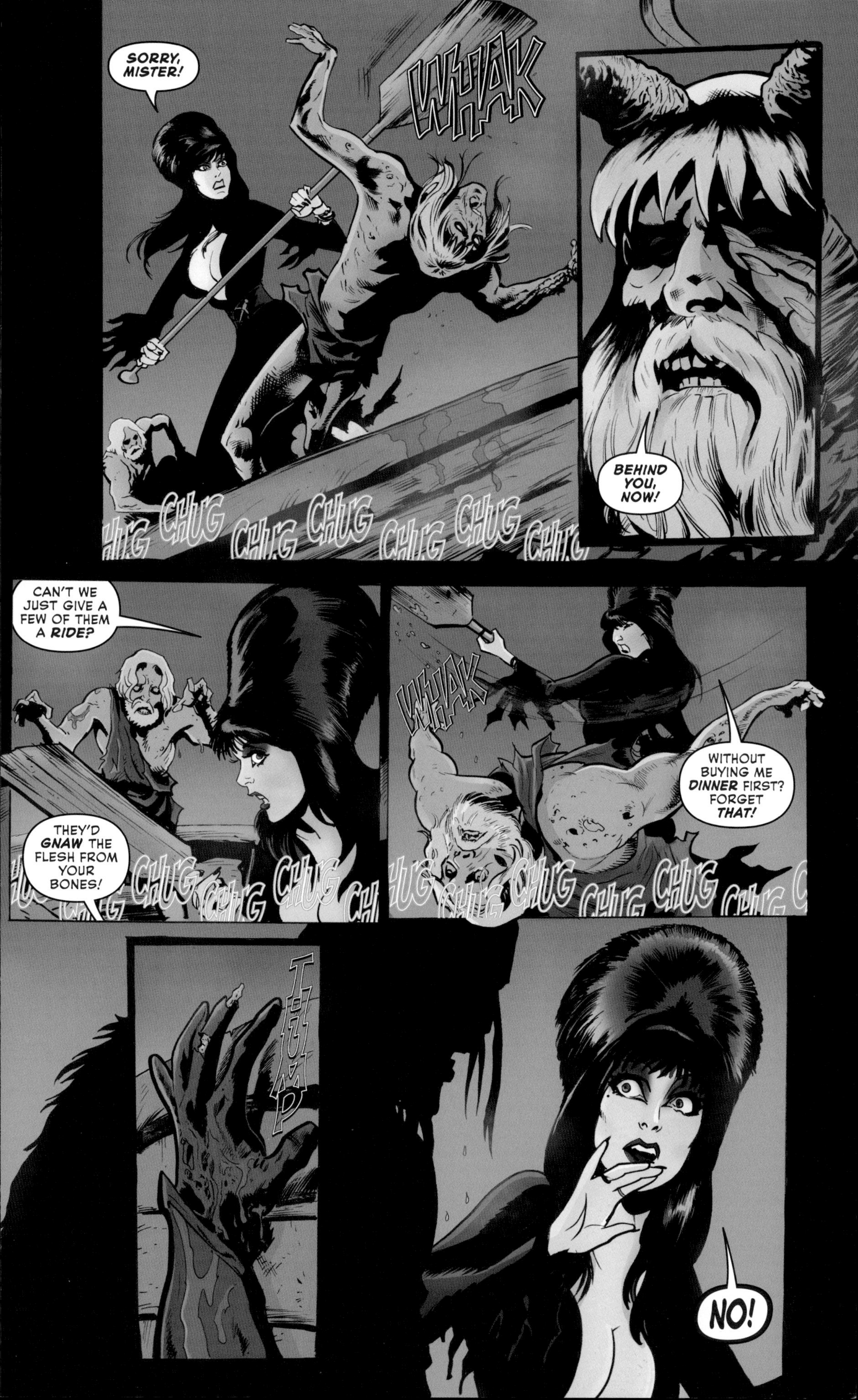
SORRY, MISTER!
WHAK
BEHIND YOU, NOW!
CHUG CHUG CHUG CHUG CHUG CHUG CHUG
CAN'T WE JUST GIVE A FEW OF THEM A RIDE?
THEY'D GNAW THE FLESH FROM YOUR BONES!
CHUG CHUG CHUG
WHAK
WITHOUT BUYING ME DINNER FIRST? FORGET THAT!
CHUG CHUG CHUG CHUG CHUG
THUMP
NO!

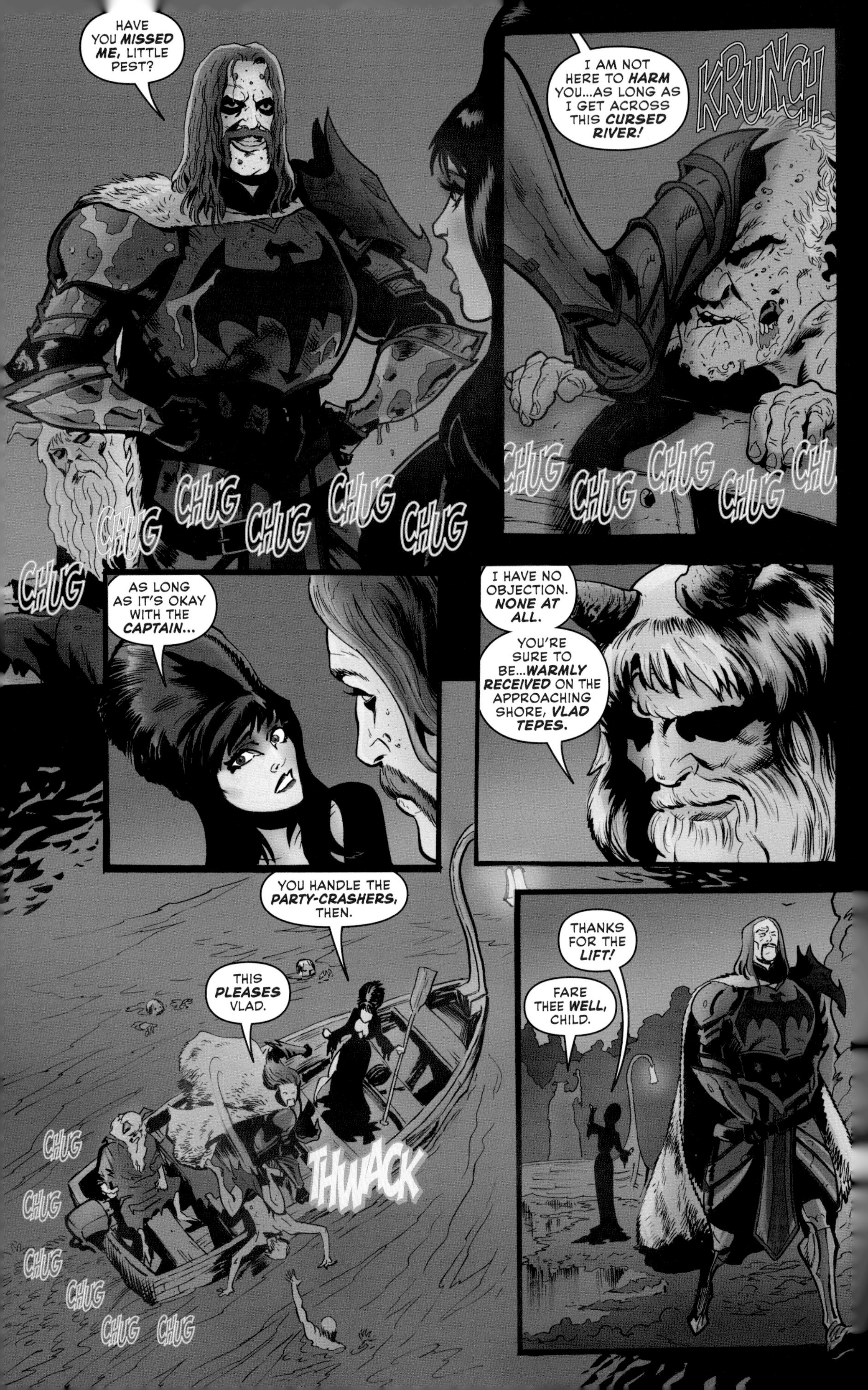
HAVE YOU MISSED ME, LITTLE PEST?
CHUG CHUG CHUG CHUG CHUG CHUG
I AM NOT HERE TO HARM YOU...AS LONG AS I GET ACROSS THIS CURSED RIVER!
KRUNCH
CHUG CHUG CHUG CHUG CHUG
AS LONG AS IT'S OKAY WITH THE CAPTAIN...
I HAVE NO OBJECTION. NONE AT ALL.
YOU'RE SURE TO BE...WARMLY RECEIVED ON THE APPROACHING SHORE, VLAD TEPES.
YOU HANDLE THE PARTY-CRASHERS, THEN.
THIS PLEASES VLAD.
THWACK
CHUG CHUG CHUG CHUG CHUG CHUG
THANKS FOR THE LIFT!
FARE THEE WELL, CHILD.

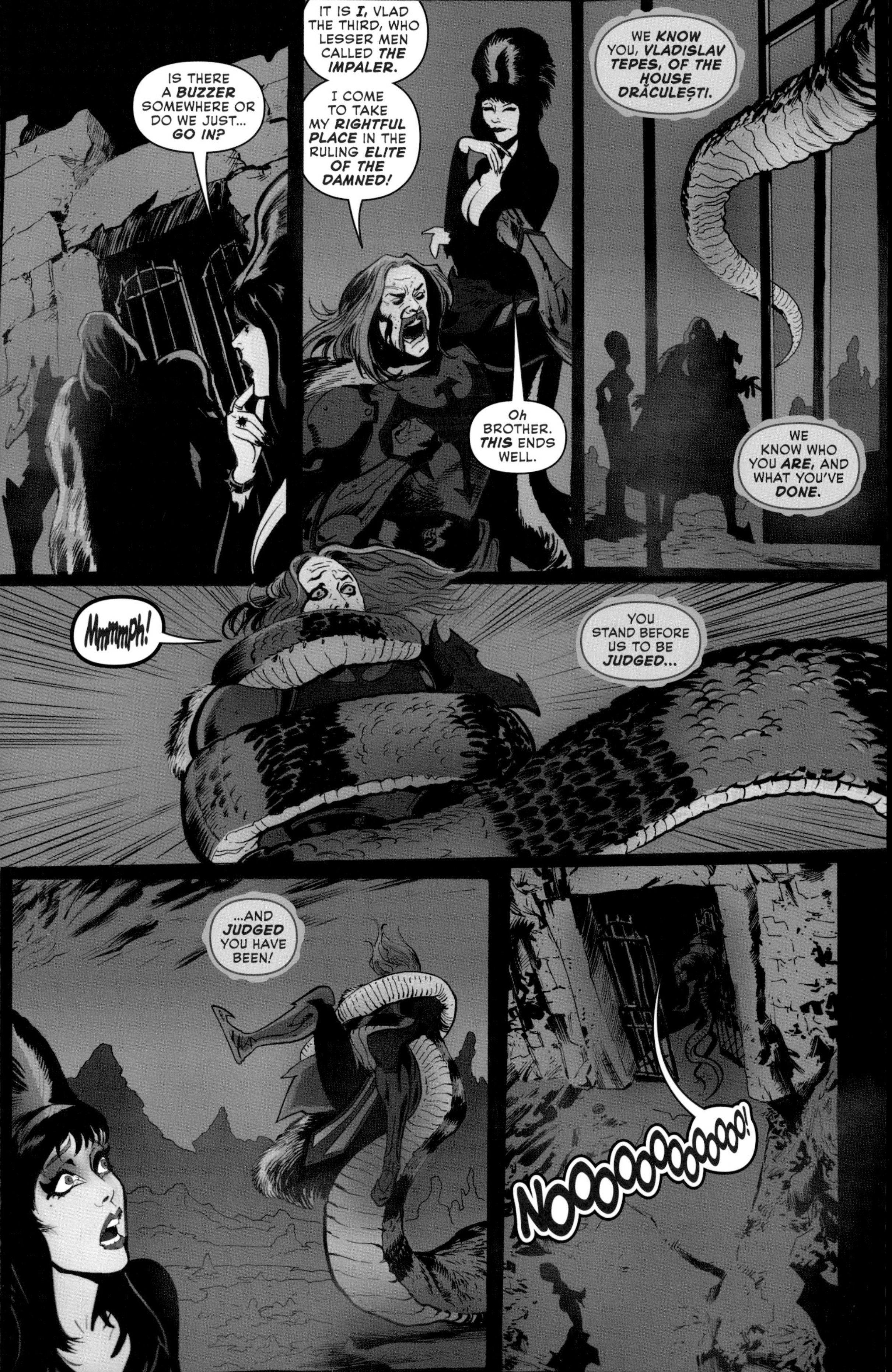
IS THERE A BUZZER SOMEWHERE OR DO WE JUST... GO IN?
IT IS I, VLAD THE THIRD, WHO LESSER MEN CALLED THE IMPALER.
I COME TO TAKE MY RIGHTFUL PLACE IN THE RULING ELITE OF THE DAMNED!
Oh BROTHER. THIS ENDS WELL.
WE KNOW YOU, VLADISLAV TEPES, OF THE HOUSE DRĂCULEȘTI.
WE KNOW WHO YOU ARE, AND WHAT YOU'VE DONE.
Mmmmph!
YOU STAND BEFORE US TO BE JUDGED...
...AND JUDGED YOU HAVE BEEN!
NOOOOOOOOOOOOO!

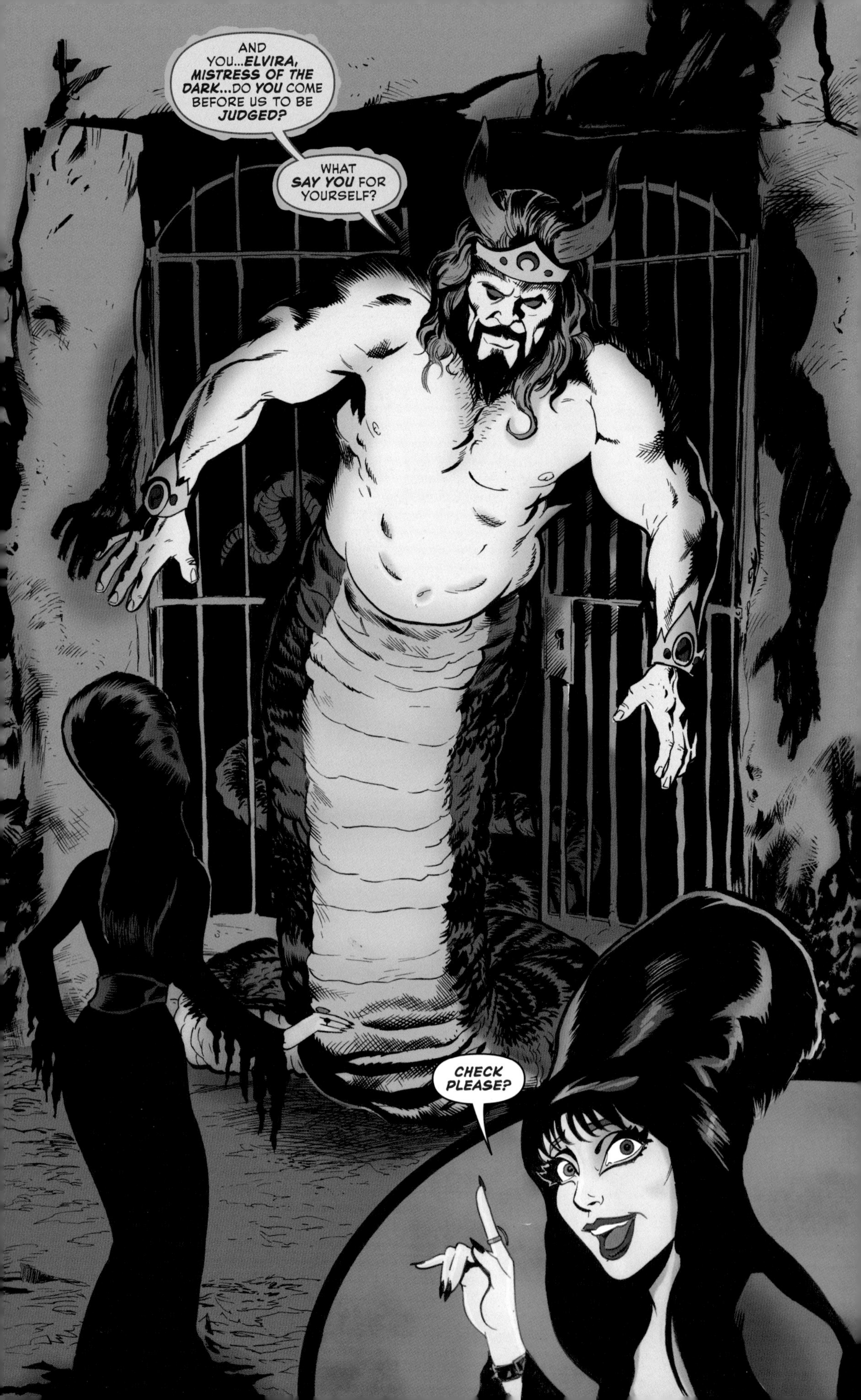
AND YOU...ELVIRA, MISTRESS OF THE DARK...DO YOU COME BEFORE US TO BE JUDGED?
WHAT SAY YOU FOR YOURSELF?
CHECK PLEASE?

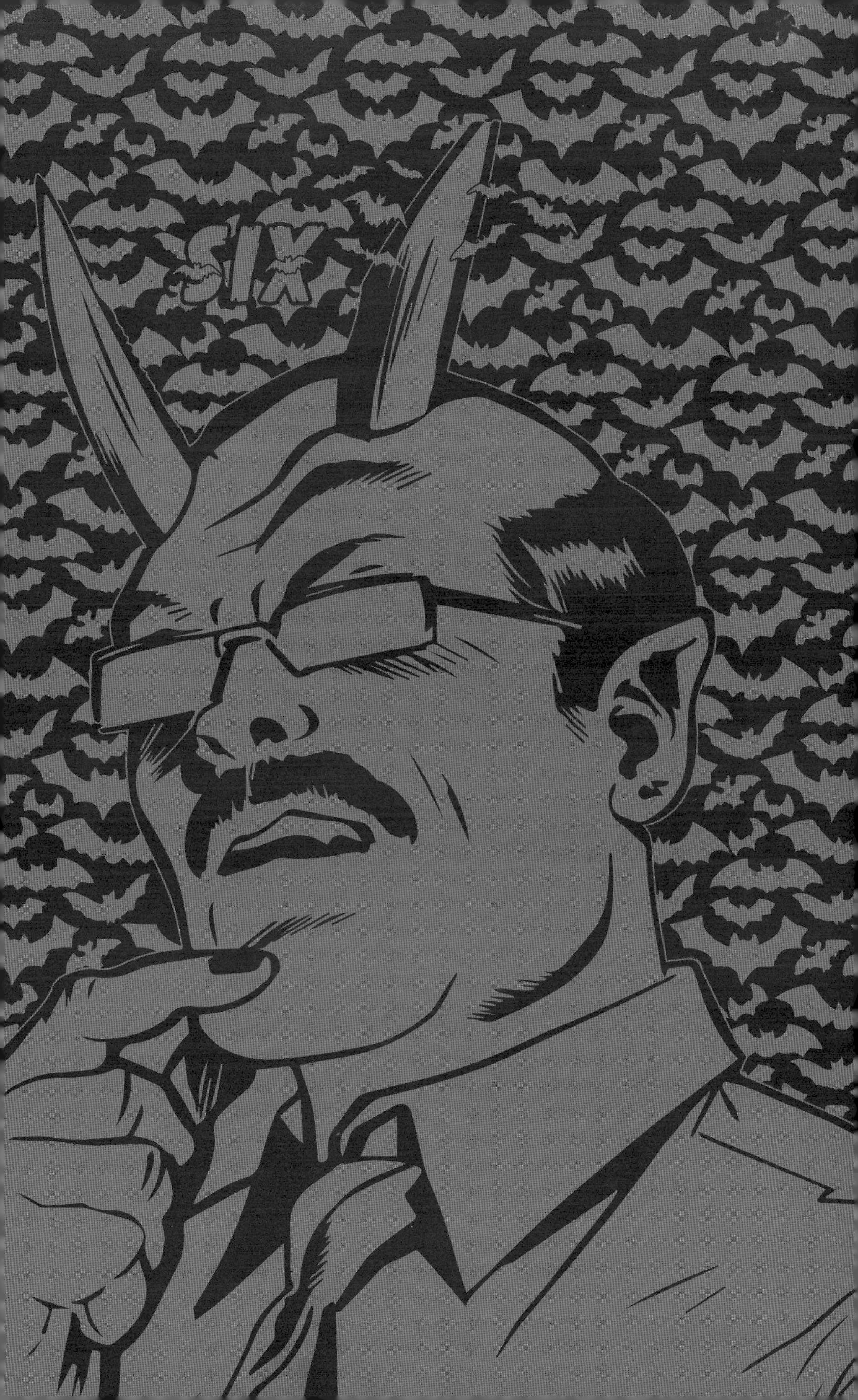
SIX

6 COVER ART: JOSEPH MICHAEL LINSNER

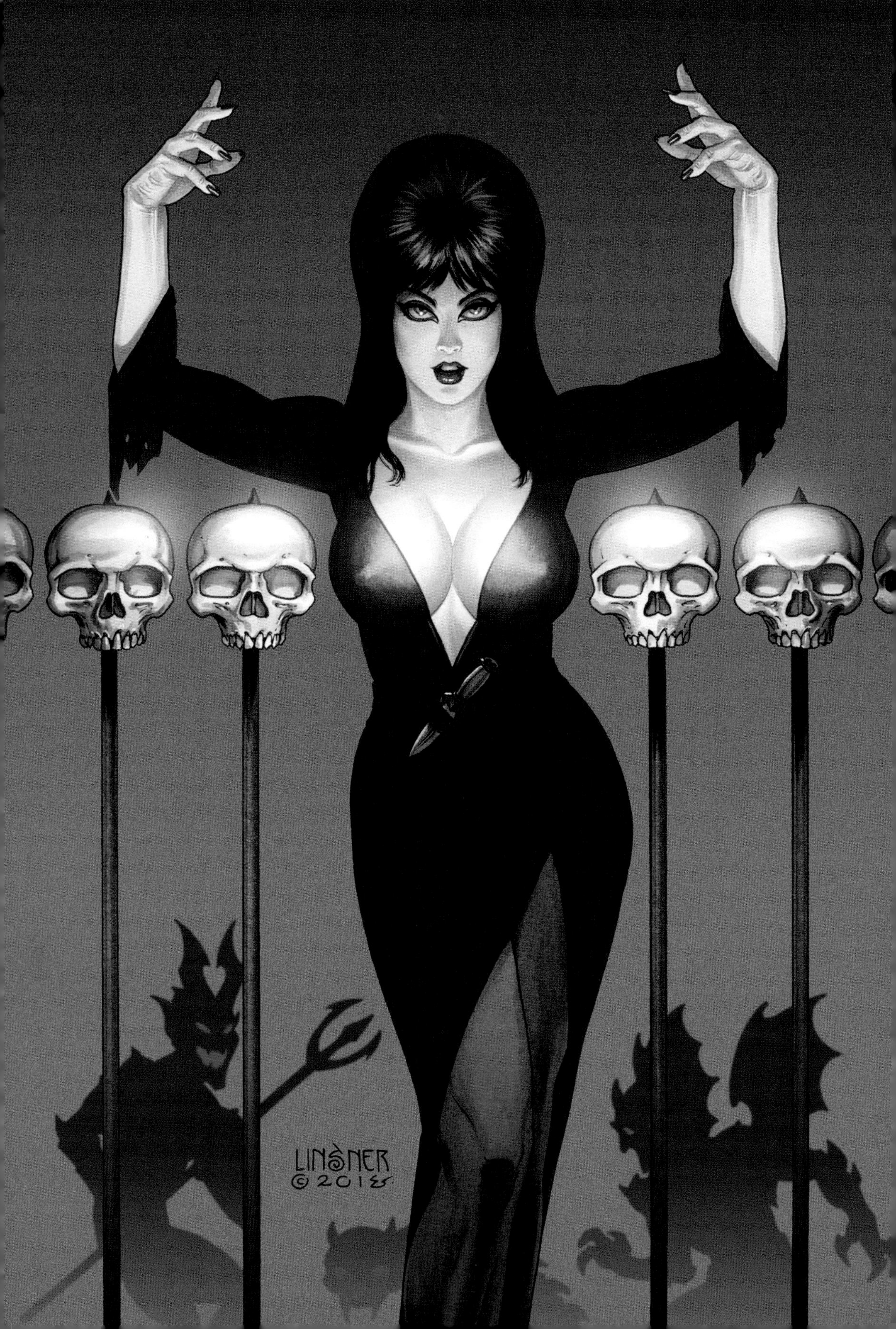
LINSNER
©2018

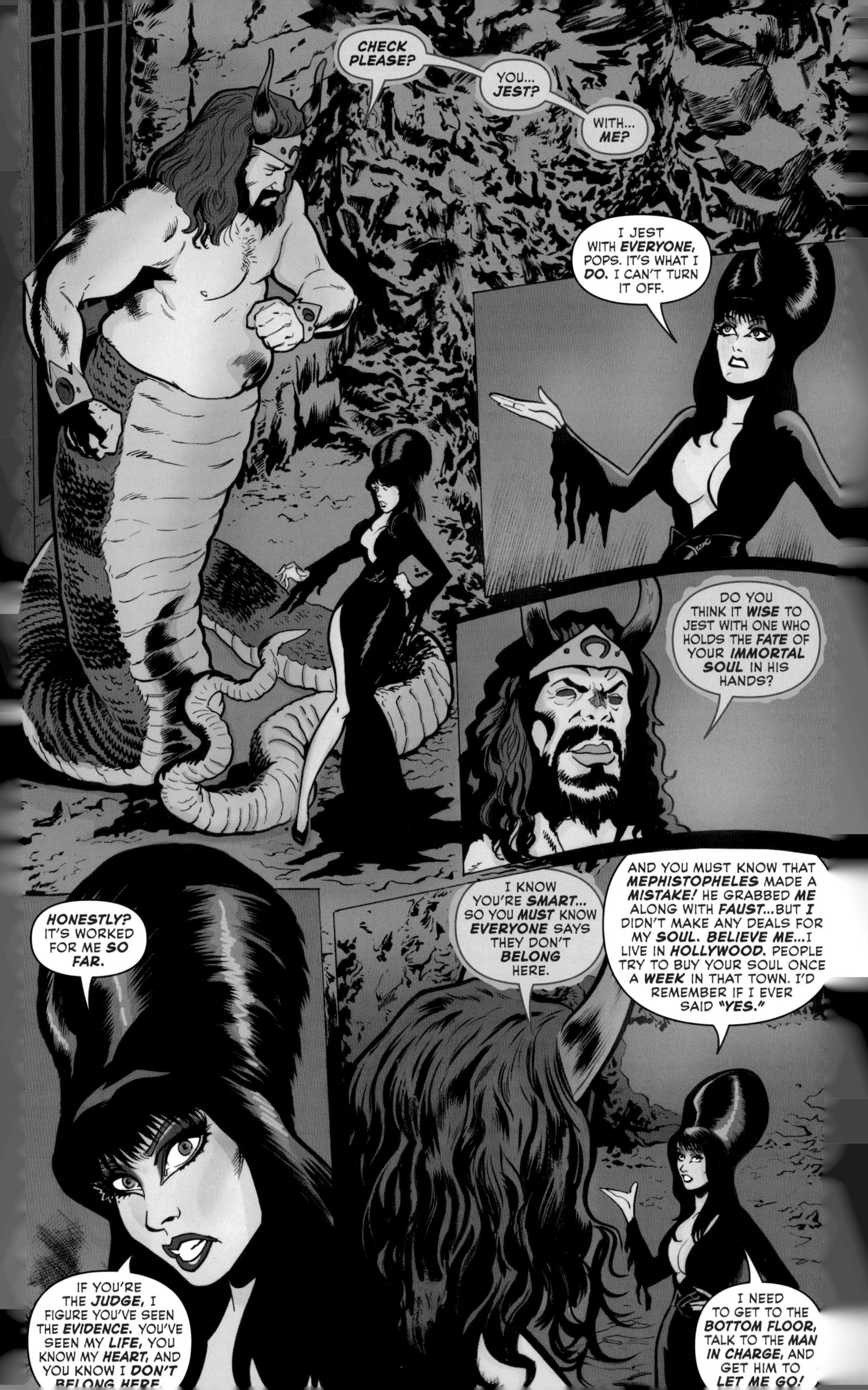
CHECK PLEASE?
YOU... JEST?
WITH... ME?
I JEST WITH EVERYONE, POPS. IT'S WHAT I DO. I CAN'T TURN IT OFF.
DO YOU THINK IT WISE TO JEST WITH ONE WHO HOLDS THE FATE OF YOUR IMMORTAL SOUL IN HIS HANDS?
HONESTLY? IT'S WORKED FOR ME SO FAR.
IF YOU'RE THE JUDGE, I FIGURE YOU'VE SEEN THE EVIDENCE. YOU'VE SEEN MY LIFE, YOU KNOW MY HEART, AND YOU KNOW I DON'T BELONG HERE.
I KNOW YOU'RE SMART... SO YOU MUST KNOW EVERYONE SAYS THEY DON'T BELONG HERE.
AND YOU MUST KNOW THAT MEPHISTOPHELES MADE A MISTAKE! HE GRABBED ME ALONG WITH FAUST...BUT I DIDN'T MAKE ANY DEALS FOR MY SOUL. BELIEVE ME...I LIVE IN HOLLYWOOD. PEOPLE TRY TO BUY YOUR SOUL ONCE A WEEK IN THAT TOWN. I'D REMEMBER IF I EVER SAID "YES."
I NEED TO GET TO THE BOTTOM FLOOR, TALK TO THE MAN IN CHARGE, AND GET HIM TO LET ME GO!

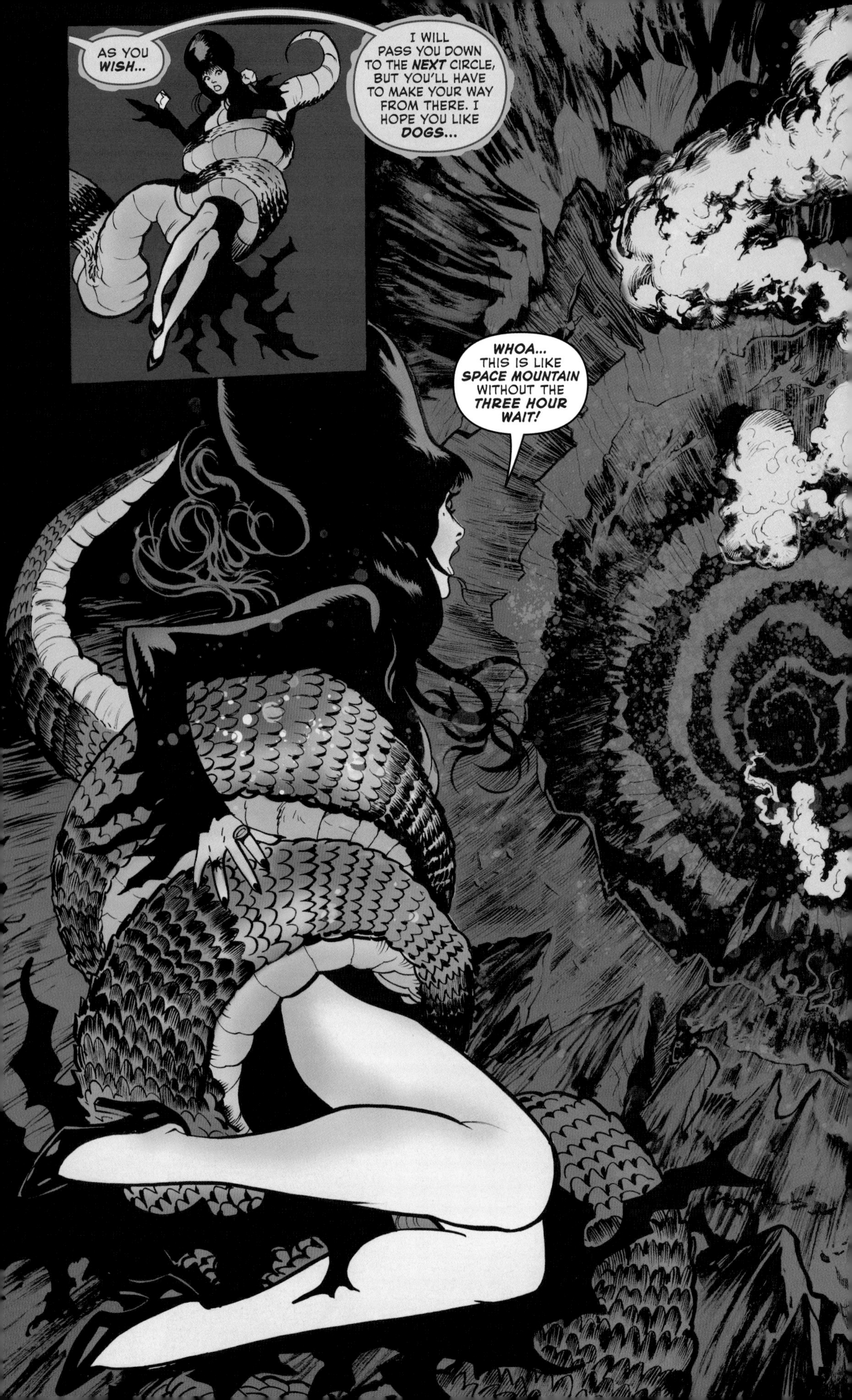
AS YOU WISH...
I WILL PASS YOU DOWN TO THE NEXT CIRCLE, BUT YOU'LL HAVE TO MAKE YOUR WAY FROM THERE. I HOPE YOU LIKE DOGS...
WHOA... THIS IS LIKE SPACE MOUNTAIN WITHOUT THE THREE HOUR WAIT!

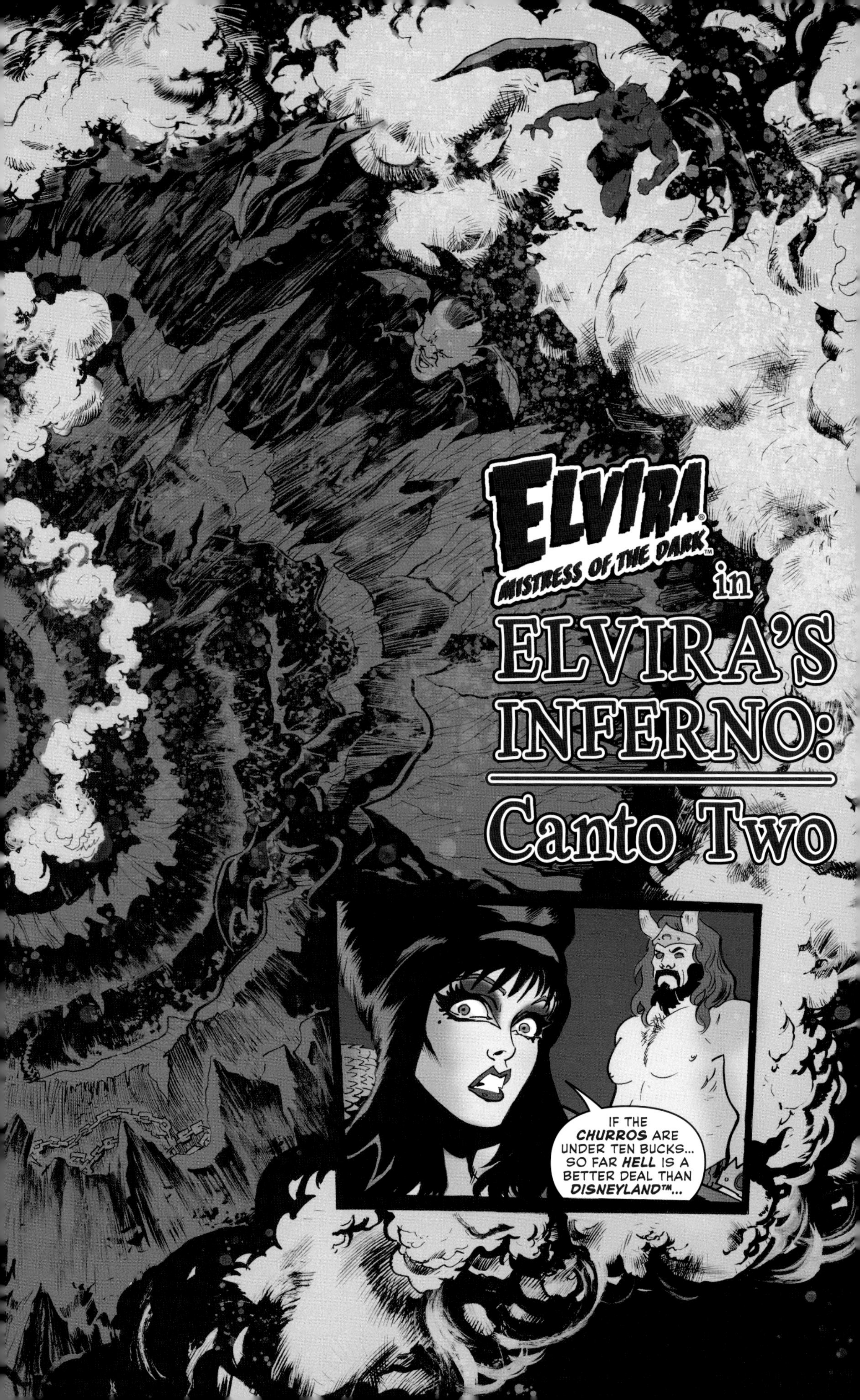
ELVIRA® MISTRESS OF THE DARK™
in
ELVIRA'S INFERNO:
Canto Two
IF THE CHURROS ARE UNDER TEN BUCKS... SO FAR HELL IS A BETTER DEAL THAN DISNEYLAND™...

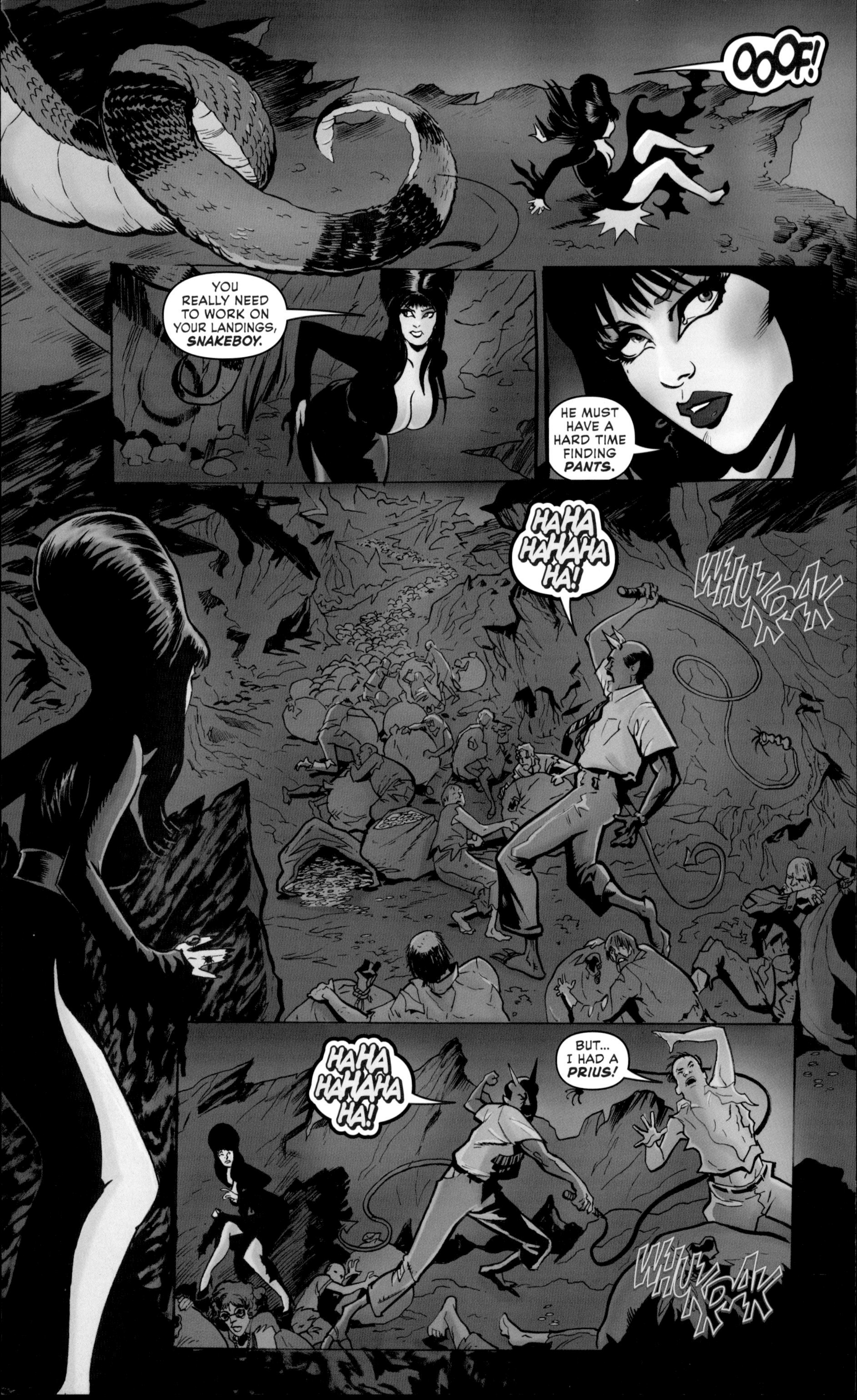
OOOF!
YOU REALLY NEED TO WORK ON YOUR LANDINGS, SNAKEBOY.
HE MUST HAVE A HARD TIME FINDING PANTS.
HAHA HAHAHA HA!
WHUKRAK
HAHA HAHAHA HA!
BUT... I HAD A PRIUS!
WHUKRAK

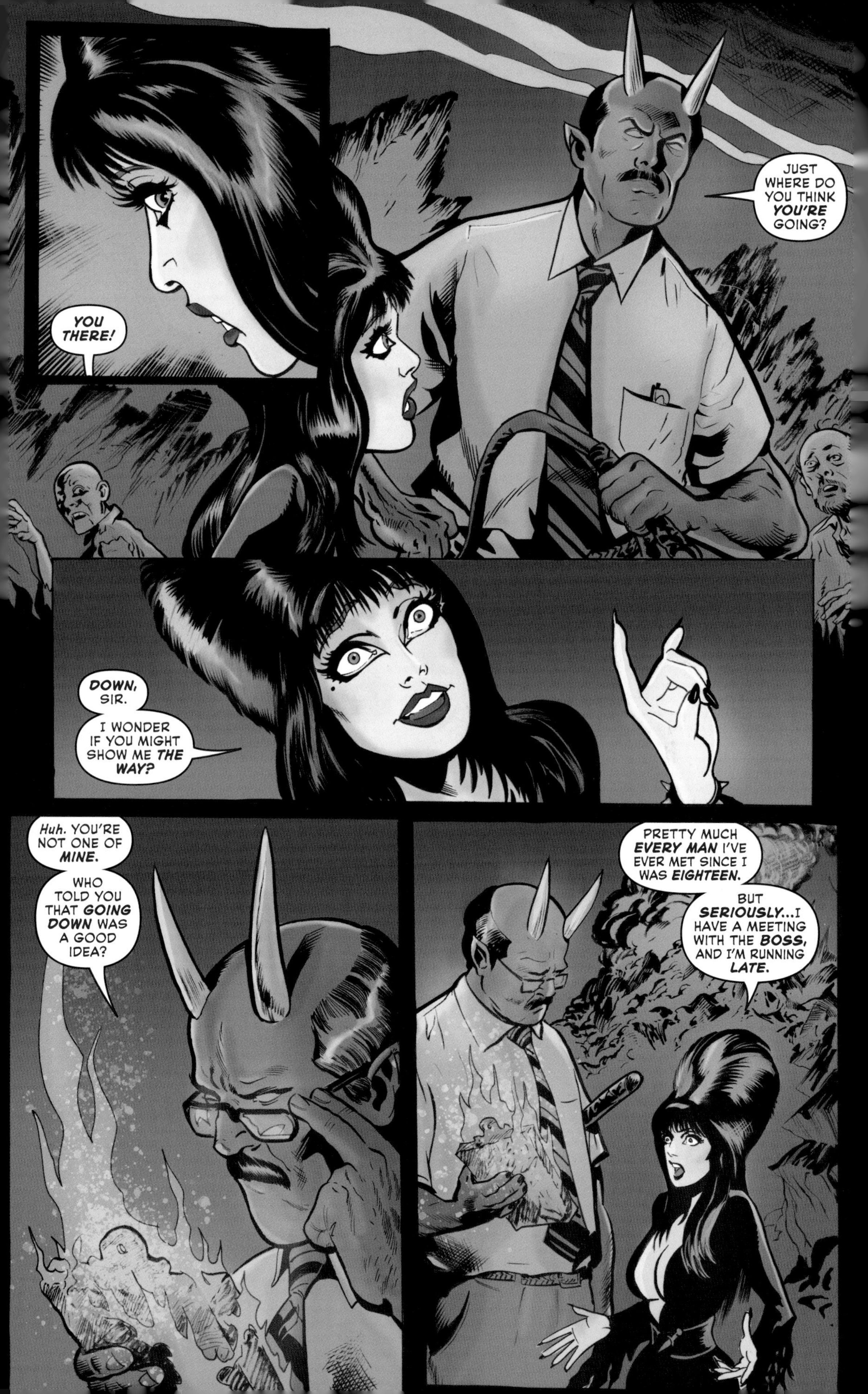
YOU THERE!
JUST WHERE DO YOU THINK YOU'RE GOING?
DOWN, SIR.
I WONDER IF YOU MIGHT SHOW ME THE WAY?
Huh. YOU'RE NOT ONE OF MINE.
WHO TOLD YOU THAT GOING DOWN WAS A GOOD IDEA?
PRETTY MUCH EVERY MAN I'VE EVER MET SINCE I WAS EIGHTEEN.
BUT SERIOUSLY...I HAVE A MEETING WITH THE BOSS, AND I'M RUNNING LATE.

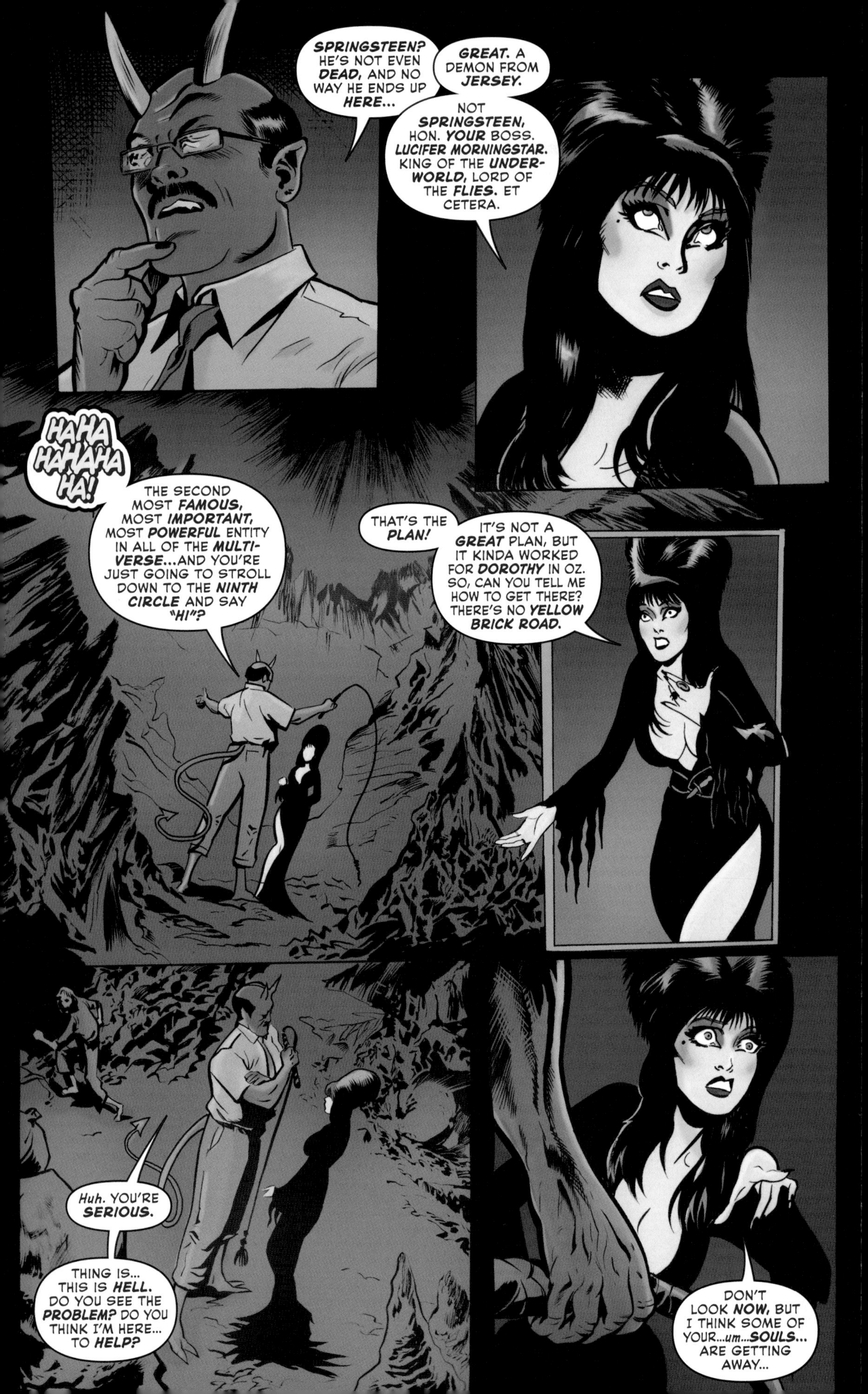
SPRINGSTEEN? HE'S NOT EVEN DEAD, AND NO WAY HE ENDS UP HERE...
GREAT. A DEMON FROM JERSEY.
NOT SPRINGSTEEN, HON. YOUR BOSS. LUCIFER MORNINGSTAR. KING OF THE UNDERWORLD, LORD OF THE FLIES. ET CETERA.
HAHA HAHAHA HA!
THE SECOND MOST FAMOUS, MOST IMPORTANT, MOST POWERFUL ENTITY IN ALL OF THE MULTIVERSE...AND YOU'RE JUST GOING TO STROLL DOWN TO THE NINTH CIRCLE AND SAY "HI"?
THAT'S THE PLAN!
IT'S NOT A GREAT PLAN, BUT IT KINDA WORKED FOR DOROTHY IN OZ. SO, CAN YOU TELL ME HOW TO GET THERE? THERE'S NO YELLOW BRICK ROAD.
Huh. YOU'RE SERIOUS.
THING IS... THIS IS HELL. DO YOU SEE THE PROBLEM? DO YOU THINK I'M HERE... TO HELP?
DON'T LOOK NOW, BUT I THINK SOME OF YOUR...um...SOULS... ARE GETTING AWAY...

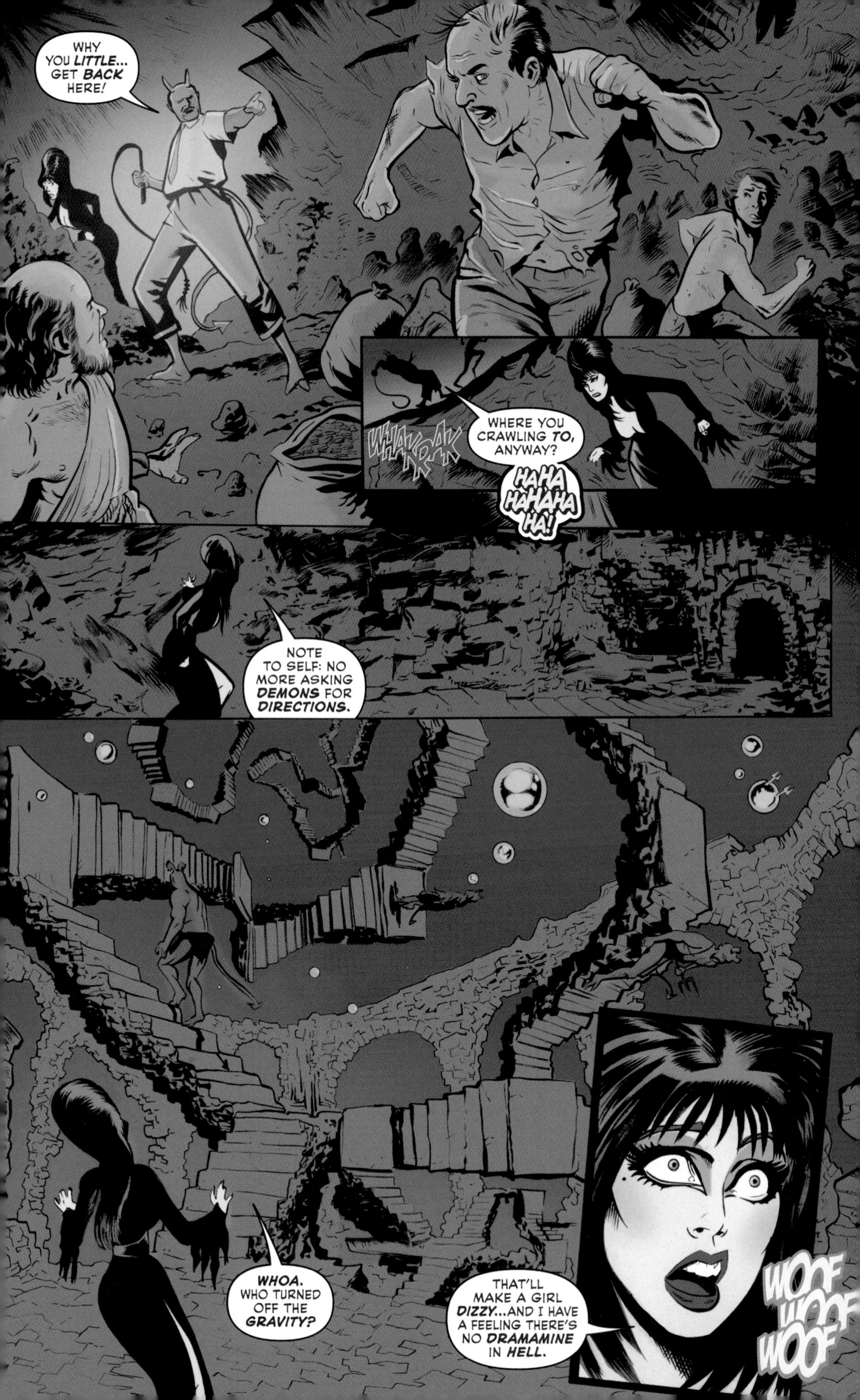
WHY YOU LITTLE... GET BACK HERE!
WHAKRAK
WHERE YOU CRAWLING TO, ANYWAY?
HAHA HAHAHA HA!
NOTE TO SELF: NO MORE ASKING DEMONS FOR DIRECTIONS.
WHOA. WHO TURNED OFF THE GRAVITY?
THAT'LL MAKE A GIRL DIZZY...AND I HAVE A FEELING THERE'S NO DRAMAMINE IN HELL.
WOOF WOOF WOOF

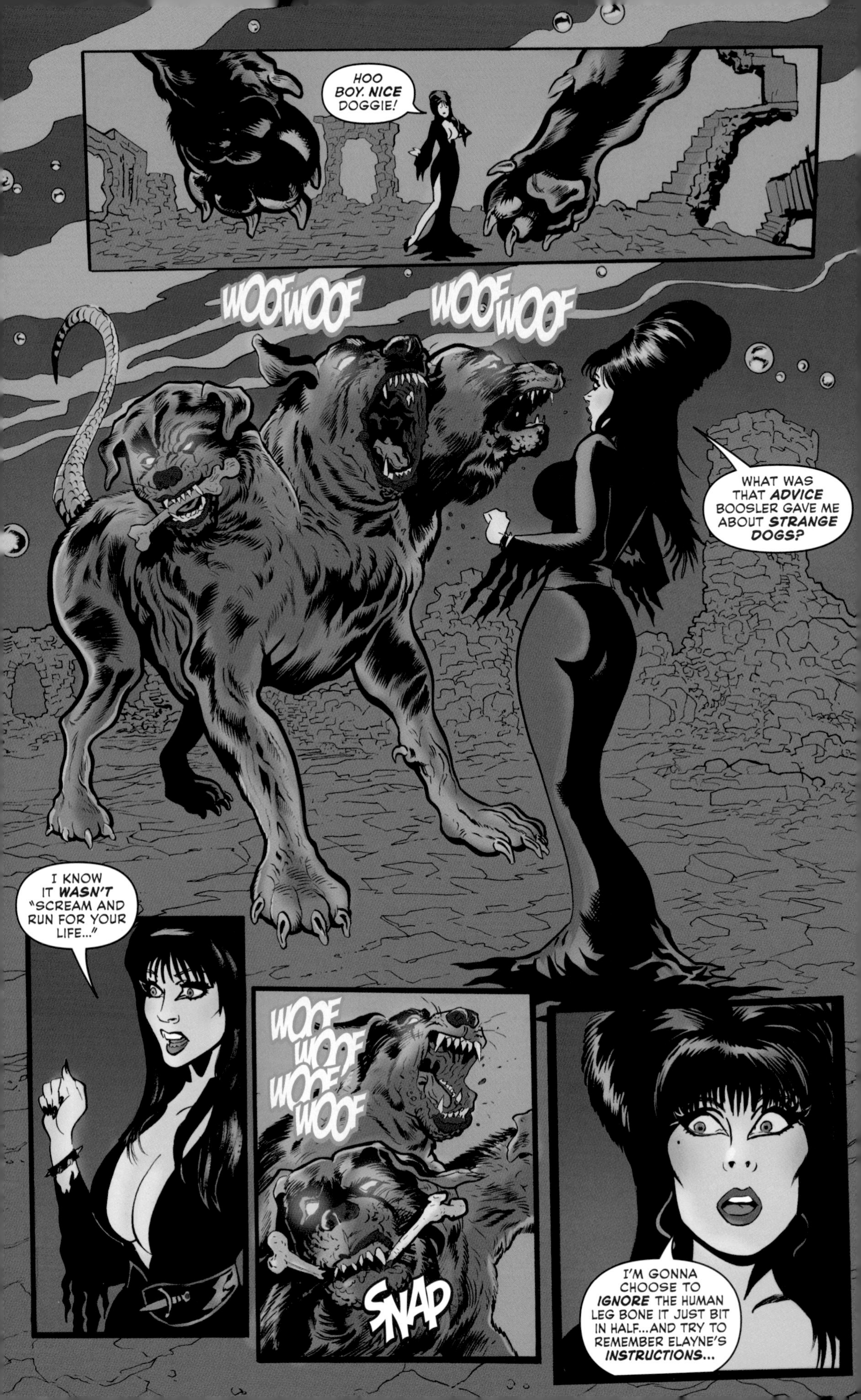

HOO BOY. NICE DOGGIE!
WOOF WOOF WOOF WOOF
WHAT WAS THAT ADVICE BOOSLER GAVE ME ABOUT STRANGE DOGS?
I KNOW IT WASN'T "SCREAM AND RUN FOR YOUR LIFE..."
WOOF WOOF WOOF WOOF
SNAP
I'M GONNA CHOOSE TO IGNORE THE HUMAN LEG BONE IT JUST BIT IN HALF...AND TRY TO REMEMBER ELAYNE'S INSTRUCTIONS...

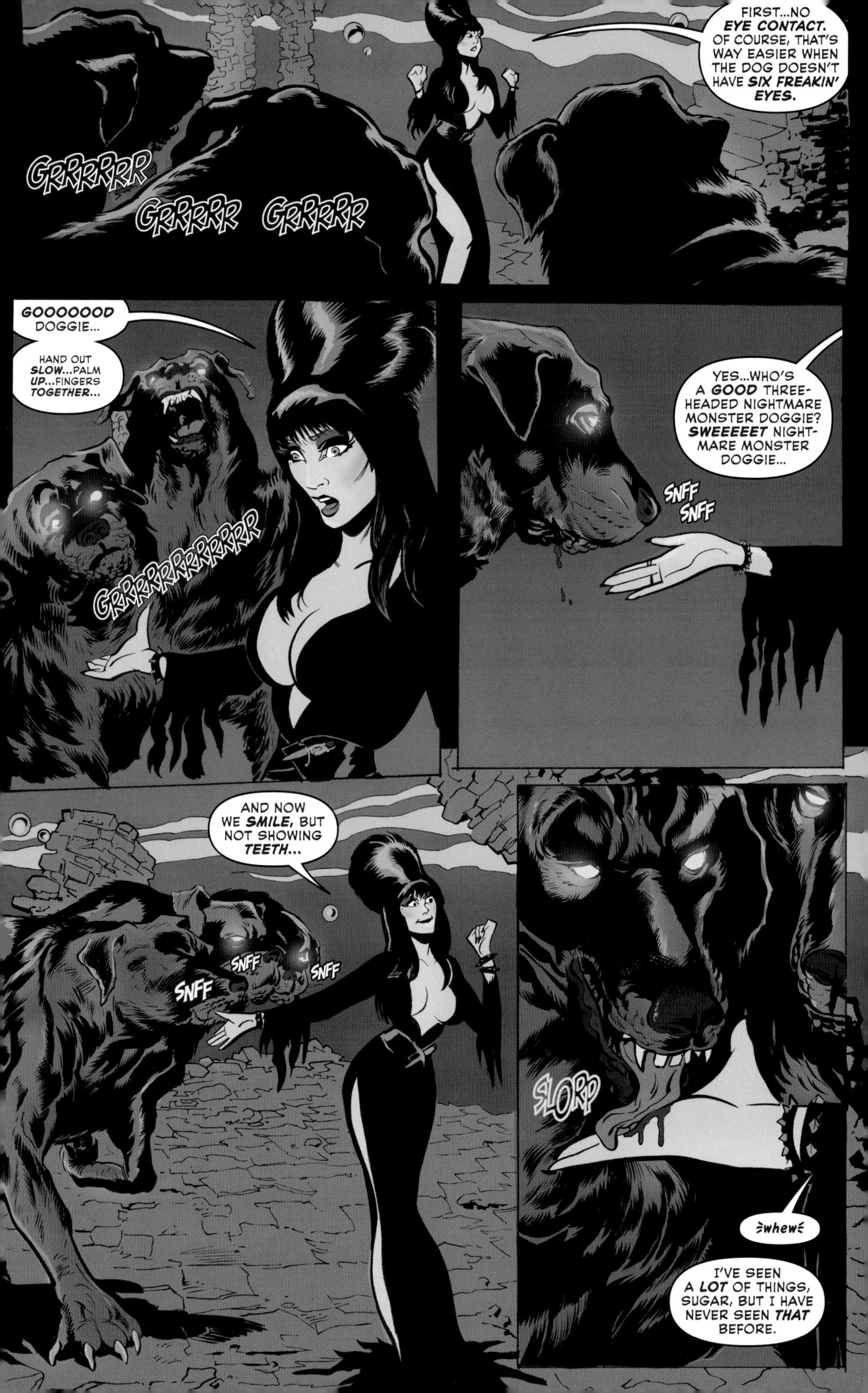
FIRST...NO EYE CONTACT. OF COURSE, THAT'S WAY EASIER WHEN THE DOG DOESN'T HAVE SIX FREAKIN' EYES.
GRRRRRR
GRRRRR GRRRRR
GOOOOOOD DOGGIE...
HAND OUT SLOW...PALM UP...FINGERS TOGETHER...
GRRRRRRRRRRRR
YES...WHO'S A GOOD THREE-HEADED NIGHTMARE MONSTER DOGGIE? SWEEEEET NIGHT-MARE MONSTER DOGGIE...
SNFF SNFF
AND NOW WE SMILE, BUT NOT SHOWING TEETH...
SNFF
SNFF
SNFF
SLORP
whew
I'VE SEEN A LOT OF THINGS, SUGAR, BUT I HAVE NEVER SEEN THAT BEFORE.

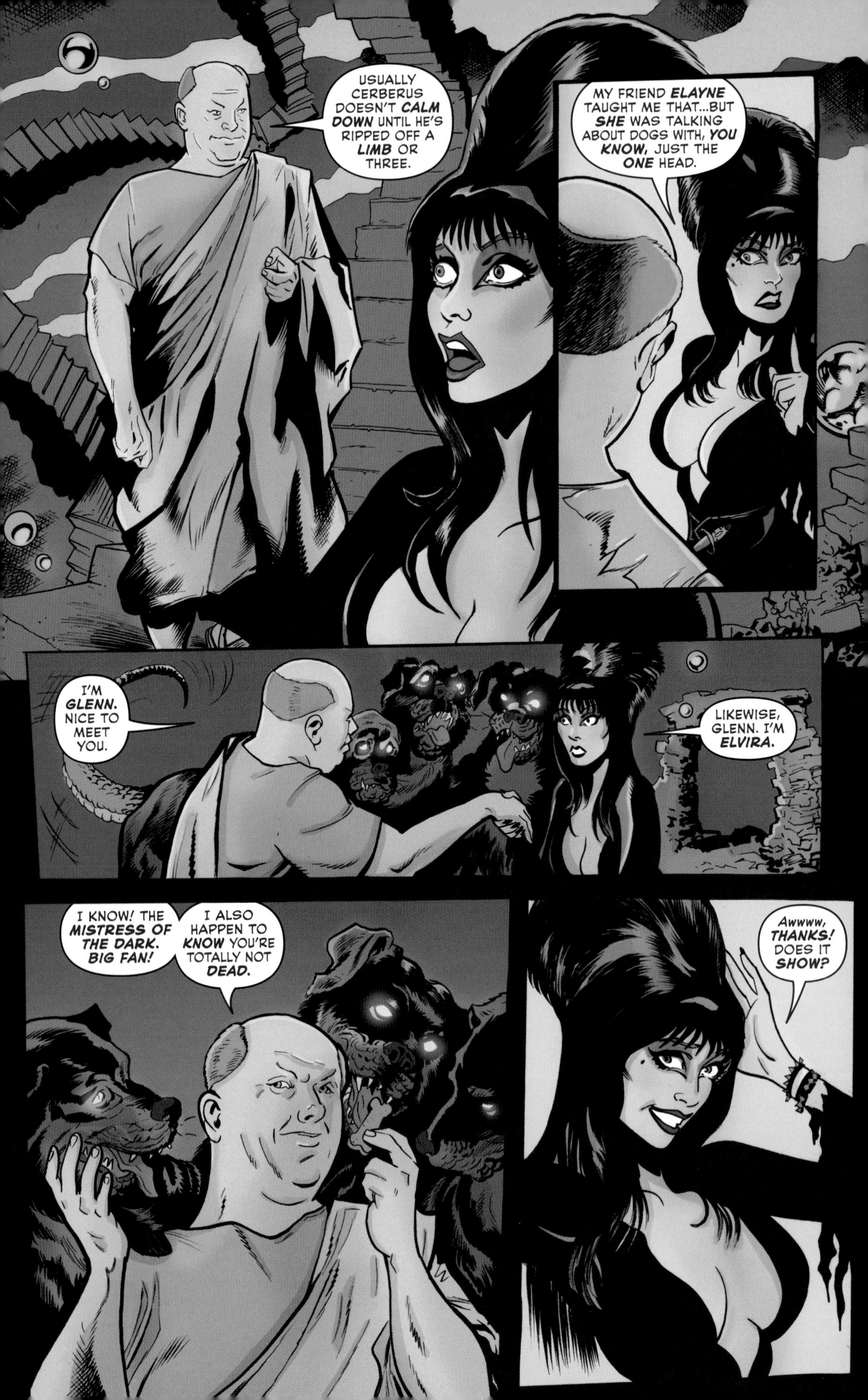
USUALLY CERBERUS DOESN'T CALM DOWN UNTIL HE'S RIPPED OFF A LIMB OR THREE.
MY FRIEND ELAYNE TAUGHT ME THAT...BUT SHE WAS TALKING ABOUT DOGS WITH, YOU KNOW, JUST THE ONE HEAD.
I'M GLENN. NICE TO MEET YOU.
LIKEWISE, GLENN. I'M ELVIRA.
I KNOW! THE MISTRESS OF THE DARK. BIG FAN!
I ALSO HAPPEN TO KNOW YOU'RE TOTALLY NOT DEAD.
Awwww, THANKS! DOES IT SHOW?

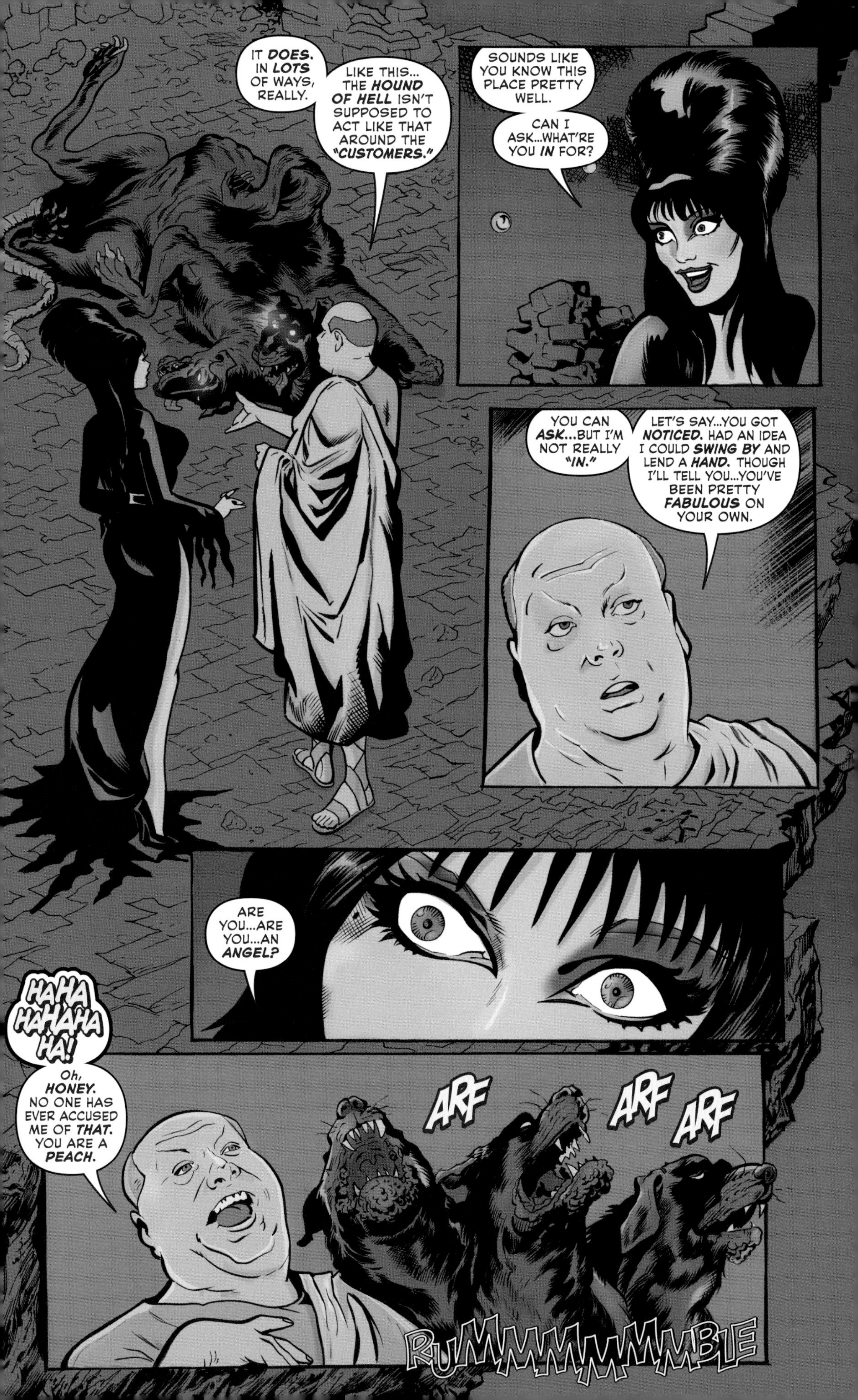
IT DOES. IN LOTS OF WAYS, REALLY.
LIKE THIS... THE HOUND OF HELL ISN'T SUPPOSED TO ACT LIKE THAT AROUND THE "CUSTOMERS."
SOUNDS LIKE YOU KNOW THIS PLACE PRETTY WELL.
CAN I ASK...WHAT'RE YOU IN FOR?
YOU CAN ASK...BUT I'M NOT REALLY "IN."
LET'S SAY...YOU GOT NOTICED. HAD AN IDEA I COULD SWING BY AND LEND A HAND. THOUGH I'LL TELL YOU...YOU'VE BEEN PRETTY FABULOUS ON YOUR OWN.
ARE YOU...ARE YOU...AN ANGEL?
HAHA HAHAHA HA!
Oh, HONEY. NO ONE HAS EVER ACCUSED ME OF THAT. YOU ARE A PEACH.
ARF
ARF
ARF
RUMMMMMMMBLE

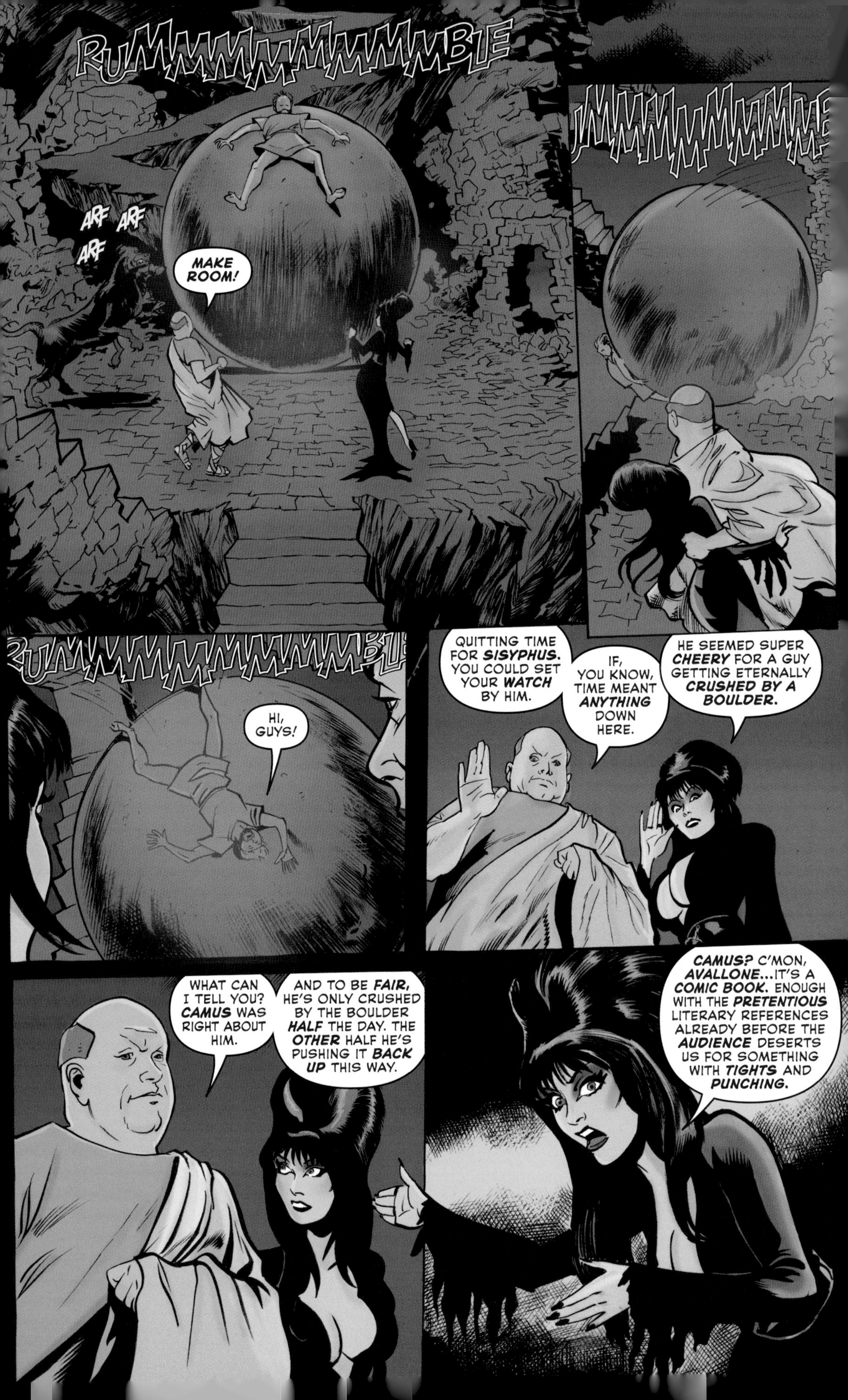
RUMMMMMMMMMBLE
ARF ARF
ARF
MAKE ROOM!
MMMMMMMMMME
RUMMMMMMMMMMBLE
HI, GUYS!
QUITTING TIME FOR SISYPHUS. YOU COULD SET YOUR WATCH BY HIM.
IF, YOU KNOW, TIME MEANT ANYTHING DOWN HERE.
HE SEEMED SUPER CHEERY FOR A GUY GETTING ETERNALLY CRUSHED BY A BOULDER.
WHAT CAN I TELL YOU? CAMUS WAS RIGHT ABOUT HIM.
AND TO BE FAIR, HE'S ONLY CRUSHED BY THE BOULDER HALF THE DAY. THE OTHER HALF HE'S PUSHING IT BACK UP THIS WAY.
CAMUS? C'MON, AVALLONE...IT'S A COMIC BOOK. ENOUGH WITH THE PRETENTIOUS LITERARY REFERENCES ALREADY BEFORE THE AUDIENCE DESERTS US FOR SOMETHING WITH TIGHTS AND PUNCHING.

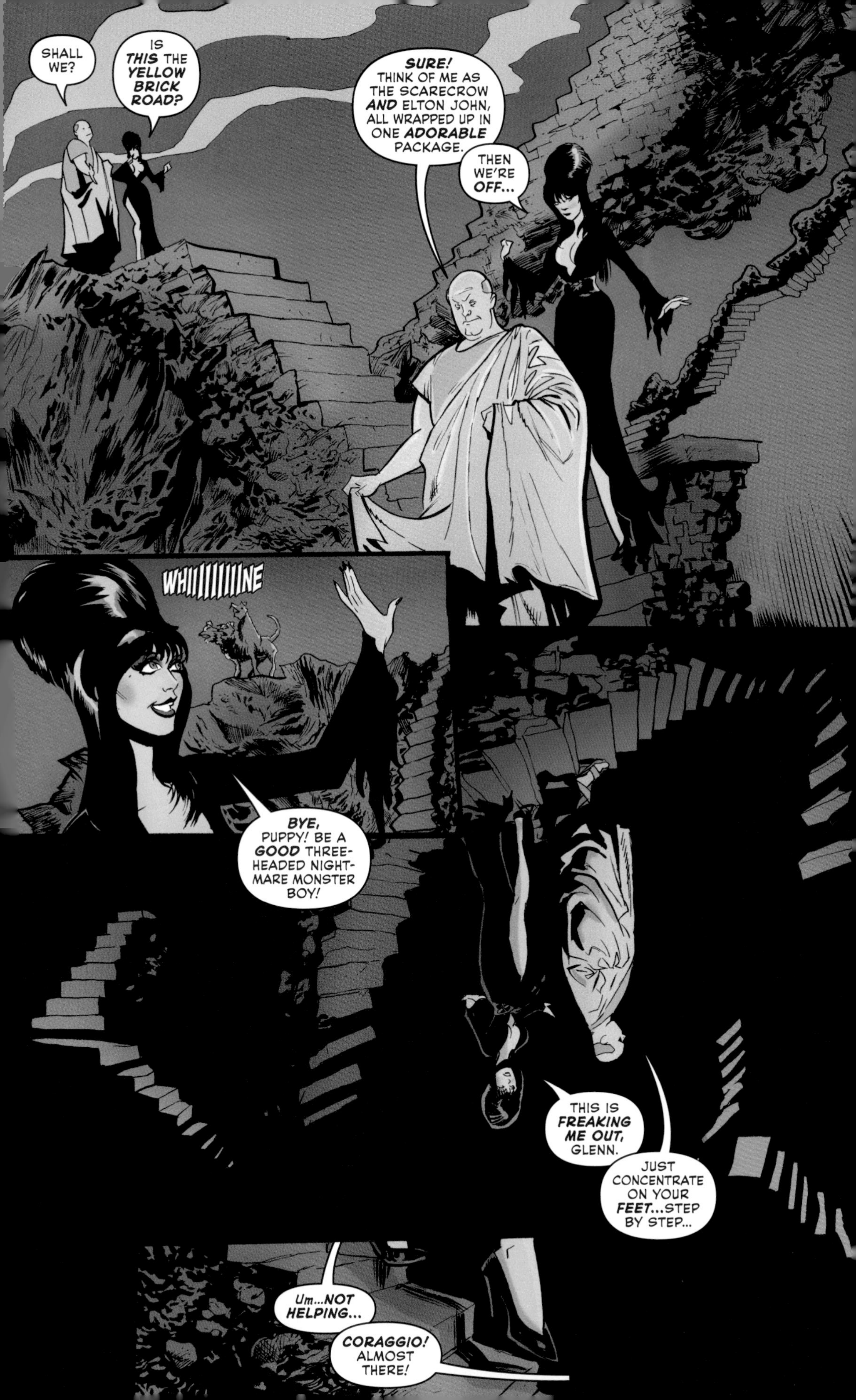
SHALL WE?
IS *THIS* THE *YELLOW BRICK ROAD?*
SURE! THINK OF ME AS THE SCARECROW *AND* ELTON JOHN, ALL WRAPPED UP IN ONE *ADORABLE* PACKAGE.
THEN WE'RE *OFF...*
WHIIIIIIIINE
BYE, PUPPY! BE A *GOOD* THREE-HEADED NIGHT-MARE MONSTER BOY!
THIS IS *FREAKING ME OUT,* GLENN.
JUST CONCENTRATE ON YOUR *FEET...*STEP BY STEP...
Um...*NOT HELPING...*
CORAGGIO! ALMOST THERE!

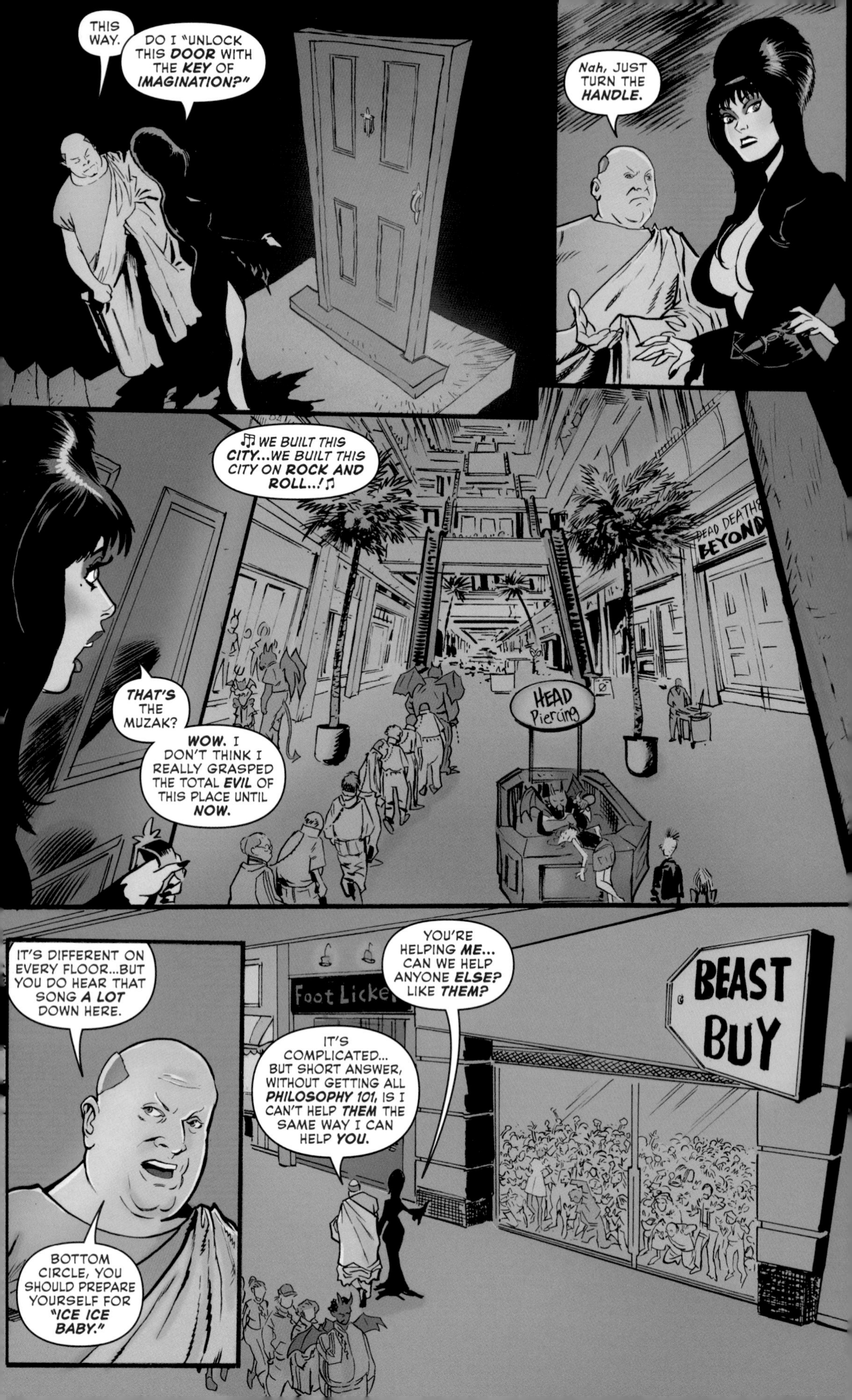
THIS WAY.
DO I "UNLOCK THIS DOOR WITH THE KEY OF IMAGINATION?"
Nah, JUST TURN THE HANDLE.
♫ WE BUILT THIS CITY...WE BUILT THIS CITY ON ROCK AND ROLL..! ♫
DEAD DEATH & BEYOND
HEAD Piercing
THAT'S THE MUZAK?
WOW. I DON'T THINK I REALLY GRASPED THE TOTAL EVIL OF THIS PLACE UNTIL NOW.
IT'S DIFFERENT ON EVERY FLOOR...BUT YOU DO HEAR THAT SONG A LOT DOWN HERE.
BOTTOM CIRCLE, YOU SHOULD PREPARE YOURSELF FOR "ICE ICE BABY."
Foot Licker
YOU'RE HELPING ME... CAN WE HELP ANYONE ELSE? LIKE THEM?
IT'S COMPLICATED... BUT SHORT ANSWER, WITHOUT GETTING ALL PHILOSOPHY 101, IS I CAN'T HELP THEM THE SAME WAY I CAN HELP YOU.
BEAST BUY

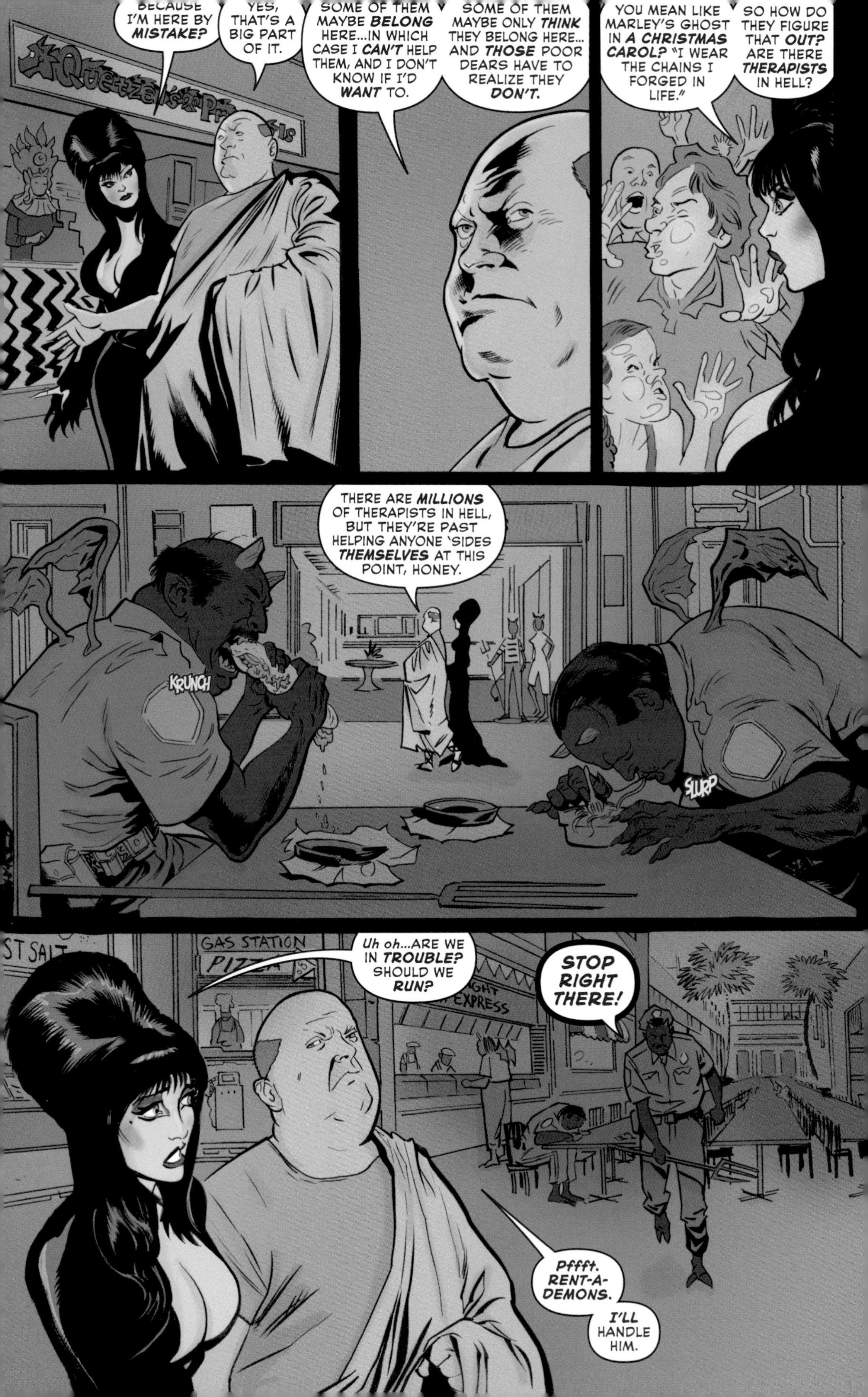
BECAUSE I'M HERE BY MISTAKE?
YES, THAT'S A BIG PART OF IT.
SOME OF THEM MAYBE BELONG HERE...IN WHICH CASE I CAN'T HELP THEM, AND I DON'T KNOW IF I'D WANT TO.
SOME OF THEM MAYBE ONLY THINK THEY BELONG HERE... AND THOSE POOR DEARS HAVE TO REALIZE THEY DON'T.
YOU MEAN LIKE MARLEY'S GHOST IN A CHRISTMAS CAROL? "I WEAR THE CHAINS I FORGED IN LIFE."
SO HOW DO THEY FIGURE THAT OUT? ARE THERE THERAPISTS IN HELL?
THERE ARE MILLIONS OF THERAPISTS IN HELL, BUT THEY'RE PAST HELPING ANYONE 'SIDES THEMSELVES AT THIS POINT, HONEY.
KRUNCH
SLURP
GAS STATION
EXPRESS
Uh oh...ARE WE IN TROUBLE? SHOULD WE RUN?
STOP RIGHT THERE!
Pffft. RENT-A-DEMONS.
I'LL HANDLE HIM.

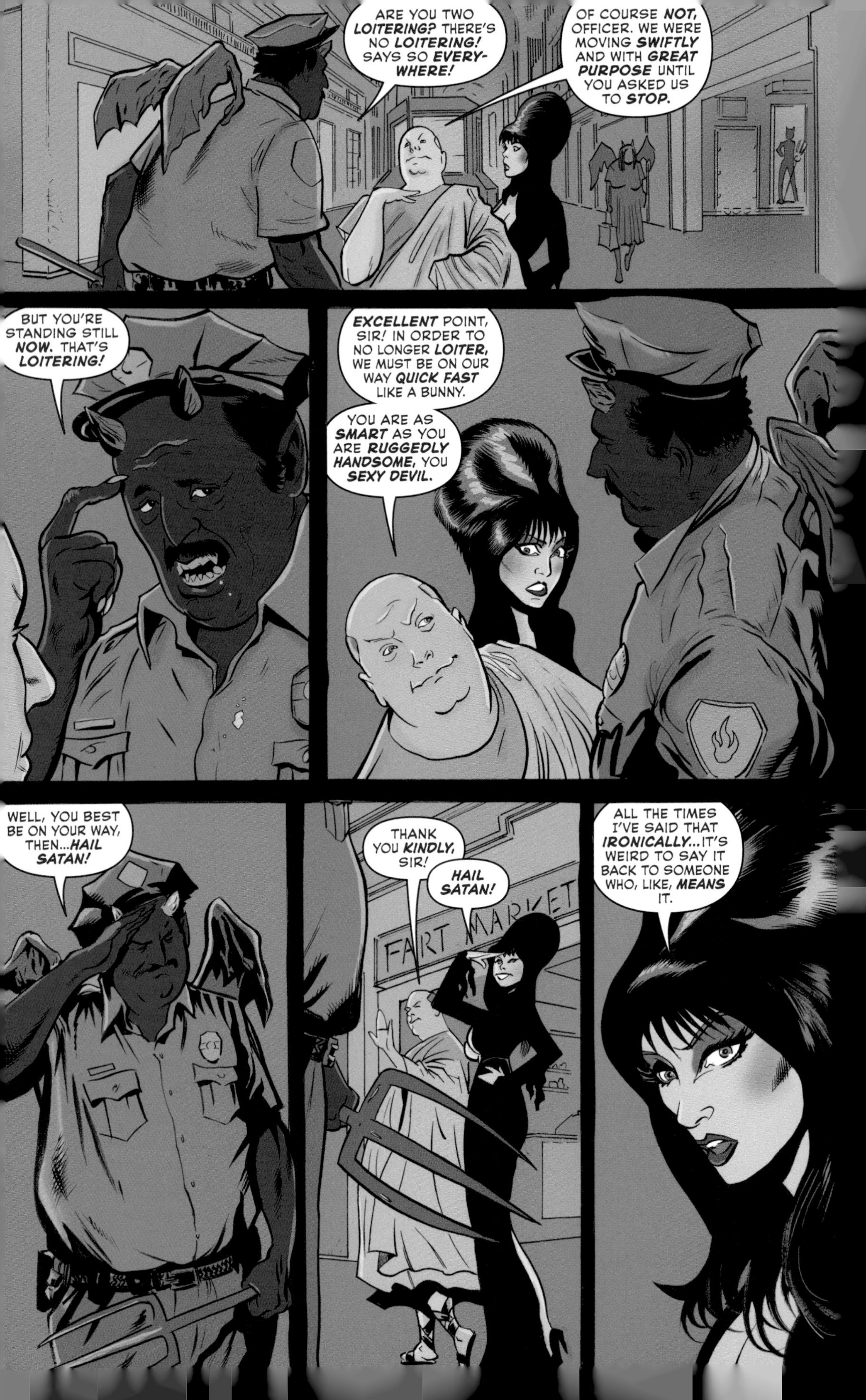
ARE YOU TWO LOITERING? THERE'S NO LOITERING! SAYS SO EVERY-WHERE!
OF COURSE NOT, OFFICER. WE WERE MOVING SWIFTLY AND WITH GREAT PURPOSE UNTIL YOU ASKED US TO STOP.
BUT YOU'RE STANDING STILL NOW. THAT'S LOITERING!
EXCELLENT POINT, SIR! IN ORDER TO NO LONGER LOITER, WE MUST BE ON OUR WAY QUICK FAST LIKE A BUNNY.
YOU ARE AS SMART AS YOU ARE RUGGEDLY HANDSOME, YOU SEXY DEVIL.
WELL, YOU BEST BE ON YOUR WAY, THEN...HAIL SATAN!
THANK YOU KINDLY, SIR!
HAIL SATAN!
FART MARKET
ALL THE TIMES I'VE SAID THAT IRONICALLY...IT'S WEIRD TO SAY IT BACK TO SOMEONE WHO, LIKE, MEANS IT.

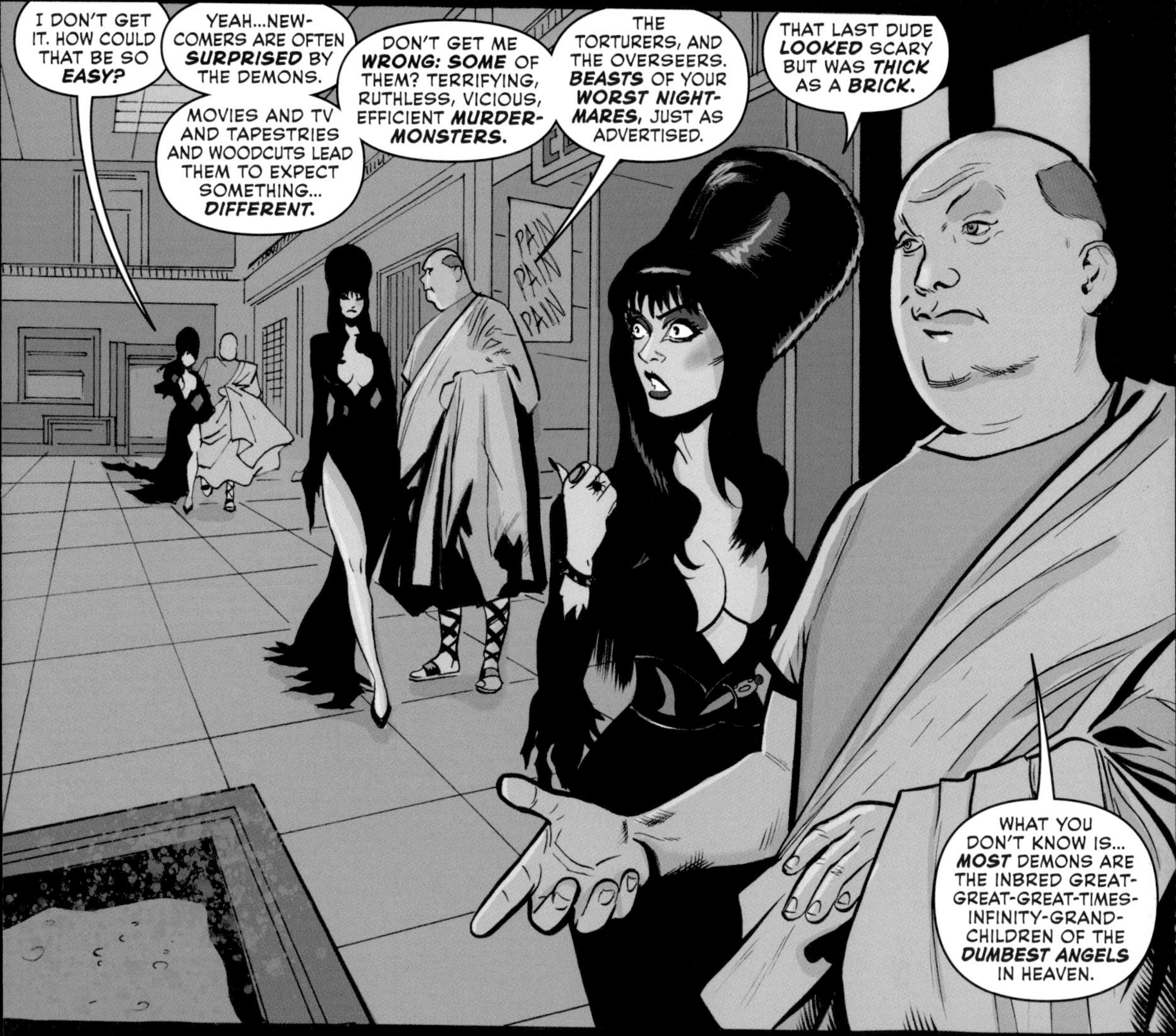
I DON'T GET IT. HOW COULD THAT BE SO **EASY?**
YEAH...NEW-COMERS ARE OFTEN **SURPRISED** BY THE DEMONS.
MOVIES AND TV AND TAPESTRIES AND WOODCUTS LEAD THEM TO EXPECT SOMETHING... **DIFFERENT.**
DON'T GET ME **WRONG: SOME** OF THEM? TERRIFYING, RUTHLESS, VICIOUS, EFFICIENT **MURDER-MONSTERS.**
THE TORTURERS, AND THE OVERSEERS. **BEASTS** OF YOUR **WORST NIGHT-MARES,** JUST AS ADVERTISED.
PAIN PAIN PAIN
THAT LAST DUDE **LOOKED** SCARY BUT WAS **THICK** AS A **BRICK.**
WHAT YOU DON'T KNOW IS... **MOST** DEMONS ARE THE INBRED GREAT-GREAT-GREAT-TIMES-INFINITY-GRAND-CHILDREN OF THE **DUMBEST ANGELS** IN HEAVEN.
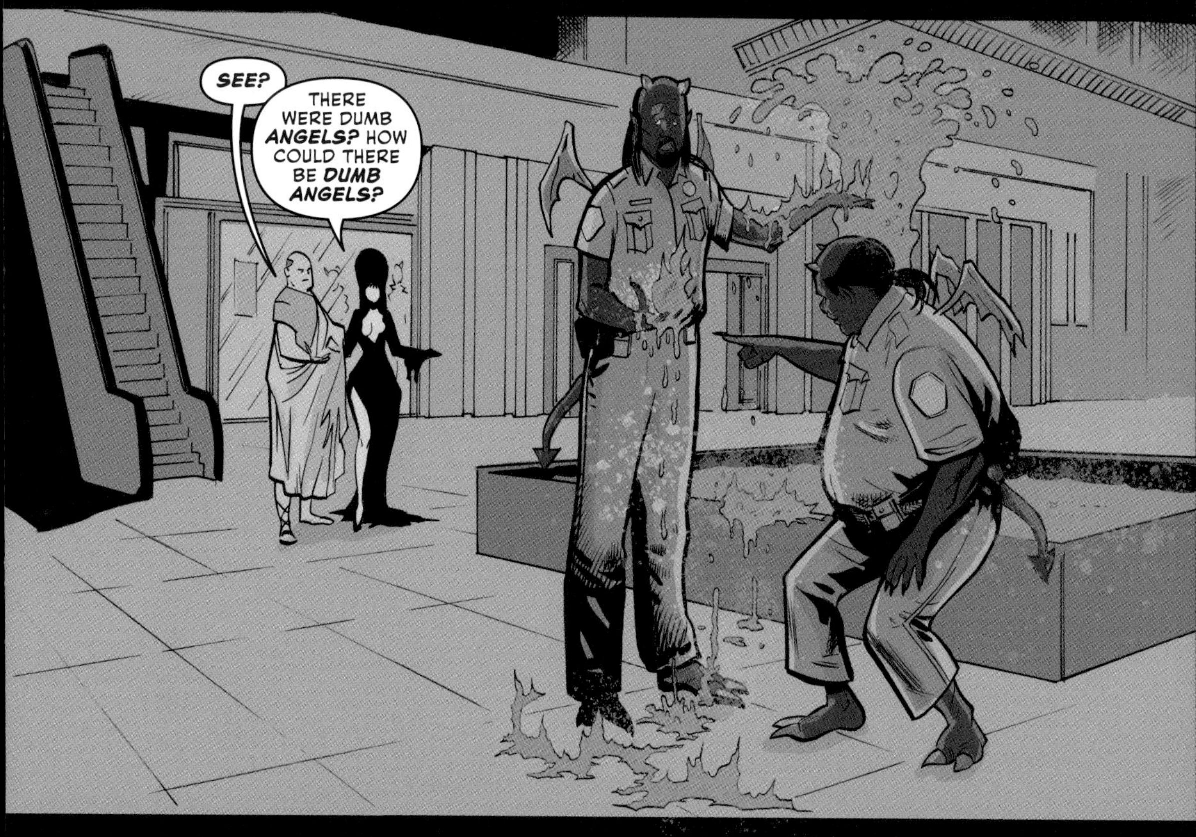
SEE?
THERE WERE DUMB **ANGELS?** HOW COULD THERE BE **DUMB ANGELS?**

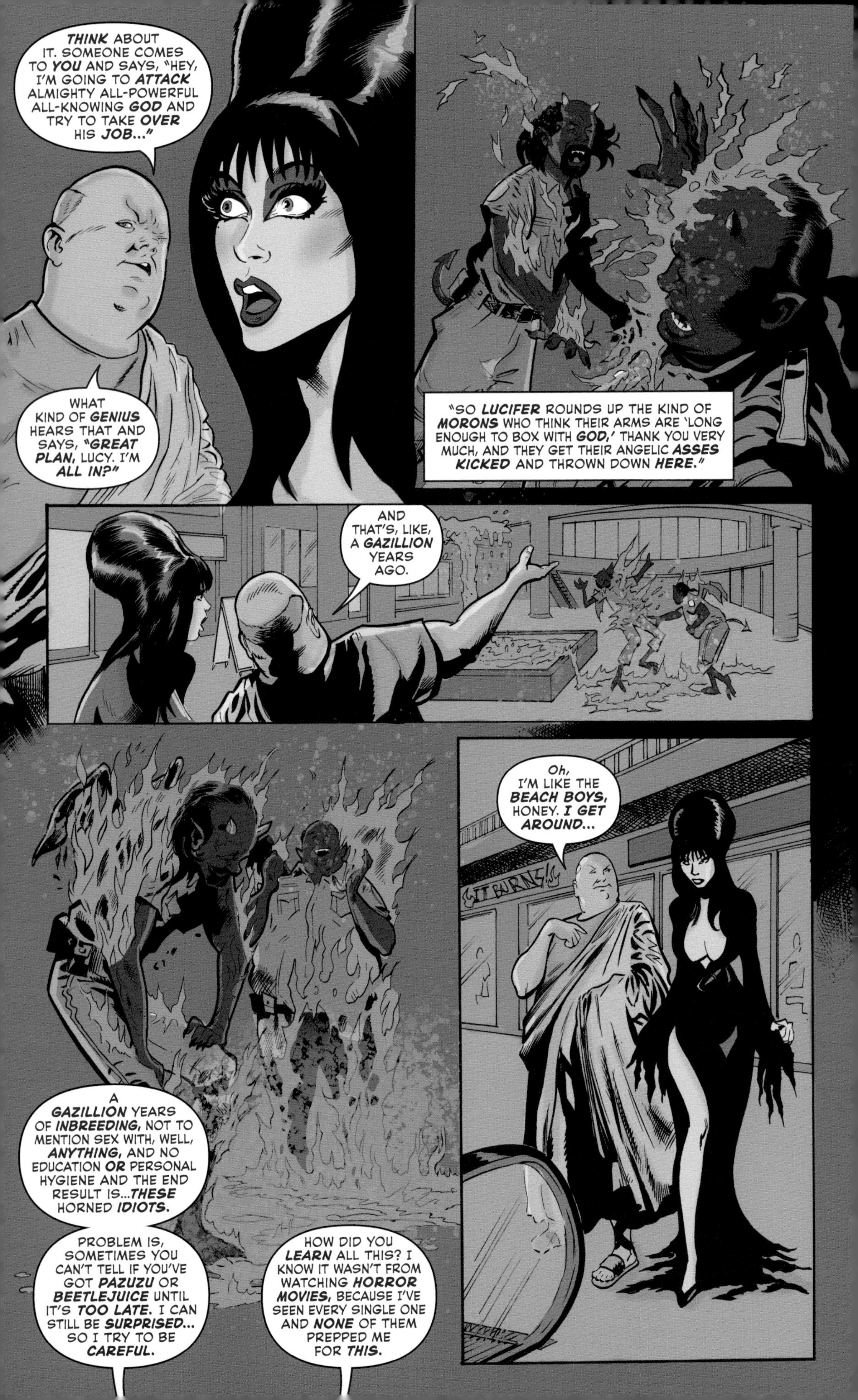
THINK ABOUT IT. SOMEONE COMES TO YOU AND SAYS, "HEY, I'M GOING TO ATTACK ALMIGHTY ALL-POWERFUL ALL-KNOWING GOD AND TRY TO TAKE OVER HIS JOB..."
WHAT KIND OF GENIUS HEARS THAT AND SAYS, "GREAT PLAN, LUCY. I'M ALL IN?"
"SO LUCIFER ROUNDS UP THE KIND OF MORONS WHO THINK THEIR ARMS ARE 'LONG ENOUGH TO BOX WITH GOD,' THANK YOU VERY MUCH, AND THEY GET THEIR ANGELIC ASSES KICKED AND THROWN DOWN HERE."
AND THAT'S, LIKE, A GAZILLION YEARS AGO.
A GAZILLION YEARS OF INBREEDING, NOT TO MENTION SEX WITH, WELL, ANYTHING, AND NO EDUCATION OR PERSONAL HYGIENE AND THE END RESULT IS...THESE HORNED IDIOTS.
PROBLEM IS, SOMETIMES YOU CAN'T TELL IF YOU'VE GOT PAZUZU OR BEETLEJUICE UNTIL IT'S TOO LATE. I CAN STILL BE SURPRISED... SO I TRY TO BE CAREFUL.
HOW DID YOU LEARN ALL THIS? I KNOW IT WASN'T FROM WATCHING HORROR MOVIES, BECAUSE I'VE SEEN EVERY SINGLE ONE AND NONE OF THEM PREPPED ME FOR THIS.
Oh, I'M LIKE THE BEACH BOYS, HONEY. I GET AROUND...
IT BURNS

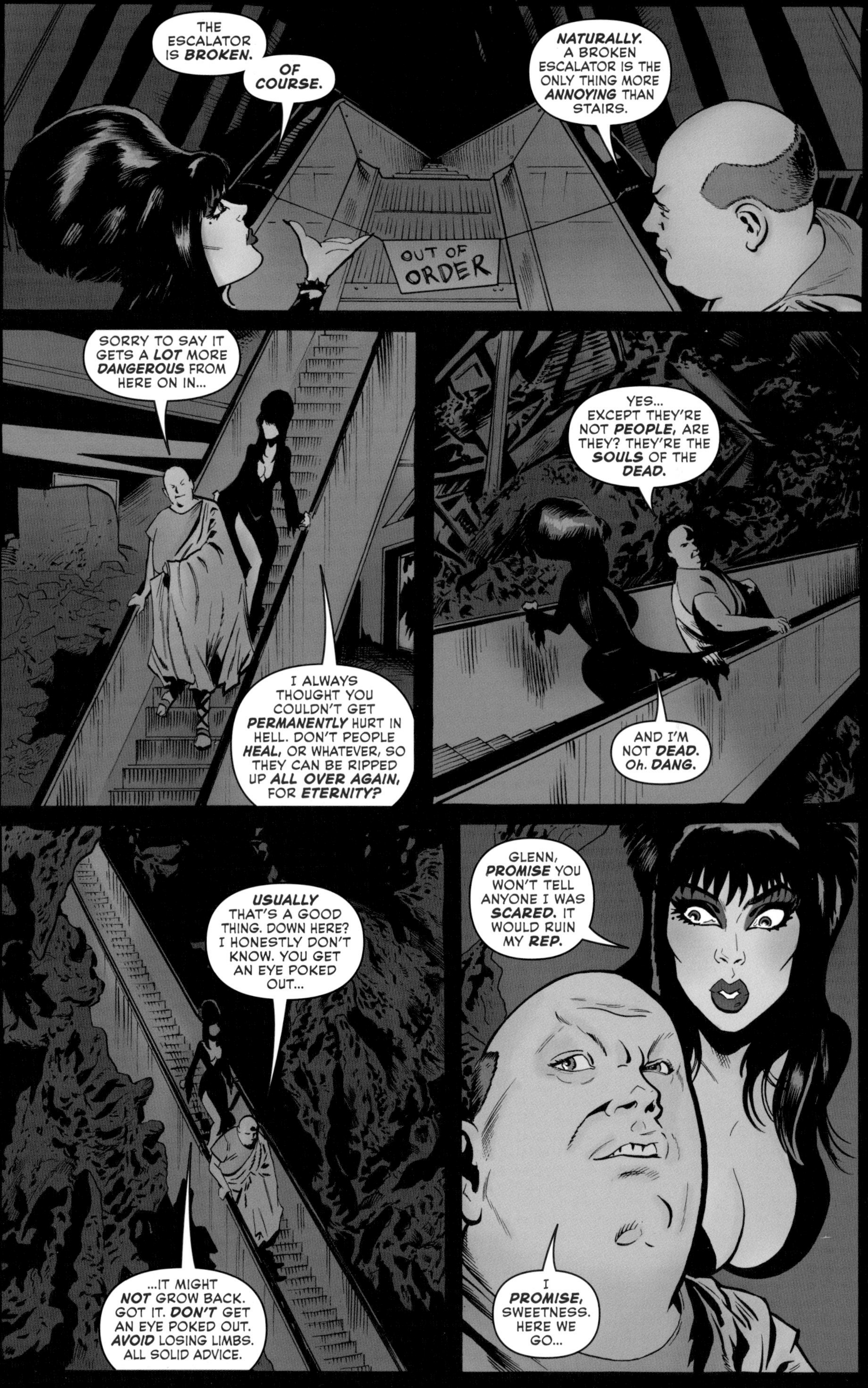
THE ESCALATOR IS **BROKEN.**
OF COURSE.
OUT OF ORDER
NATURALLY. A BROKEN ESCALATOR IS THE ONLY THING MORE ***ANNOYING*** THAN STAIRS.
SORRY TO SAY IT GETS A ***LOT*** MORE ***DANGEROUS*** FROM HERE ON IN...
I ALWAYS THOUGHT YOU COULDN'T GET ***PERMANENTLY*** HURT IN HELL. DON'T PEOPLE ***HEAL,*** OR WHATEVER, SO THEY CAN BE RIPPED UP ***ALL OVER AGAIN,*** FOR ***ETERNITY?***
YES... EXCEPT THEY'RE NOT ***PEOPLE,*** ARE THEY? THEY'RE THE ***SOULS*** OF THE ***DEAD.***
AND I'M NOT ***DEAD.*** *Oh.* ***DANG.***
USUALLY THAT'S A GOOD THING. DOWN HERE? I HONESTLY DON'T KNOW. YOU GET AN EYE POKED OUT...
...IT MIGHT ***NOT*** GROW BACK.
GOT IT. ***DON'T*** GET AN EYE POKED OUT. ***AVOID*** LOSING LIMBS. ALL SOLID ADVICE.
GLENN, ***PROMISE*** YOU WON'T TELL ANYONE I WAS ***SCARED.*** IT WOULD RUIN MY ***REP.***
I ***PROMISE,*** SWEETNESS. HERE WE GO...

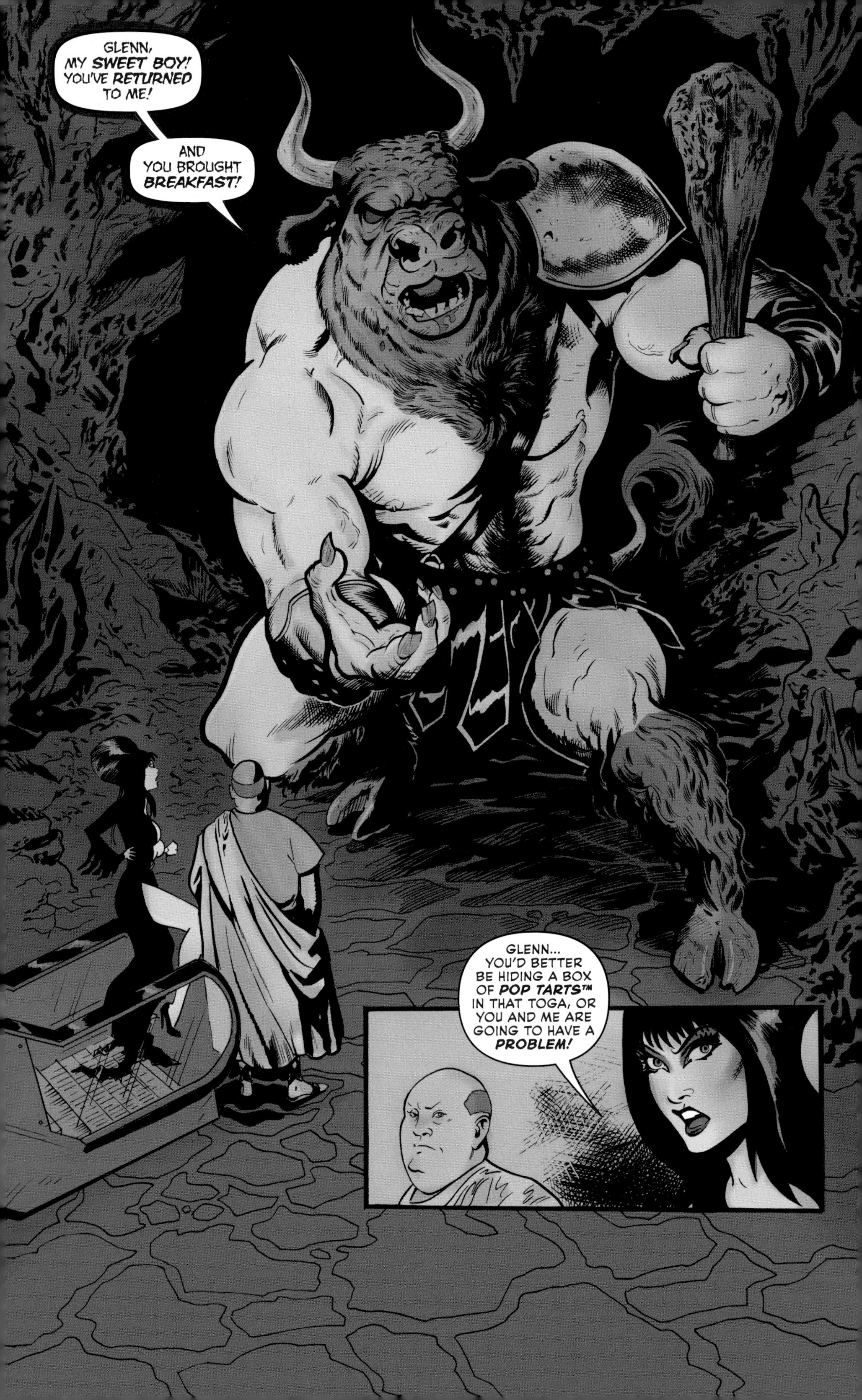
GLENN, MY SWEET BOY! YOU'VE RETURNED TO ME!
AND YOU BROUGHT BREAKFAST!
GLENN... YOU'D BETTER BE HIDING A BOX OF POP TARTS™ IN THAT TOGA, OR YOU AND ME ARE GOING TO HAVE A PROBLEM!

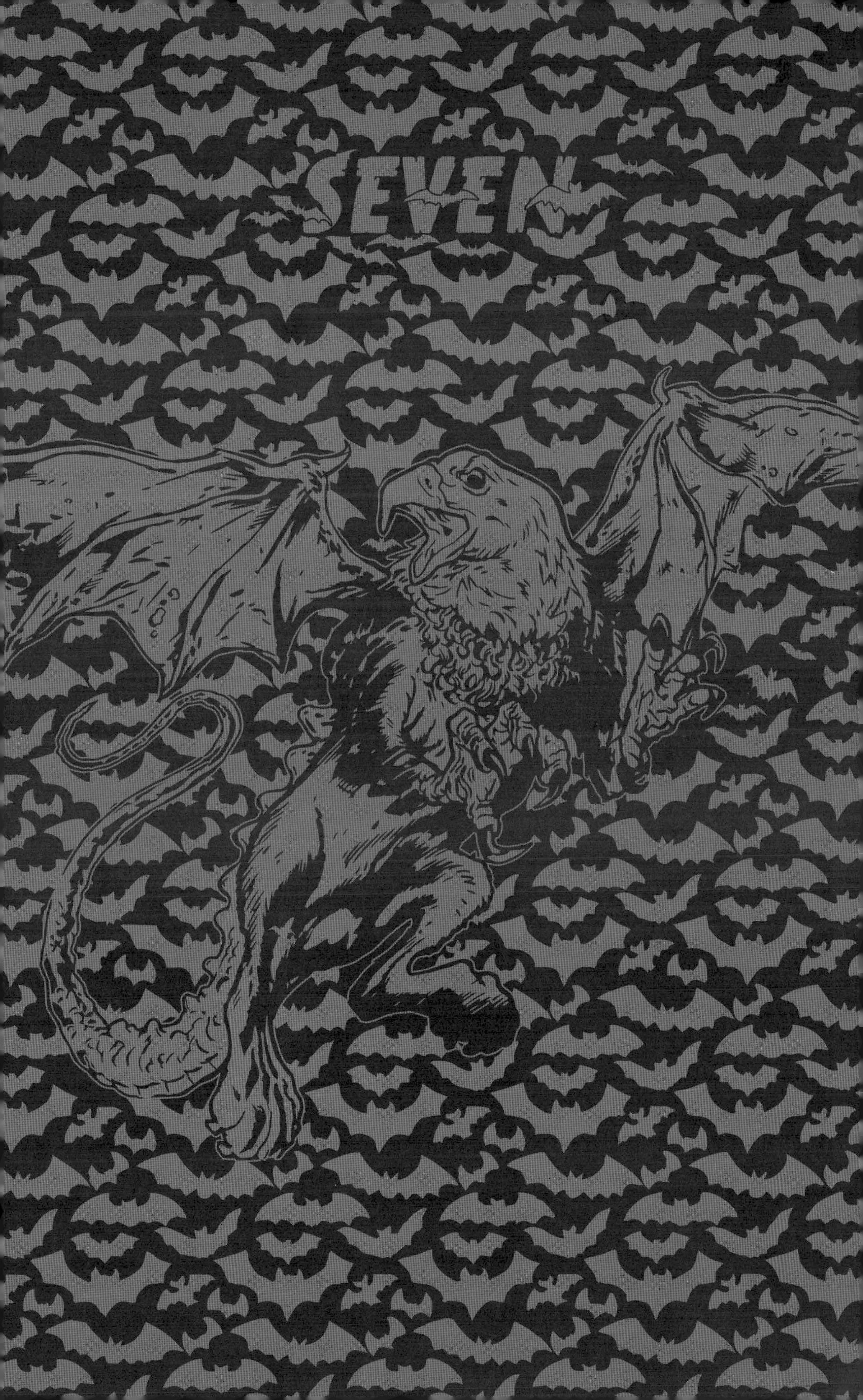
SEVEN

7

COVER ART: LUCIO PARRILLO

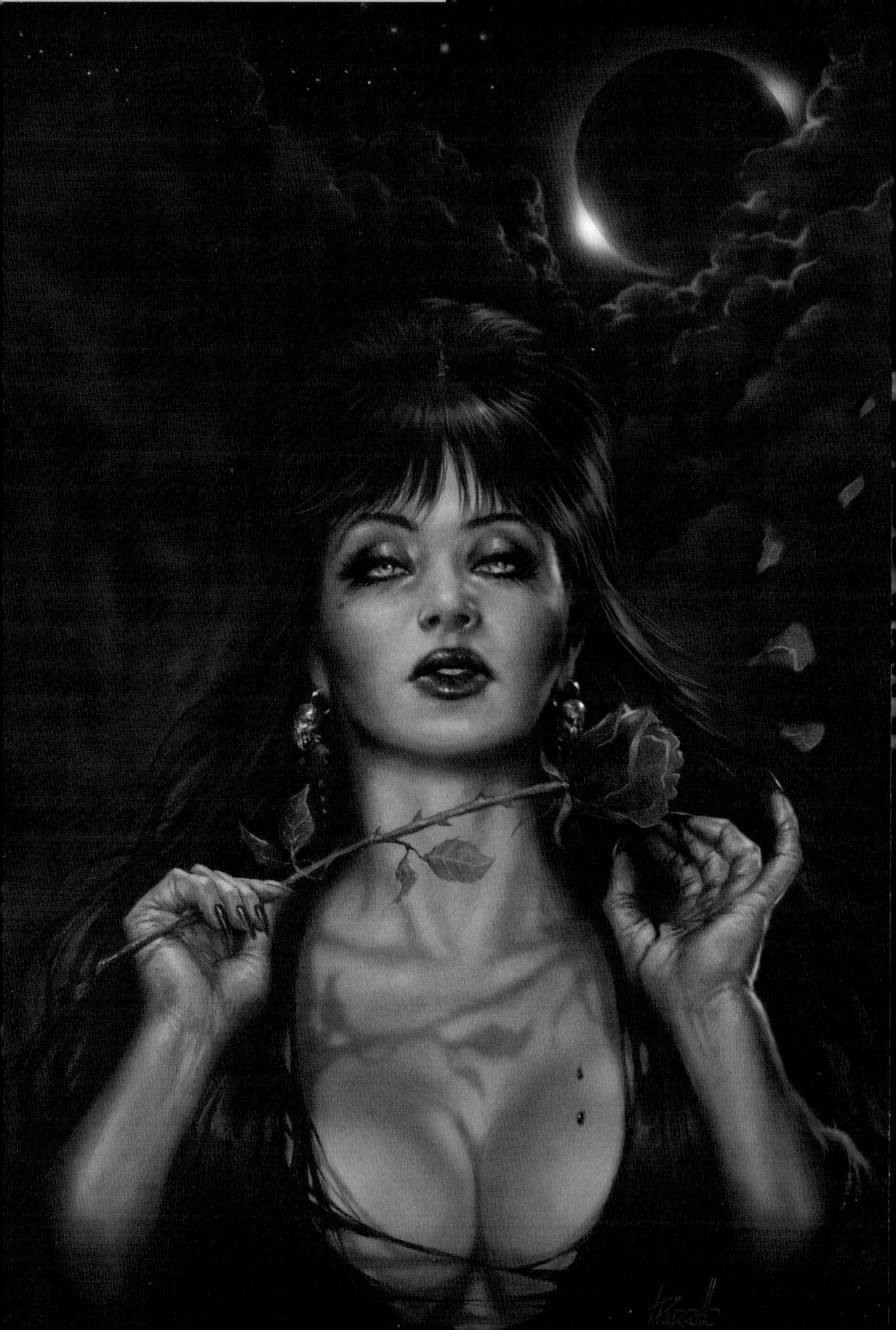

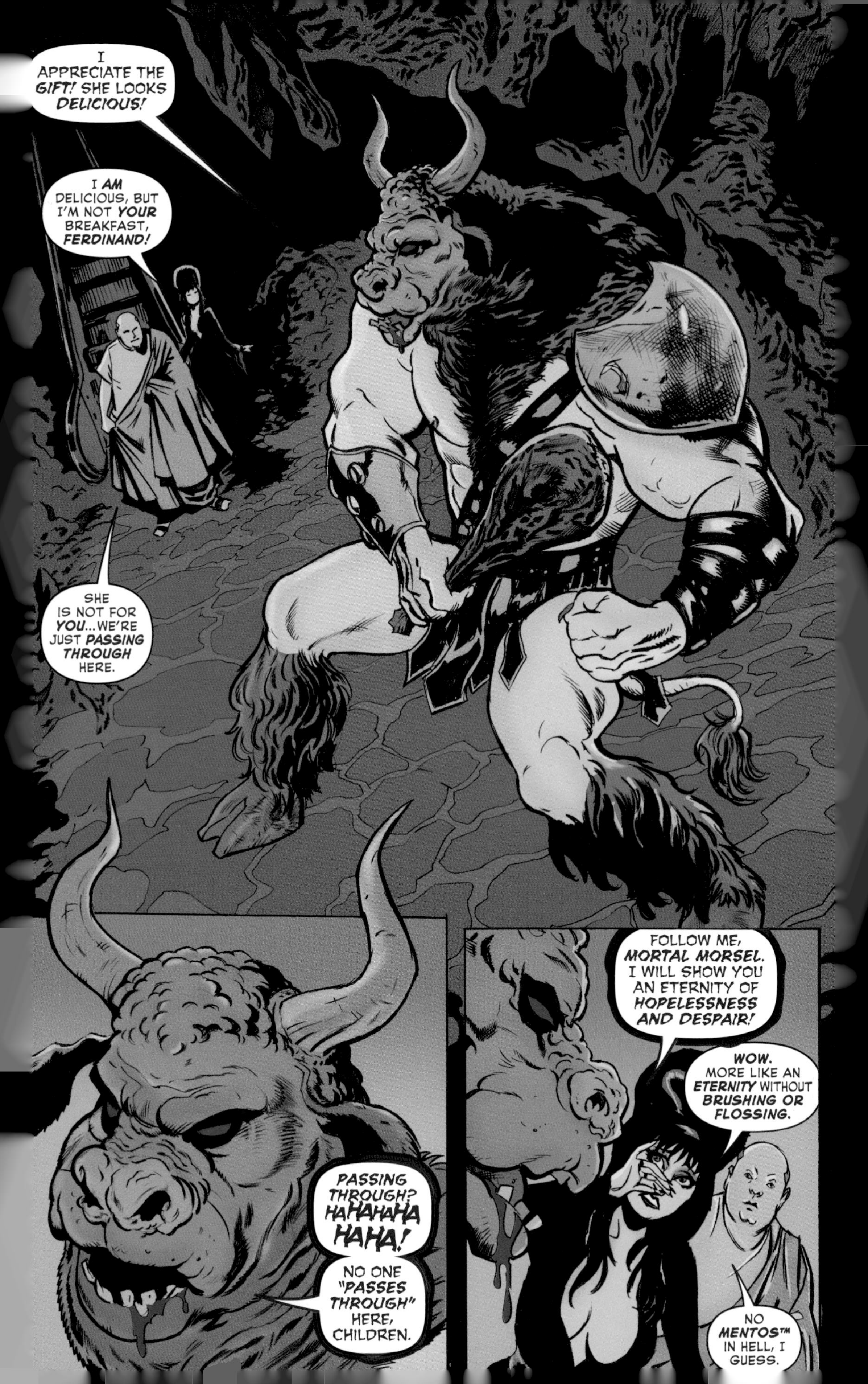
I APPRECIATE THE GIFT! SHE LOOKS DELICIOUS!
I AM DELICIOUS, BUT I'M NOT YOUR BREAKFAST, FERDINAND!
SHE IS NOT FOR YOU...WE'RE JUST PASSING THROUGH HERE.
PASSING THROUGH? HAHAHAHA HAHA!
NO ONE "PASSES THROUGH" HERE, CHILDREN.
FOLLOW ME, MORTAL MORSEL. I WILL SHOW YOU AN ETERNITY OF HOPELESSNESS AND DESPAIR!
WOW. MORE LIKE AN ETERNITY WITHOUT BRUSHING OR FLOSSING.
NO MENTOS™ IN HELL, I GUESS.

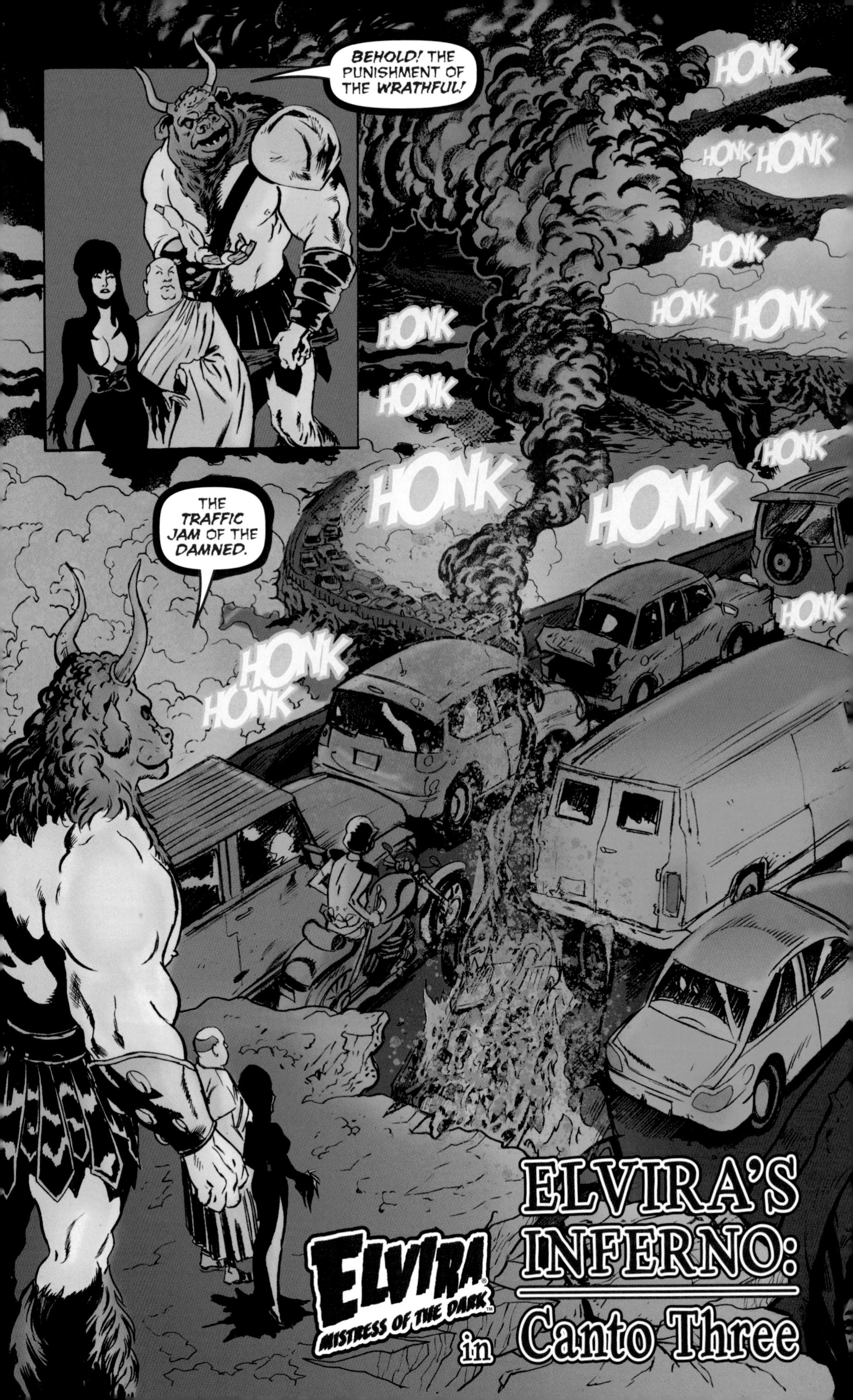
BEHOLD! THE PUNISHMENT OF THE WRATHFUL!
HONK
HONK HONK
HONK
HONK HONK
HONK
HONK
HONK
HONK
HONK
THE TRAFFIC JAM OF THE DAMNED.
HONK
HONK
HONK
ELVIRA MISTRESS OF THE DARK in
ELVIRA'S INFERNO:
Canto Three

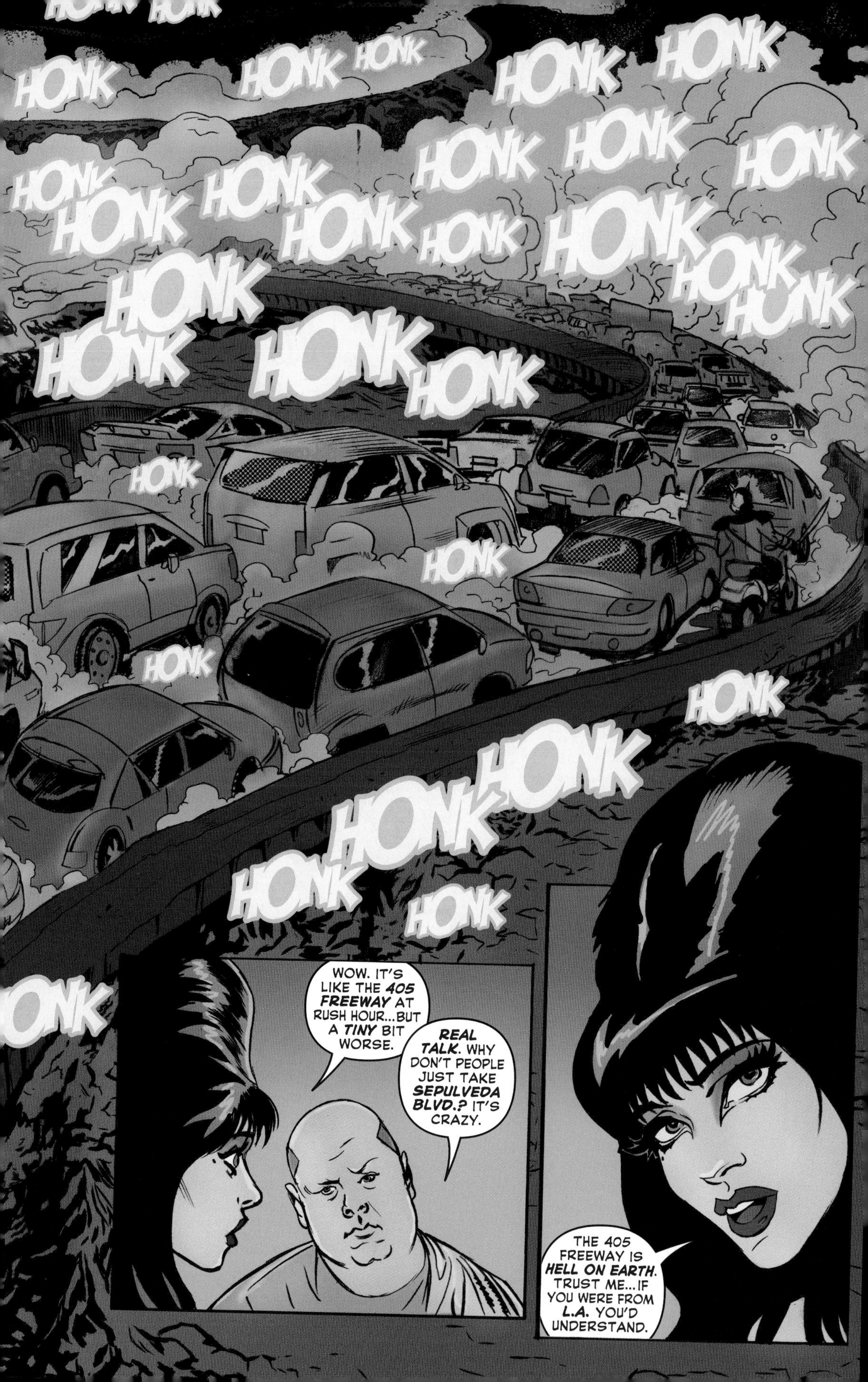
HONK HONK
HONK HONK HONK HONK HONK
HONK HONK HONK
HONK HONK HONK HONK HONK HONK
HONK HONK HONK HONK
HONK HONK HONK
HONK HONK HONK
HONK HONK HONK
HONK HONK HONK
ONK
WOW. IT'S LIKE THE 405 FREEWAY AT RUSH HOUR...BUT A TINY BIT WORSE.
REAL TALK. WHY DON'T PEOPLE JUST TAKE SEPULVEDA BLVD.? IT'S CRAZY.
THE 405 FREEWAY IS HELL ON EARTH. TRUST ME...IF YOU WERE FROM L.A. YOU'D UNDERSTAND.

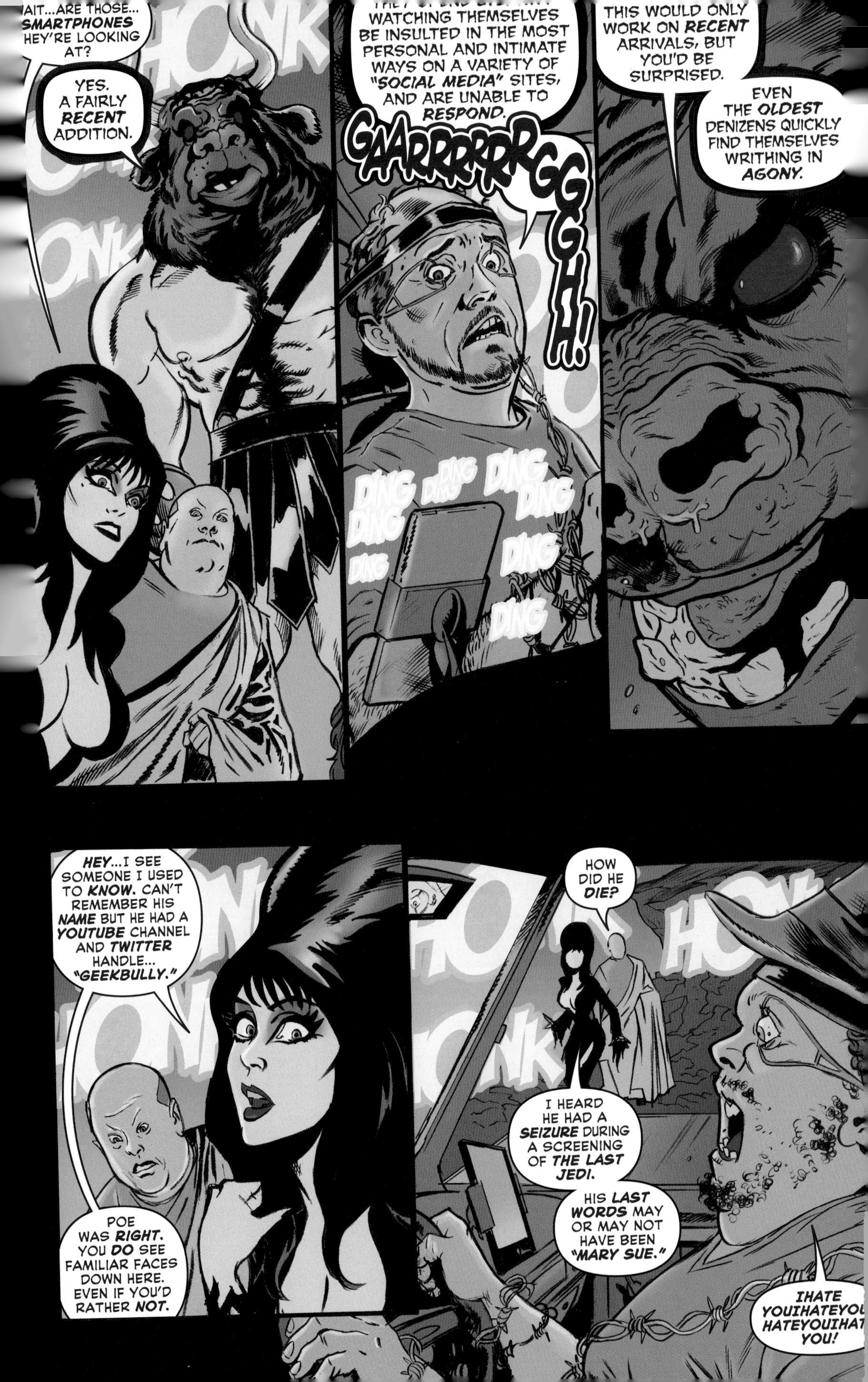
AIT...ARE THOSE... SMARTPHONES HEY'RE LOOKING AT?
YES. A FAIRLY RECENT ADDITION.
WATCHING THEMSELVES BE INSULTED IN THE MOST PERSONAL AND INTIMATE WAYS ON A VARIETY OF "SOCIAL MEDIA" SITES, AND ARE UNABLE TO RESPOND.
GAARRRRRRRGGGHH!
DING DING DING DING DING DING DING DING DING
THIS WOULD ONLY WORK ON RECENT ARRIVALS, BUT YOU'D BE SURPRISED.
EVEN THE OLDEST DENIZENS QUICKLY FIND THEMSELVES WRITHING IN AGONY.
HEY...I SEE SOMEONE I USED TO KNOW. CAN'T REMEMBER HIS NAME BUT HE HAD A YOUTUBE CHANNEL AND TWITTER HANDLE... "GEEKBULLY."
POE WAS RIGHT. YOU DO SEE FAMILIAR FACES DOWN HERE. EVEN IF YOU'D RATHER NOT.
HOW DID HE DIE?
I HEARD HE HAD A SEIZURE DURING A SCREENING OF THE LAST JEDI.
HIS LAST WORDS MAY OR MAY NOT HAVE BEEN "MARY SUE."
IHATE YOUIHATEYOU HATEYOUIHAT YOU!

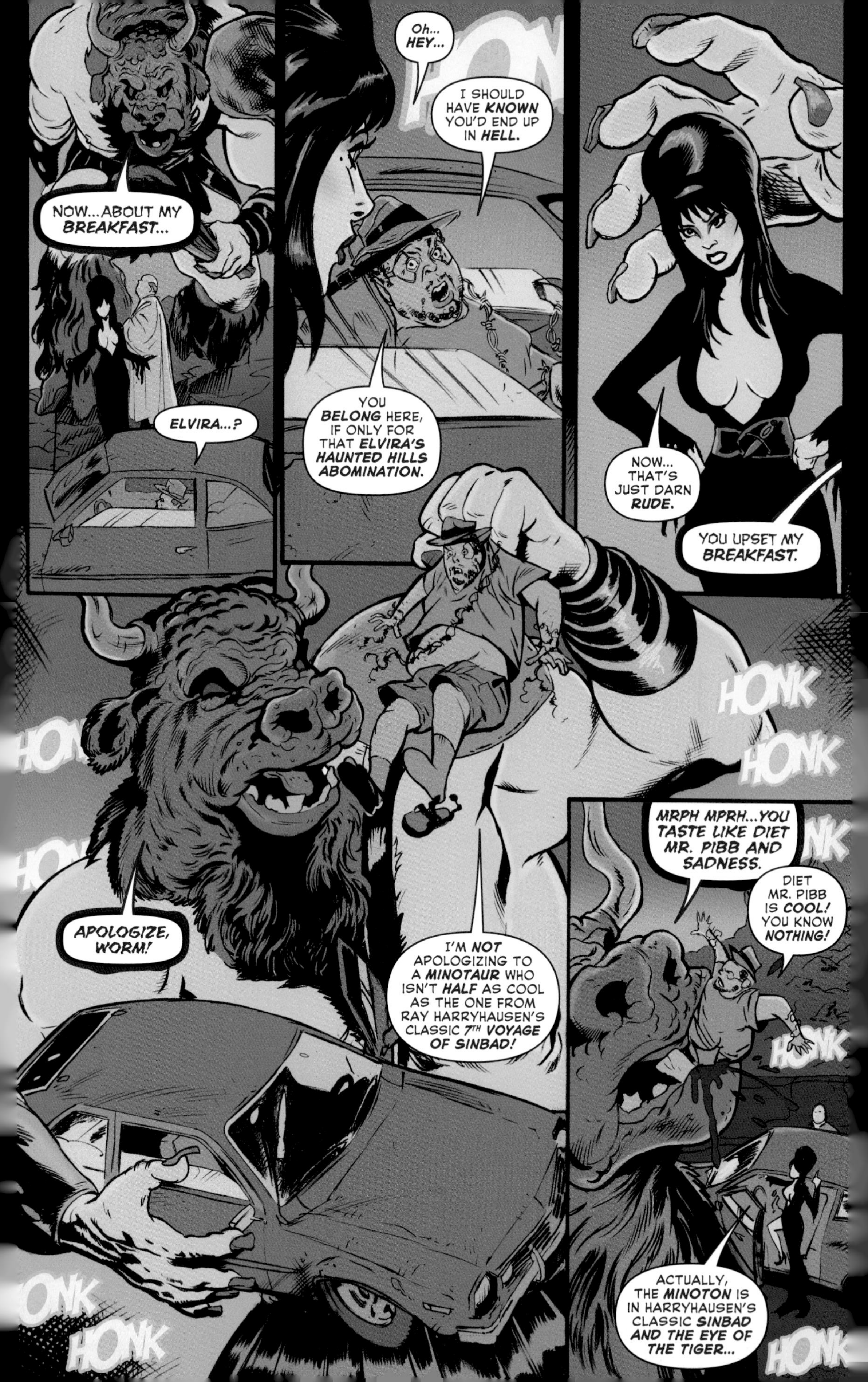

NOW...ABOUT MY BREAKFAST...
ELVIRA...?
Oh... HEY...
I SHOULD HAVE KNOWN YOU'D END UP IN HELL.
YOU BELONG HERE, IF ONLY FOR THAT ELVIRA'S HAUNTED HILLS ABOMINATION.
NOW... THAT'S JUST DARN RUDE.
YOU UPSET MY BREAKFAST.
HONK
HONK
HONK
APOLOGIZE, WORM!
I'M NOT APOLOGIZING TO A MINOTAUR WHO ISN'T HALF AS COOL AS THE ONE FROM RAY HARRYHAUSEN'S CLASSIC 7TH VOYAGE OF SINBAD!
MRPH MPRH...YOU TASTE LIKE DIET MR. PIBB AND SADNESS.
DIET MR. PIBB IS COOL! YOU KNOW NOTHING!
HONK
ACTUALLY, THE MINOTON IS IN HARRYHAUSEN'S CLASSIC SINBAD AND THE EYE OF THE TIGER...
HONK
HONK

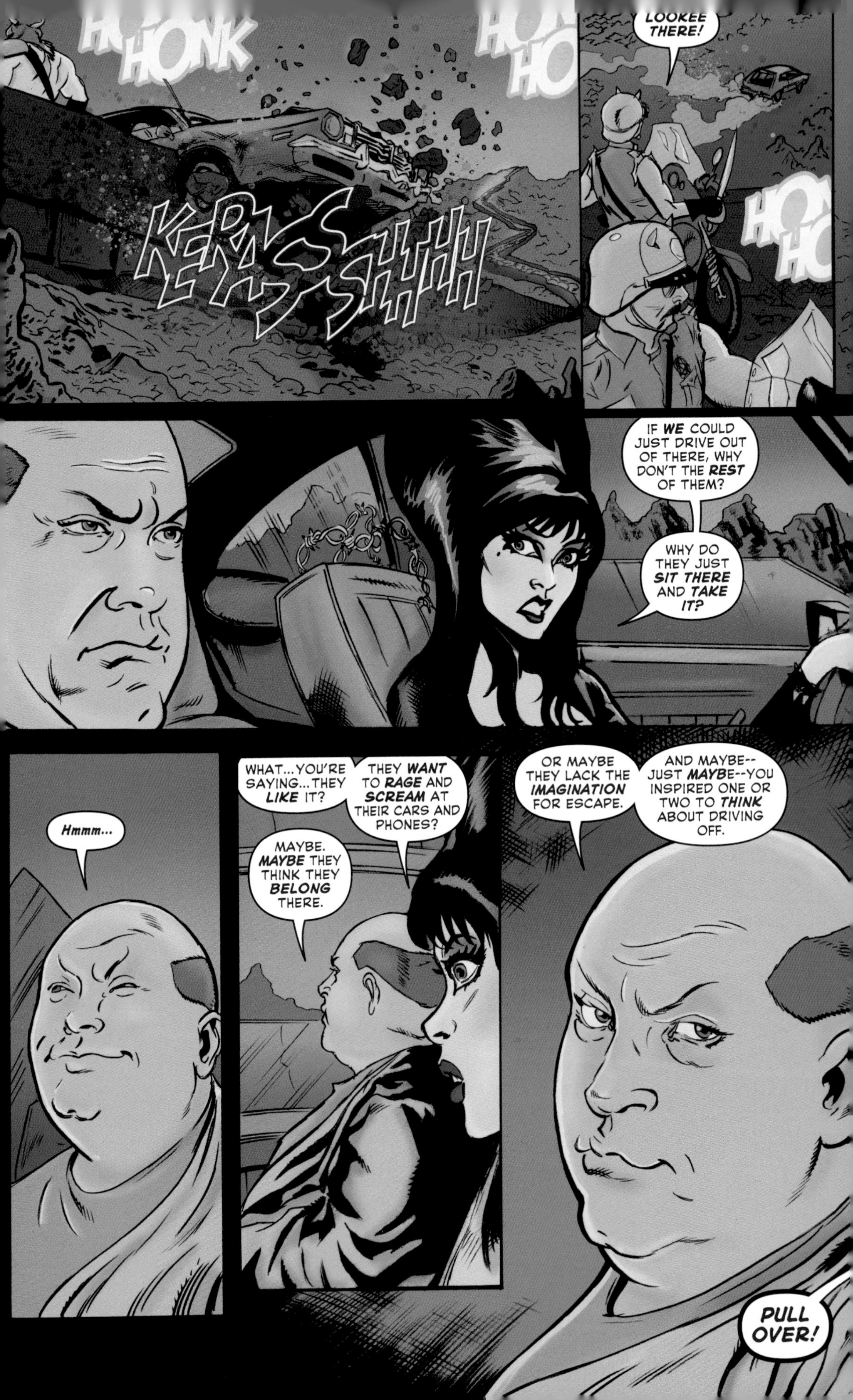
HONK HONK
LOOKEE THERE!
HONK HONK
KERASHHH
HONK HONK
IF WE COULD JUST DRIVE OUT OF THERE, WHY DON'T THE REST OF THEM?
WHY DO THEY JUST SIT THERE AND TAKE IT?
Hmmm...
WHAT...YOU'RE SAYING...THEY LIKE IT?
THEY WANT TO RAGE AND SCREAM AT THEIR CARS AND PHONES?
MAYBE. MAYBE THEY THINK THEY BELONG THERE.
OR MAYBE THEY LACK THE IMAGINATION FOR ESCAPE.
AND MAYBE--JUST MAYBE--YOU INSPIRED ONE OR TWO TO THINK ABOUT DRIVING OFF.
PULL OVER!

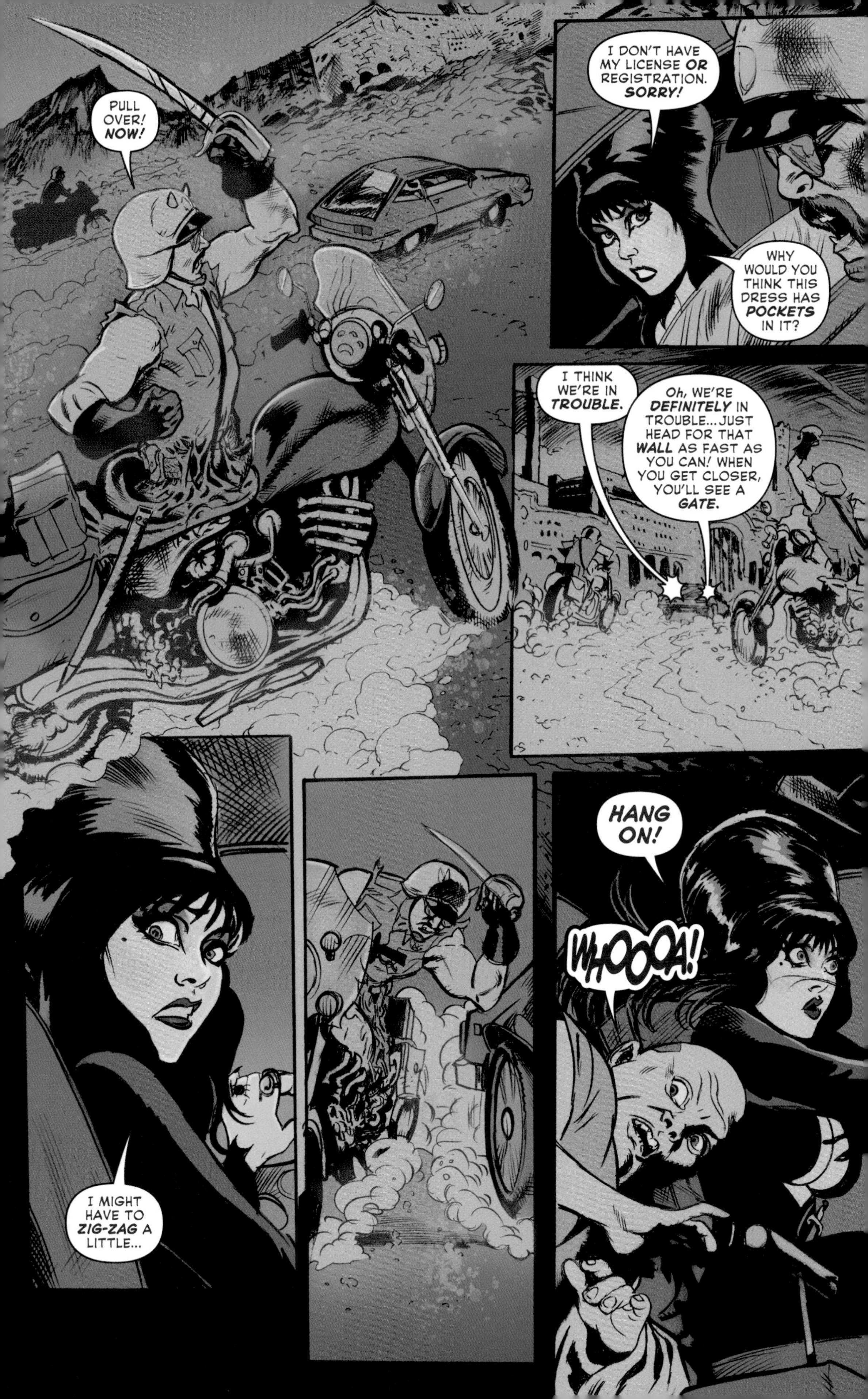

PULL OVER! NOW!
I DON'T HAVE MY LICENSE OR REGISTRATION. SORRY!
WHY WOULD YOU THINK THIS DRESS HAS POCKETS IN IT?
I THINK WE'RE IN TROUBLE.
Oh, WE'RE DEFINITELY IN TROUBLE...JUST HEAD FOR THAT WALL AS FAST AS YOU CAN! WHEN YOU GET CLOSER, YOU'LL SEE A GATE.
I MIGHT HAVE TO ZIG-ZAG A LITTLE...
HANG ON!
WHOOOA!

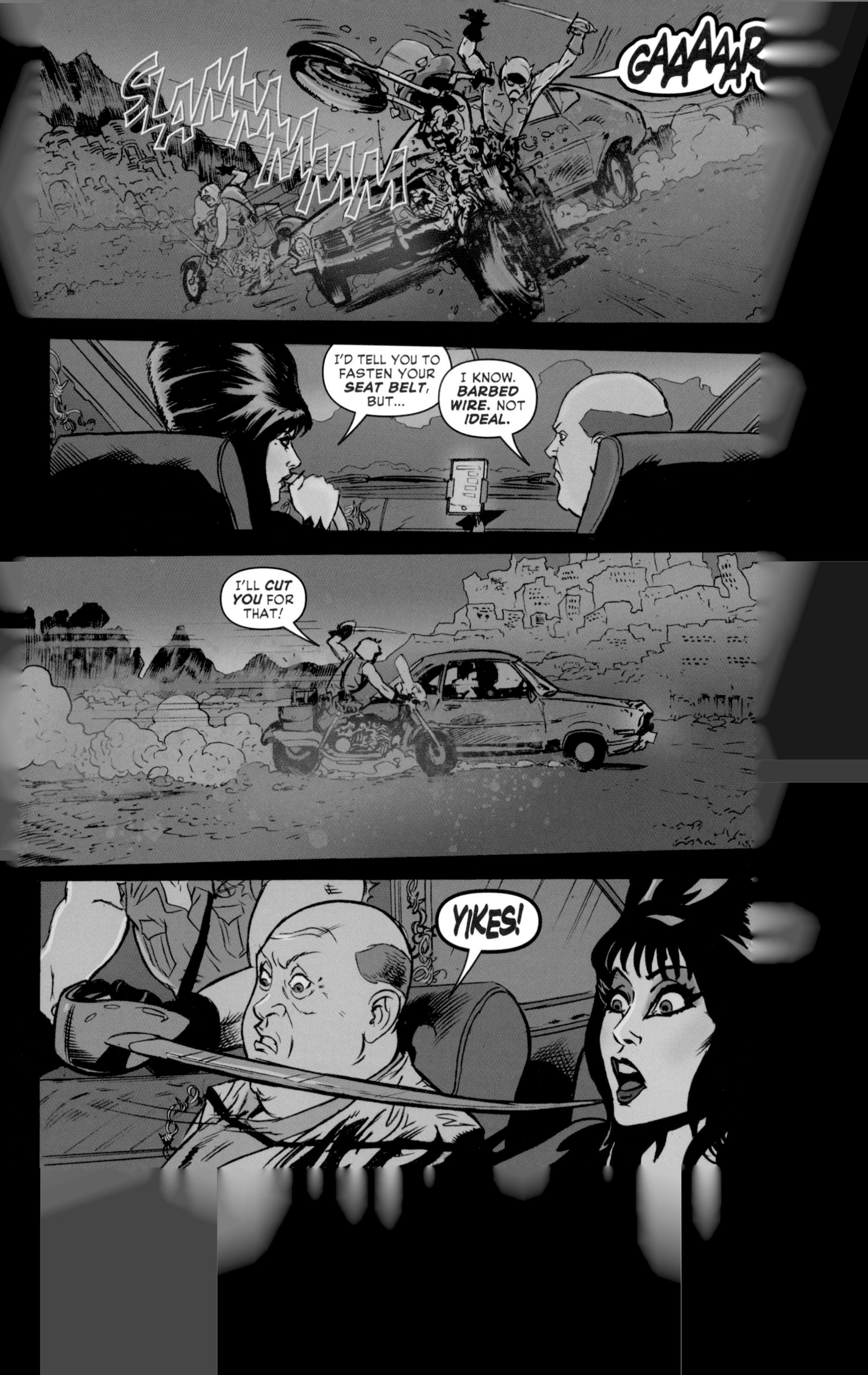
SLAMMMMMMM
GAAAAAR
I'D TELL YOU TO FASTEN YOUR **SEAT BELT**, BUT...
I KNOW. **BARBED WIRE.** NOT **IDEAL.**
I'LL **CUT YOU** FOR THAT!
YIKES!

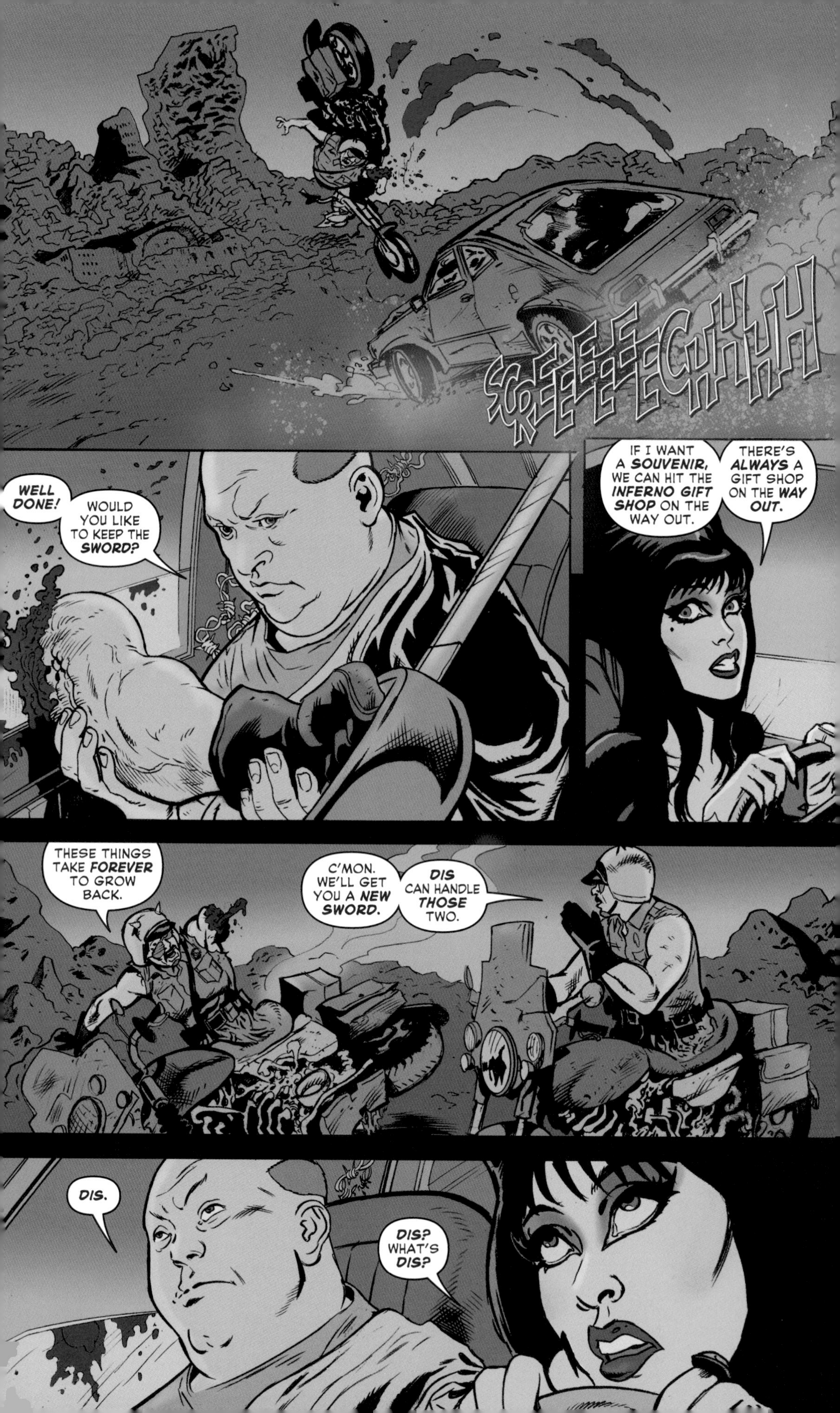
SCREEEEEECHHHHH
WELL DONE!
WOULD YOU LIKE TO KEEP THE SWORD?
IF I WANT A SOUVENIR, WE CAN HIT THE INFERNO GIFT SHOP ON THE WAY OUT.
THERE'S ALWAYS A GIFT SHOP ON THE WAY OUT.
THESE THINGS TAKE FOREVER TO GROW BACK.
C'MON. WE'LL GET YOU A NEW SWORD.
DIS CAN HANDLE THOSE TWO.
DIS.
DIS? WHAT'S DIS?

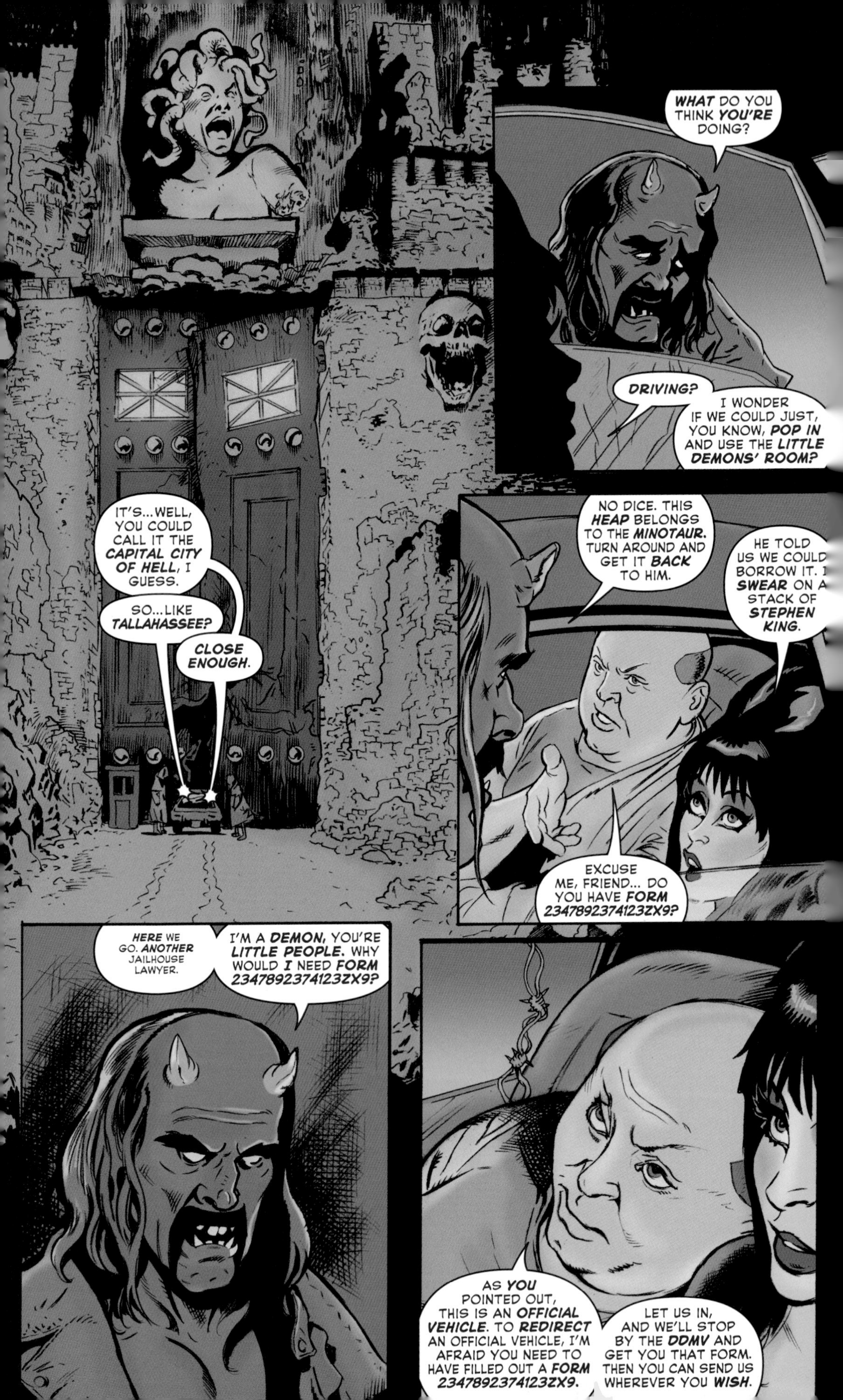
IT'S...WELL, YOU COULD CALL IT THE CAPITAL CITY OF HELL, I GUESS.
SO...LIKE TALLAHASSEE?
CLOSE ENOUGH.
WHAT DO YOU THINK YOU'RE DOING?
DRIVING?
I WONDER IF WE COULD JUST, YOU KNOW, POP IN AND USE THE LITTLE DEMONS' ROOM?
NO DICE. THIS HEAP BELONGS TO THE MINOTAUR. TURN AROUND AND GET IT BACK TO HIM.
HE TOLD US WE COULD BORROW IT. I SWEAR ON A STACK OF STEPHEN KING.
EXCUSE ME, FRIEND... DO YOU HAVE FORM 2347892374123ZX9?
HERE WE GO. ANOTHER JAILHOUSE LAWYER.
I'M A DEMON, YOU'RE LITTLE PEOPLE. WHY WOULD I NEED FORM 2347892374123ZX9?
AS YOU POINTED OUT, THIS IS AN OFFICIAL VEHICLE. TO REDIRECT AN OFFICIAL VEHICLE, I'M AFRAID YOU NEED TO HAVE FILLED OUT A FORM 2347892374123ZX9.
LET US IN, AND WE'LL STOP BY THE DDMV AND GET YOU THAT FORM. THEN YOU CAN SEND US WHEREVER YOU WISH.

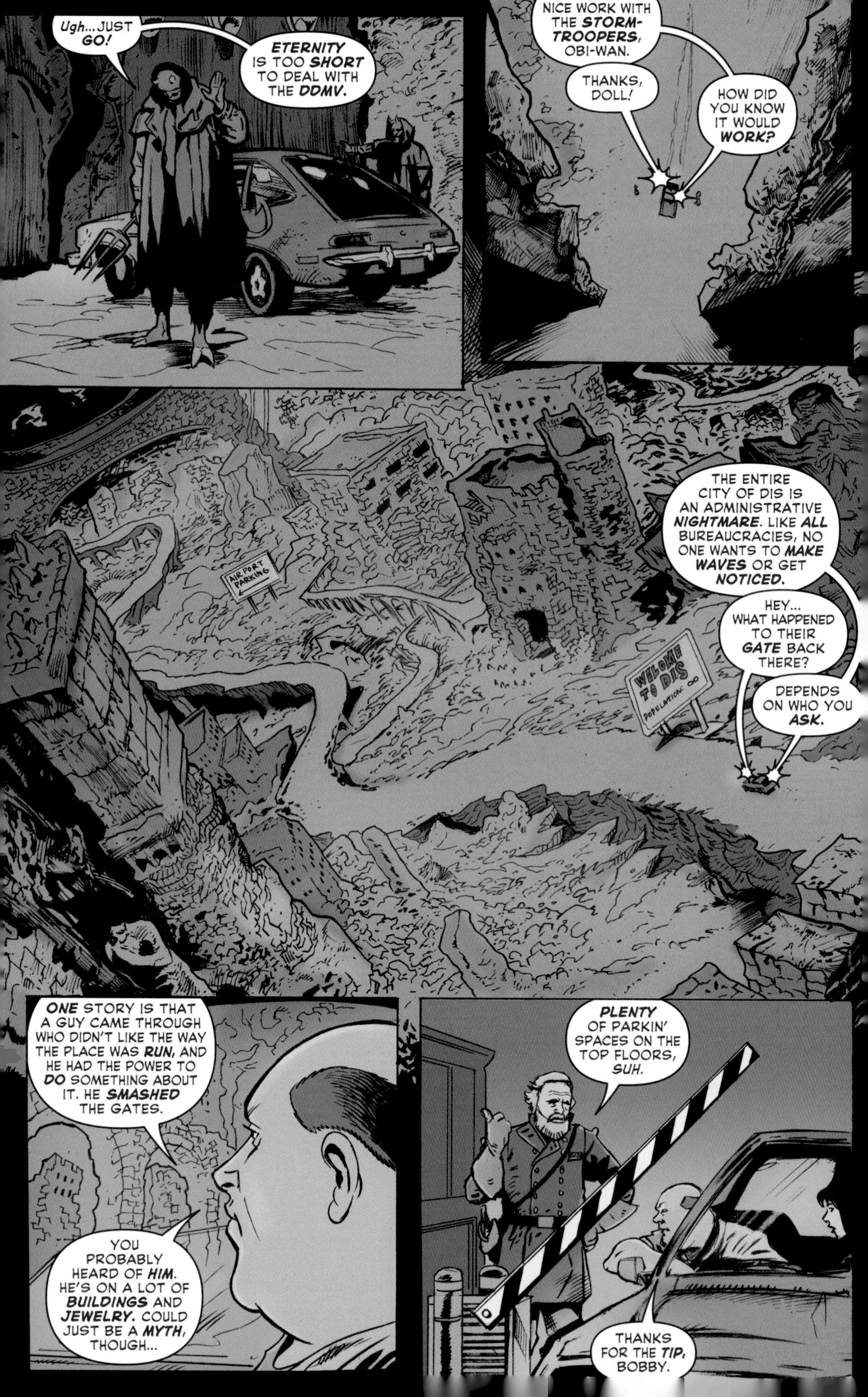

Ugh... JUST GO!
ETERNITY IS TOO SHORT TO DEAL WITH THE DDMV.
NICE WORK WITH THE STORM-TROOPERS, OBI-WAN.
THANKS, DOLL!
HOW DID YOU KNOW IT WOULD WORK?
AIRPORT PARKING
WELCOME TO DIS
POPULATION: ∞
THE ENTIRE CITY OF DIS IS AN ADMINISTRATIVE NIGHTMARE. LIKE ALL BUREAUCRACIES, NO ONE WANTS TO MAKE WAVES OR GET NOTICED.
HEY... WHAT HAPPENED TO THEIR GATE BACK THERE?
DEPENDS ON WHO YOU ASK.
ONE STORY IS THAT A GUY CAME THROUGH WHO DIDN'T LIKE THE WAY THE PLACE WAS RUN, AND HE HAD THE POWER TO DO SOMETHING ABOUT IT. HE SMASHED THE GATES.
YOU PROBABLY HEARD OF HIM. HE'S ON A LOT OF BUILDINGS AND JEWELRY. COULD JUST BE A MYTH, THOUGH...
PLENTY OF PARKIN' SPACES ON THE TOP FLOORS, SUH.
THANKS FOR THE TIP, BOBBY.

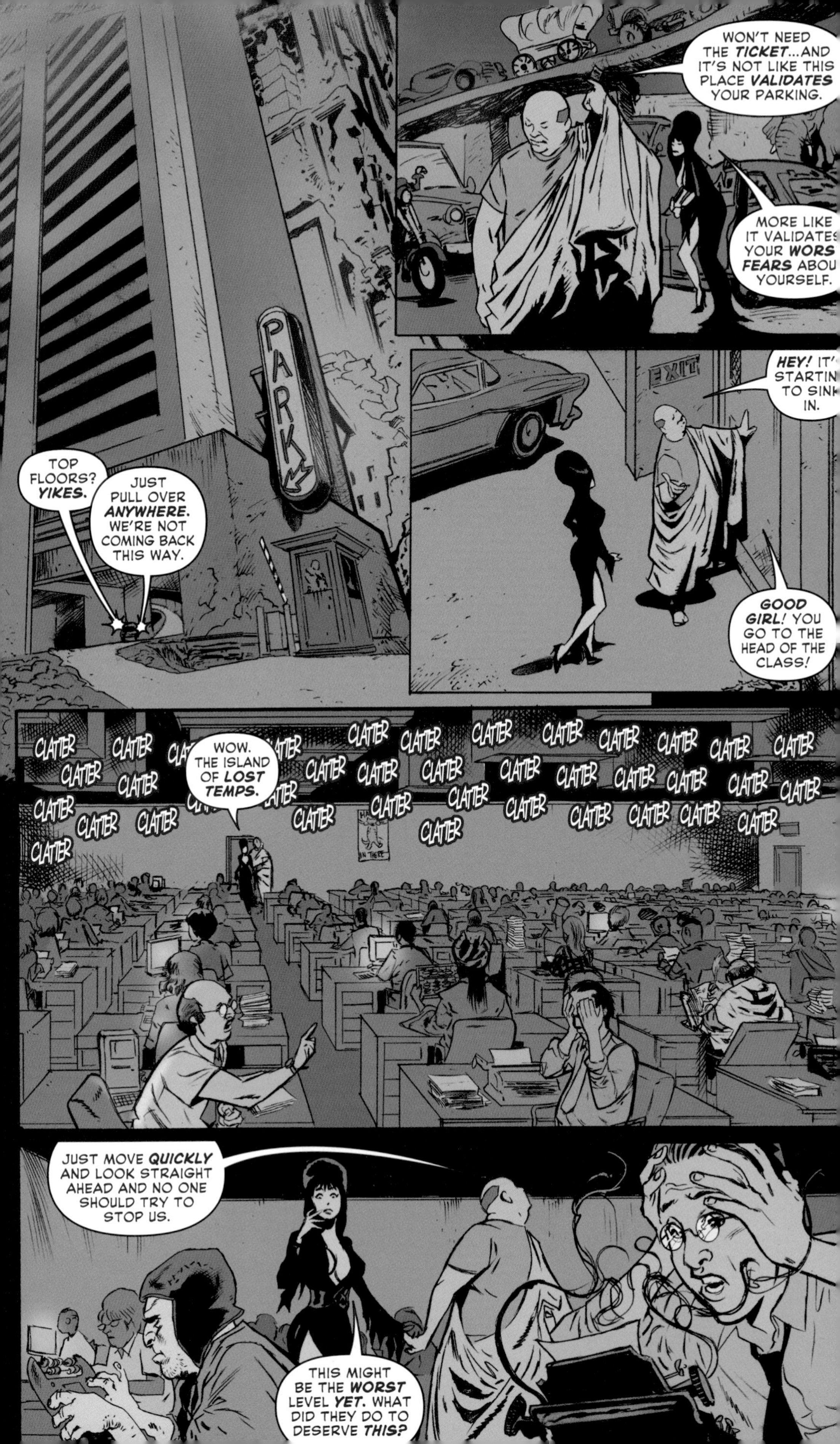

TOP FLOORS? **YIKES.**
JUST PULL OVER **ANYWHERE.** WE'RE NOT COMING BACK THIS WAY.
PARK
WON'T NEED THE **TICKET**...AND IT'S NOT LIKE THIS PLACE **VALIDATES** YOUR PARKING.
MORE LIKE IT VALIDATES YOUR **WORS** **FEARS** ABOU YOURSELF.
EXIT
HEY! IT' STARTIN TO SINK IN.
GOOD GIRL! YOU GO TO THE HEAD OF THE CLASS!
CLATTER CLATTER CLATTER CLATTER CLATTER CLATTER CLATTER CLATTER CLATTER CLATTER
WOW. THE ISLAND OF **LOST TEMPS.**
JUST MOVE **QUICKLY** AND LOOK STRAIGHT AHEAD AND NO ONE SHOULD TRY TO STOP US.
THIS MIGHT BE THE **WORST** LEVEL **YET.** WHAT DID THEY DO TO DESERVE **THIS?**

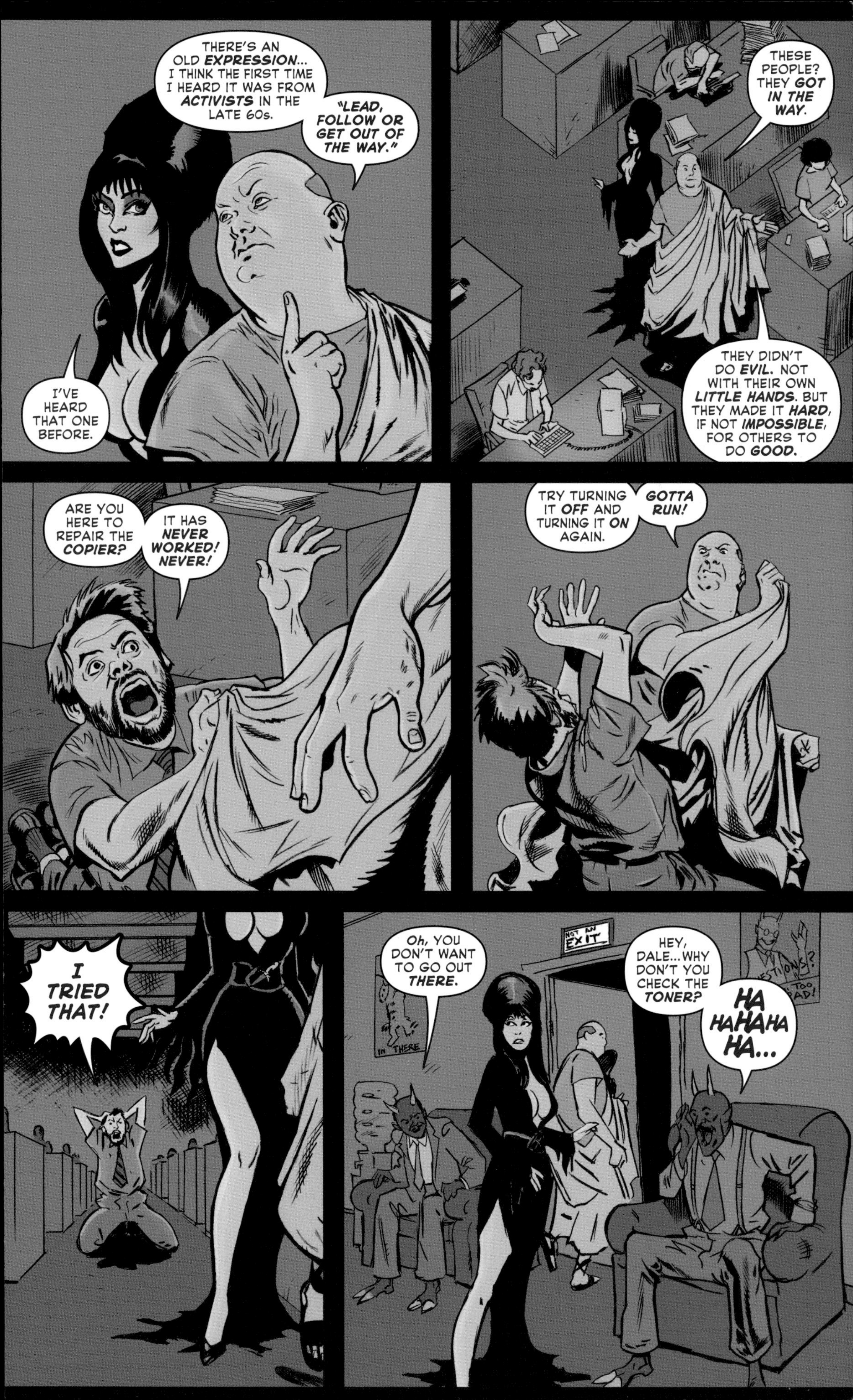

THERE'S AN OLD EXPRESSION... I THINK THE FIRST TIME I HEARD IT WAS FROM ACTIVISTS IN THE LATE 60s.
"LEAD, FOLLOW OR GET OUT OF THE WAY."
I'VE HEARD THAT ONE BEFORE.
THESE PEOPLE? THEY GOT IN THE WAY.
THEY DIDN'T DO EVIL. NOT WITH THEIR OWN LITTLE HANDS. BUT THEY MADE IT HARD, IF NOT IMPOSSIBLE, FOR OTHERS TO DO GOOD.
ARE YOU HERE TO REPAIR THE COPIER?
IT HAS NEVER WORKED! NEVER!
TRY TURNING IT OFF AND TURNING IT ON AGAIN.
GOTTA RUN!
I TRIED THAT!
NOT AN EXIT
IN THERE
Oh, YOU DON'T WANT TO GO OUT THERE.
HEY, DALE... WHY DON'T YOU CHECK THE TONER?
HA HAHAHA HA...

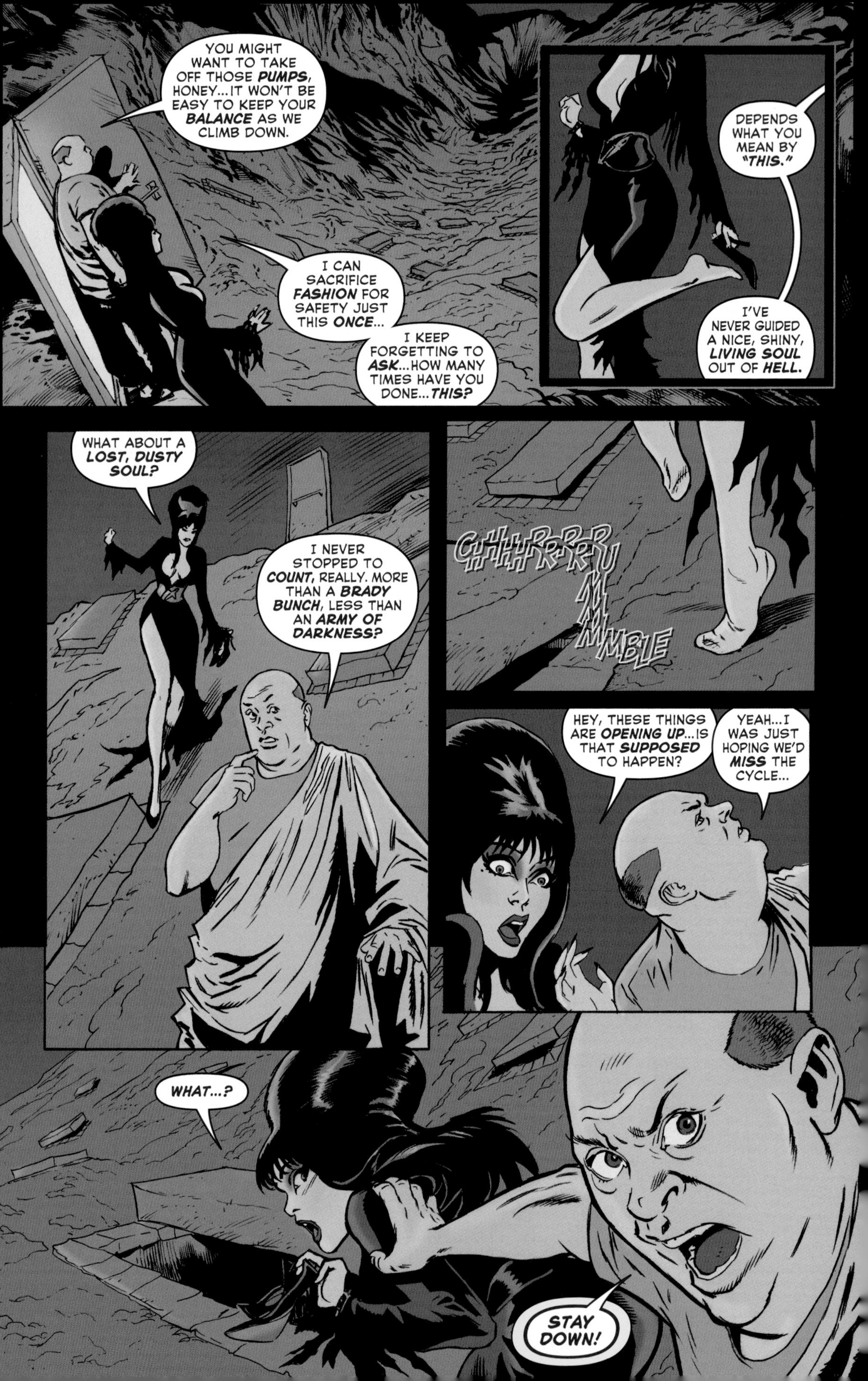

YOU MIGHT WANT TO TAKE OFF THOSE PUMPS, HONEY...IT WON'T BE EASY TO KEEP YOUR BALANCE AS WE CLIMB DOWN.
I CAN SACRIFICE FASHION FOR SAFETY JUST THIS ONCE...
I KEEP FORGETTING TO ASK...HOW MANY TIMES HAVE YOU DONE...THIS?
DEPENDS WHAT YOU MEAN BY "THIS."
I'VE NEVER GUIDED A NICE, SHINY, LIVING SOUL OUT OF HELL.
WHAT ABOUT A LOST, DUSTY SOUL?
I NEVER STOPPED TO COUNT, REALLY. MORE THAN A BRADY BUNCH, LESS THAN AN ARMY OF DARKNESS?
CHHHRRRRUMMMBLE
HEY, THESE THINGS ARE OPENING UP...IS THAT SUPPOSED TO HAPPEN?
YEAH...I WAS JUST HOPING WE'D MISS THE CYCLE...
WHAT...?
STAY DOWN!

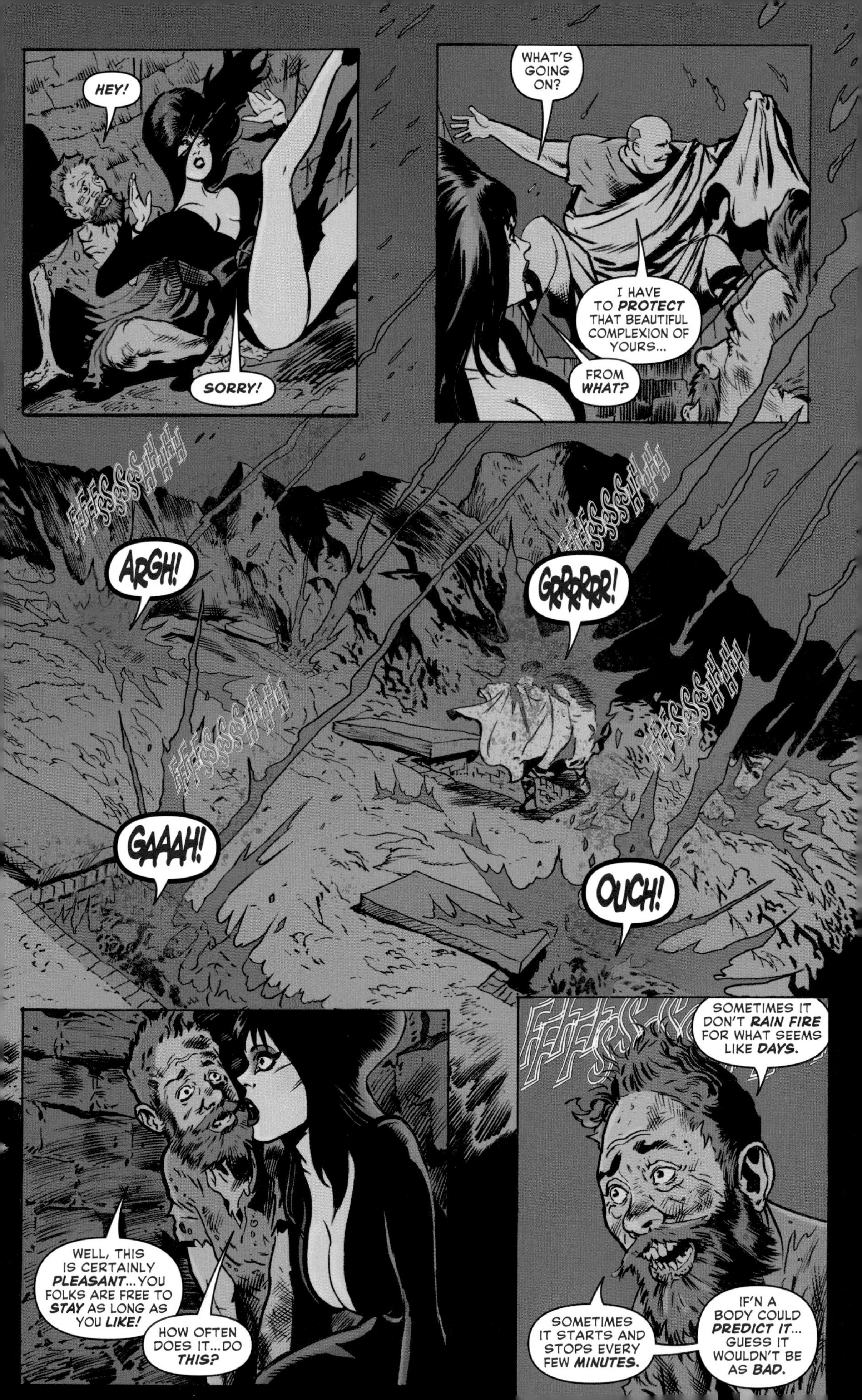
HEY!
SORRY!
WHAT'S GOING ON?
I HAVE TO PROTECT THAT BEAUTIFUL COMPLEXION OF YOURS...
FROM WHAT?
FFFSSSSSHHHH
ARGH!
GRRRRRR!
FFFSSSSSHHHH
FFFSSSSSHHHH
GAAAH!
FFFSSSSSHHHH
OUCH!
WELL, THIS IS CERTAINLY PLEASANT...YOU FOLKS ARE FREE TO STAY AS LONG AS YOU LIKE!
HOW OFTEN DOES IT...DO THIS?
SOMETIMES IT DON'T RAIN FIRE FOR WHAT SEEMS LIKE DAYS.
SOMETIMES IT STARTS AND STOPS EVERY FEW MINUTES.
IF'N A BODY COULD PREDICT IT... GUESS IT WOULDN'T BE AS BAD.

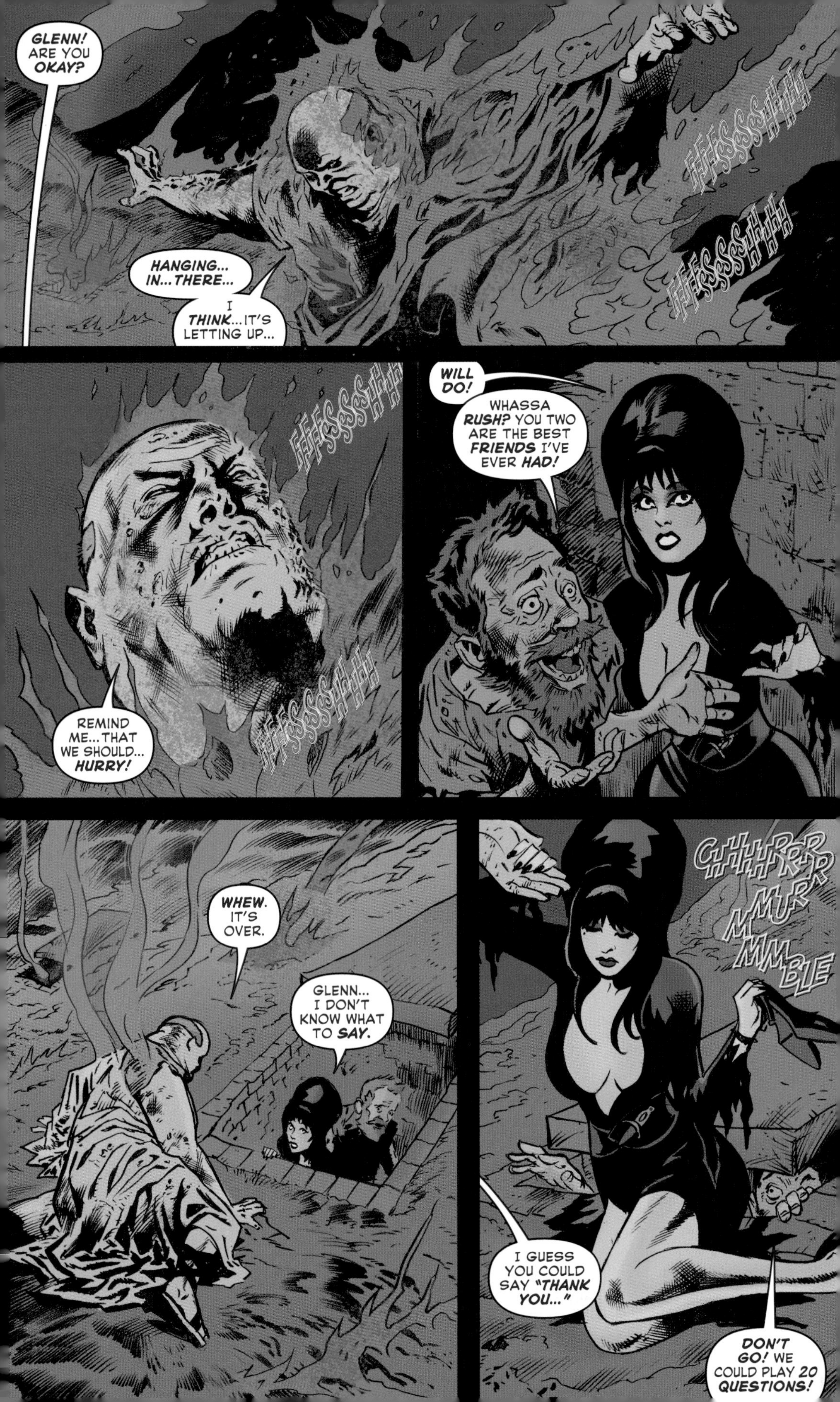

GLENN! ARE YOU OKAY?
HANGING... IN...THERE...
I THINK...IT'S LETTING UP...
FFFSSSSHHHH
FFFSSSSHHHH
FFFSSSSHHHH
REMIND ME...THAT WE SHOULD... HURRY!
FFFSSSSHHHH
WILL DO!
WHASSA RUSH? YOU TWO ARE THE BEST FRIENDS I'VE EVER HAD!
WHEW. IT'S OVER.
GLENN... I DON'T KNOW WHAT TO SAY.
GHHHRRR
MMUR MMMBLE
I GUESS YOU COULD SAY "THANK YOU..."
DON'T GO! WE COULD PLAY 20 QUESTIONS!

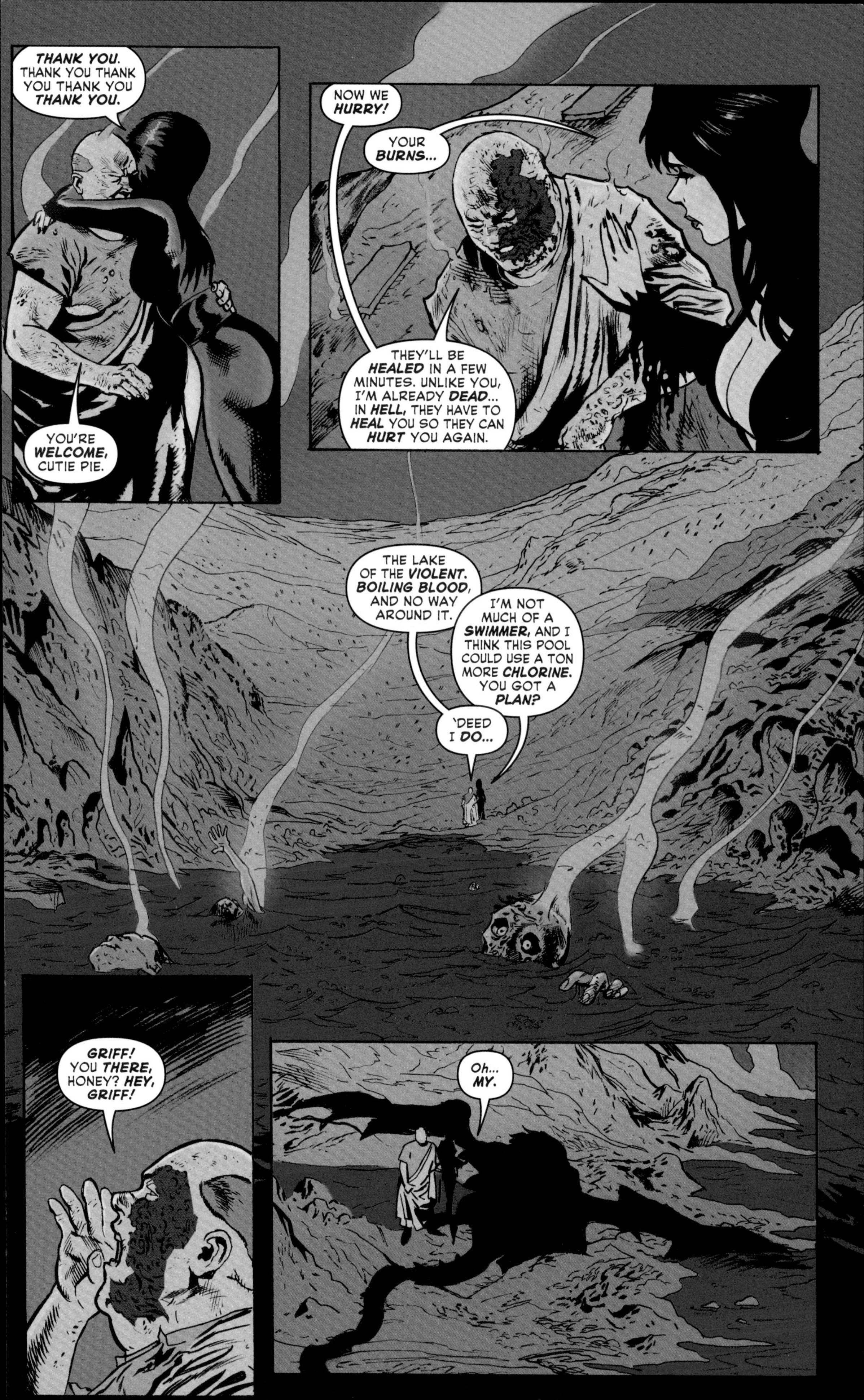
THANK YOU. THANK YOU THANK YOU THANK YOU THANK YOU.
YOU'RE WELCOME, CUTIE PIE.
NOW WE HURRY!
YOUR BURNS...
THEY'LL BE HEALED IN A FEW MINUTES. UNLIKE YOU, I'M ALREADY DEAD... IN HELL, THEY HAVE TO HEAL YOU SO THEY CAN HURT YOU AGAIN.
THE LAKE OF THE VIOLENT. BOILING BLOOD, AND NO WAY AROUND IT.
I'M NOT MUCH OF A SWIMMER, AND I THINK THIS POOL COULD USE A TON MORE CHLORINE. YOU GOT A PLAN?
'DEED I DO...
GRIFF! YOU THERE, HONEY? HEY, GRIFF!
Oh... MY.

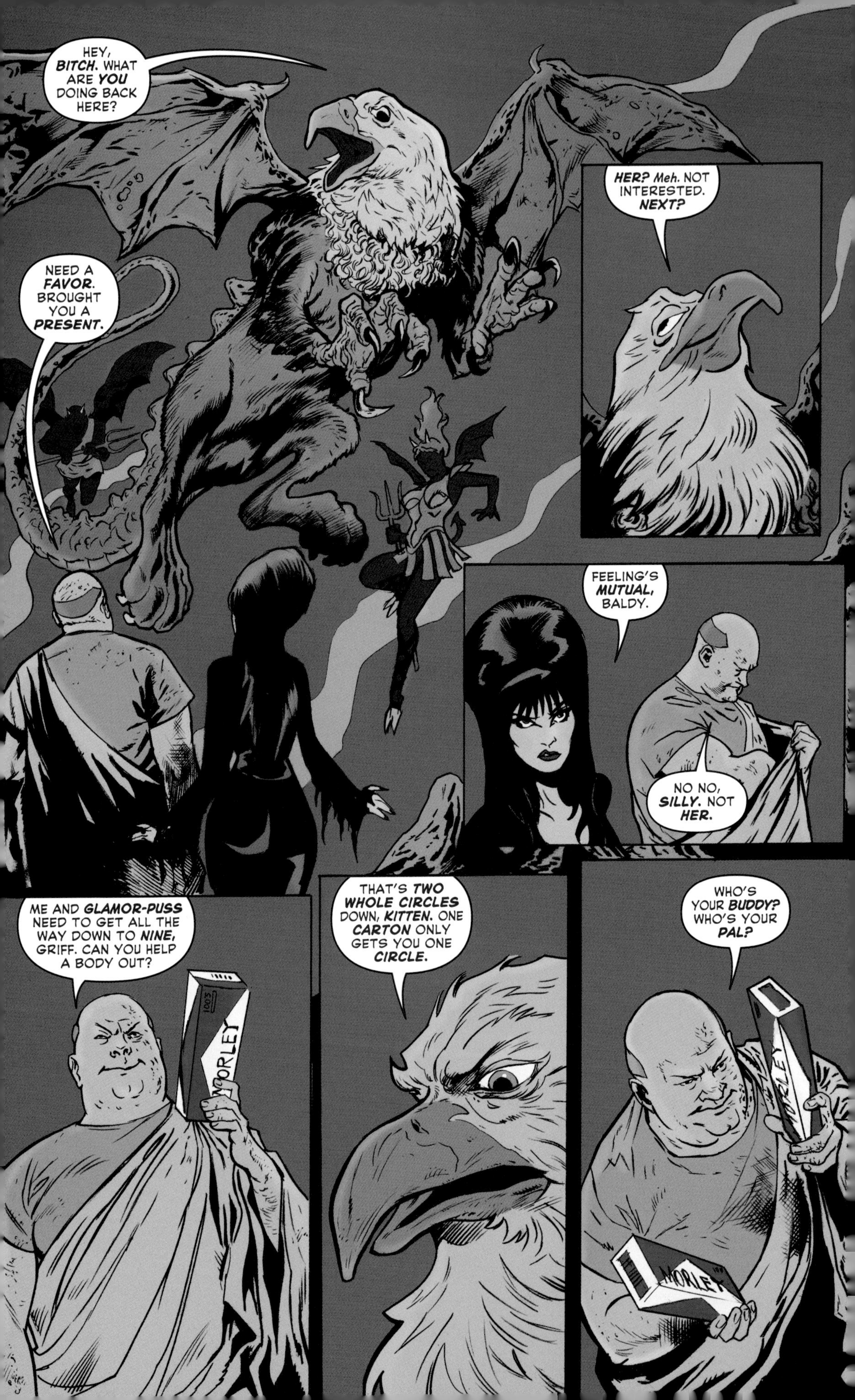
HEY, BITCH. WHAT ARE YOU DOING BACK HERE?
NEED A FAVOR. BROUGHT YOU A PRESENT.
HER? Meh. NOT INTERESTED. NEXT?
FEELING'S MUTUAL, BALDY.
NO NO, SILLY. NOT HER.
ME AND GLAMOR-PUSS NEED TO GET ALL THE WAY DOWN TO NINE, GRIFF. CAN YOU HELP A BODY OUT?
MORLEY
THAT'S TWO WHOLE CIRCLES DOWN, KITTEN. ONE CARTON ONLY GETS YOU ONE CIRCLE.
WHO'S YOUR BUDDY? WHO'S YOUR PAL?
MORLEY
MORLEY

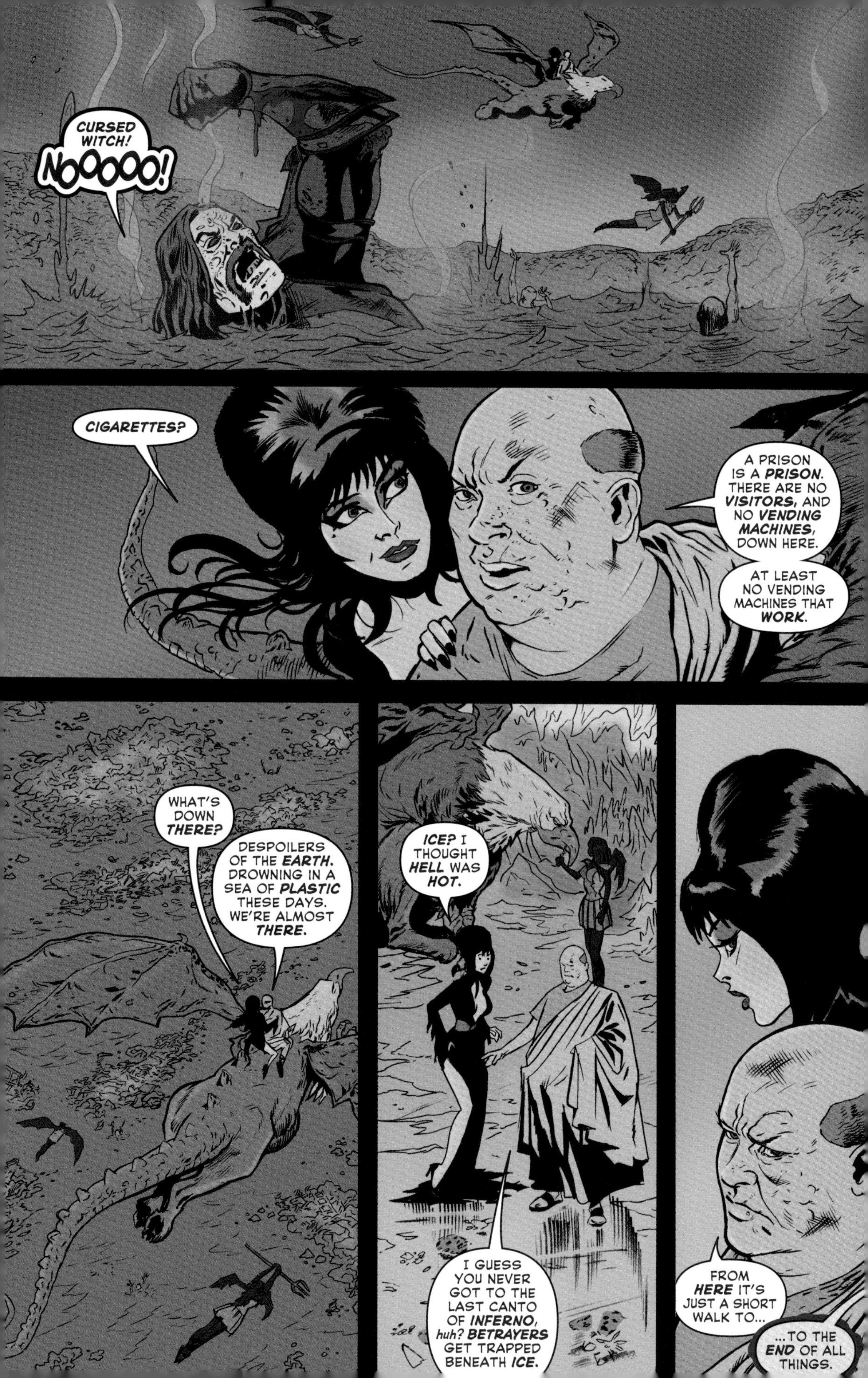
CURSED WITCH!
NOOOOO!
CIGARETTES?
A PRISON IS A PRISON. THERE ARE NO VISITORS, AND NO VENDING MACHINES, DOWN HERE.
AT LEAST NO VENDING MACHINES THAT WORK.
WHAT'S DOWN THERE?
DESPOILERS OF THE EARTH. DROWNING IN A SEA OF PLASTIC THESE DAYS. WE'RE ALMOST THERE.
ICE? I THOUGHT HELL WAS HOT.
I GUESS YOU NEVER GOT TO THE LAST CANTO OF INFERNO, huh? BETRAYERS GET TRAPPED BENEATH ICE.
FROM HERE IT'S JUST A SHORT WALK TO...
...TO THE END OF ALL THINGS.

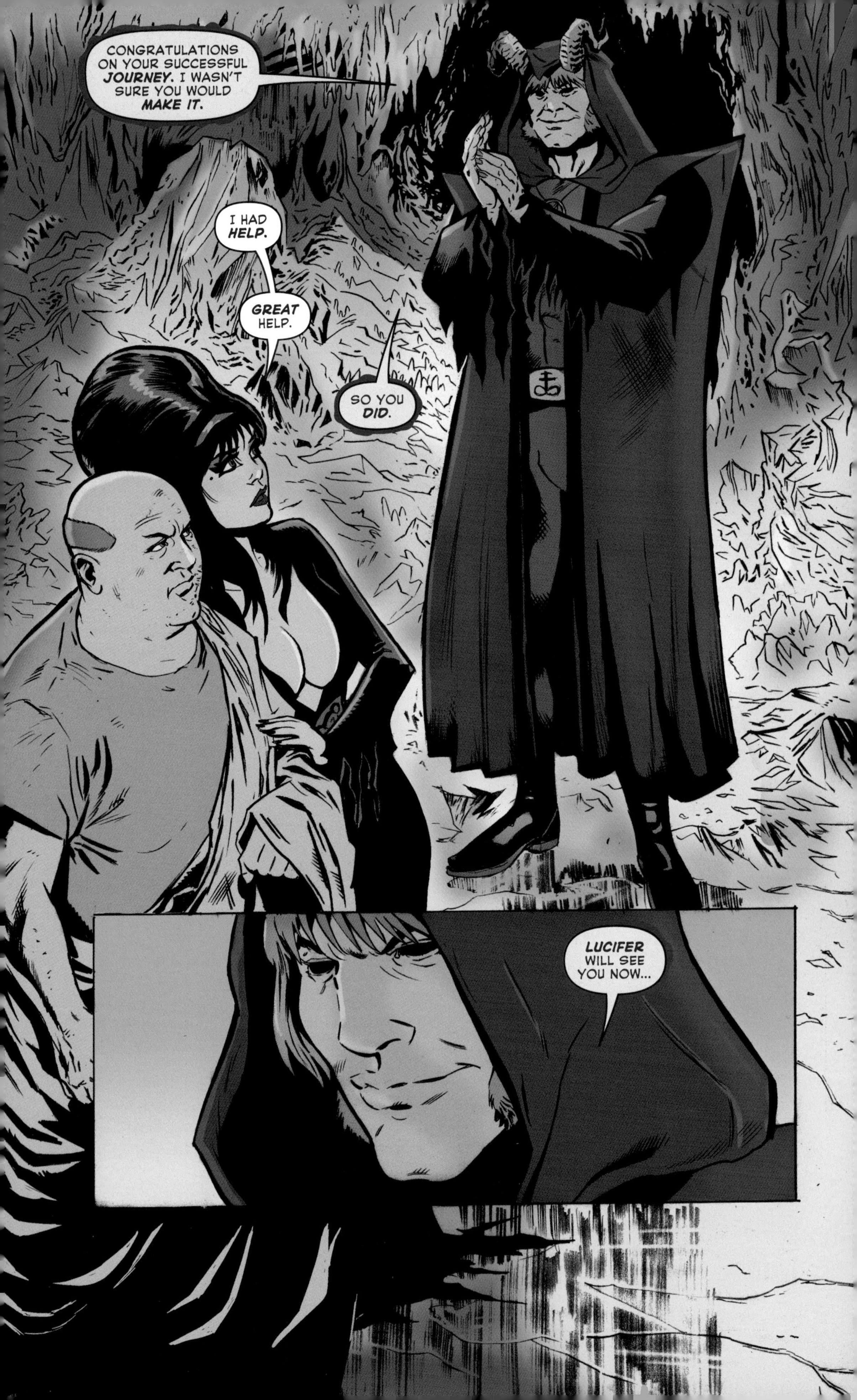
CONGRATULATIONS ON YOUR SUCCESSFUL JOURNEY. I WASN'T SURE YOU WOULD MAKE IT.
I HAD HELP.
GREAT HELP.
SO YOU DID.
LUCIFER WILL SEE YOU NOW...

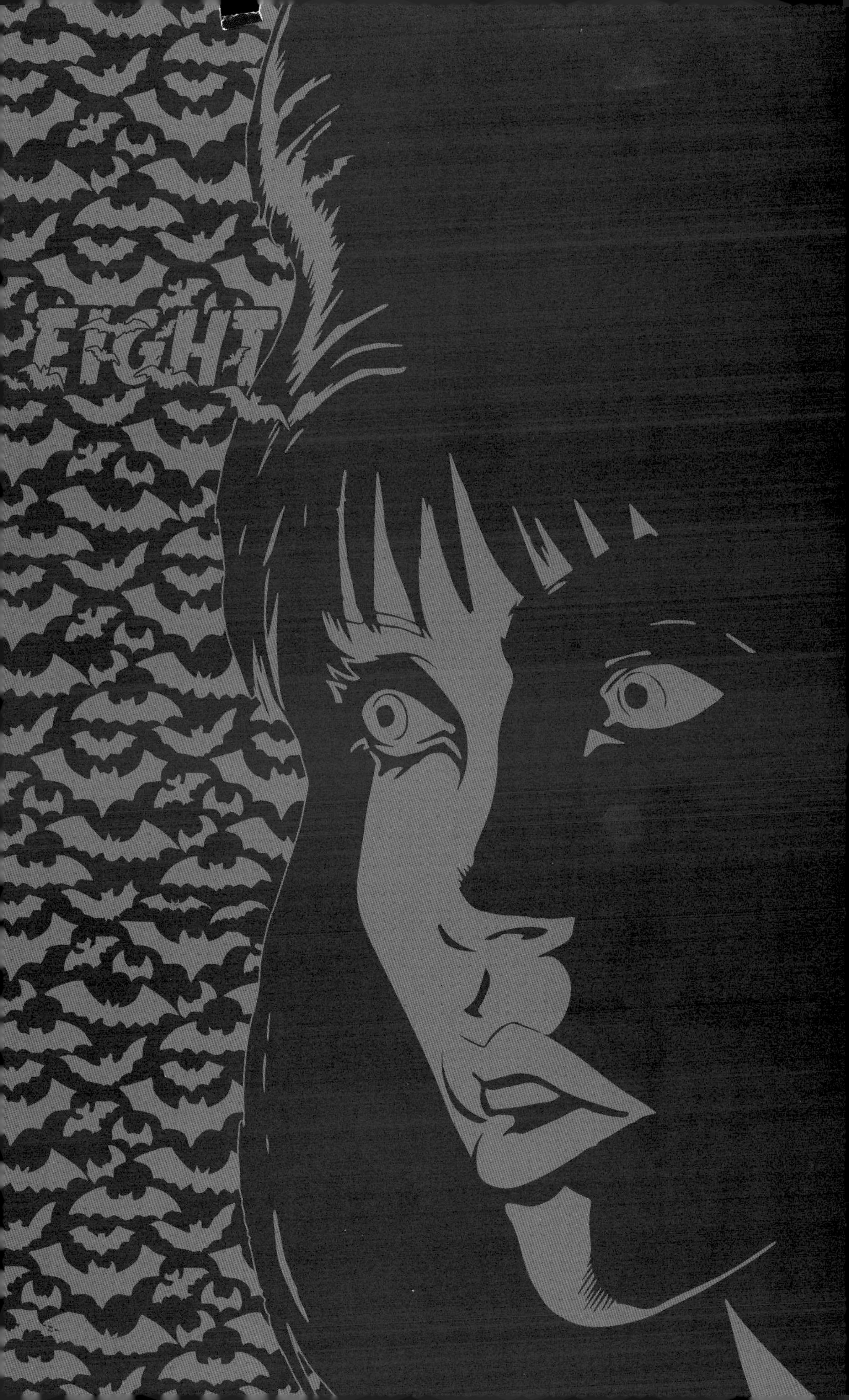
EIGHT

8 COVER ART: JOE JUSKO

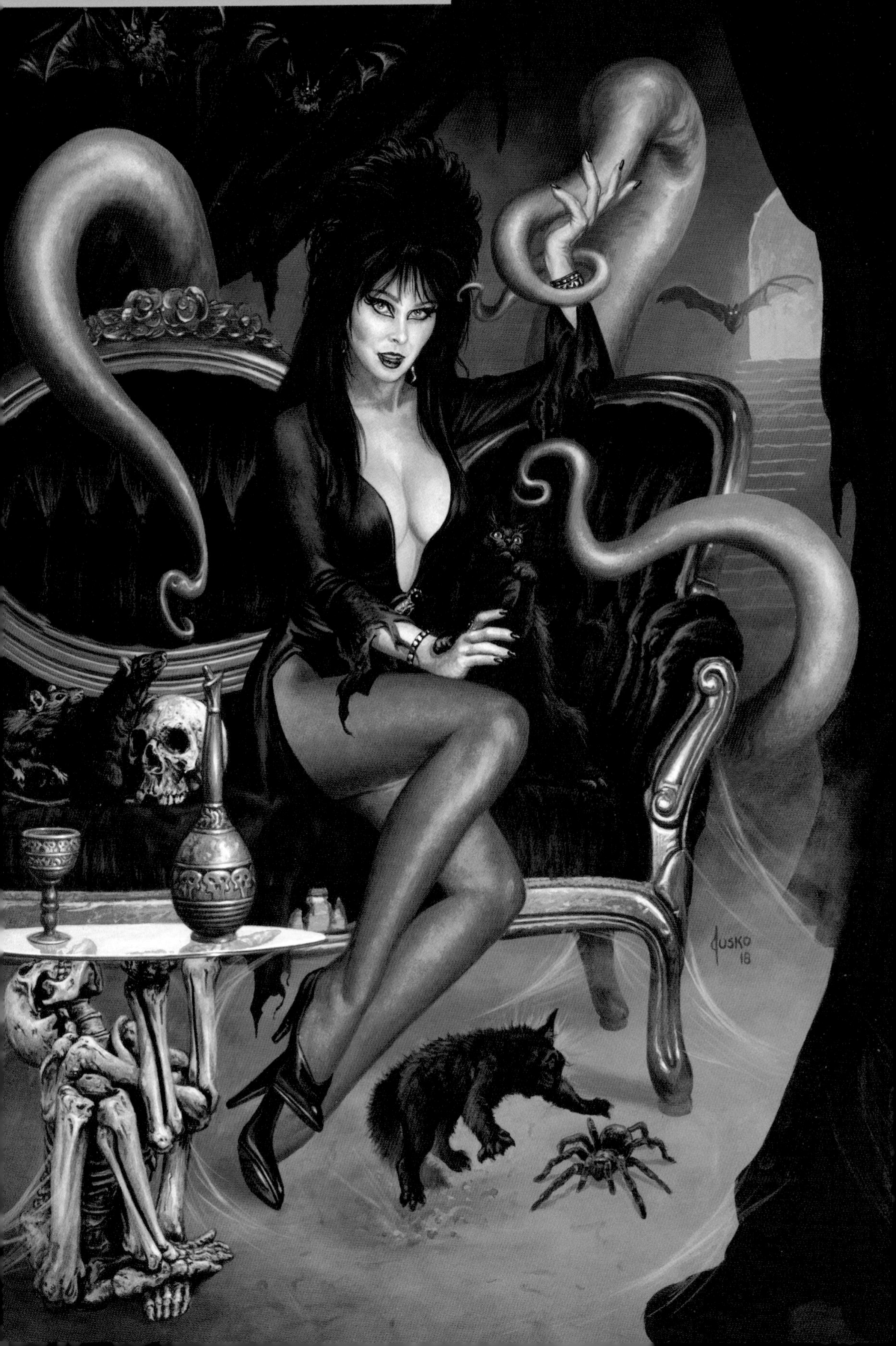
JUSKO
18

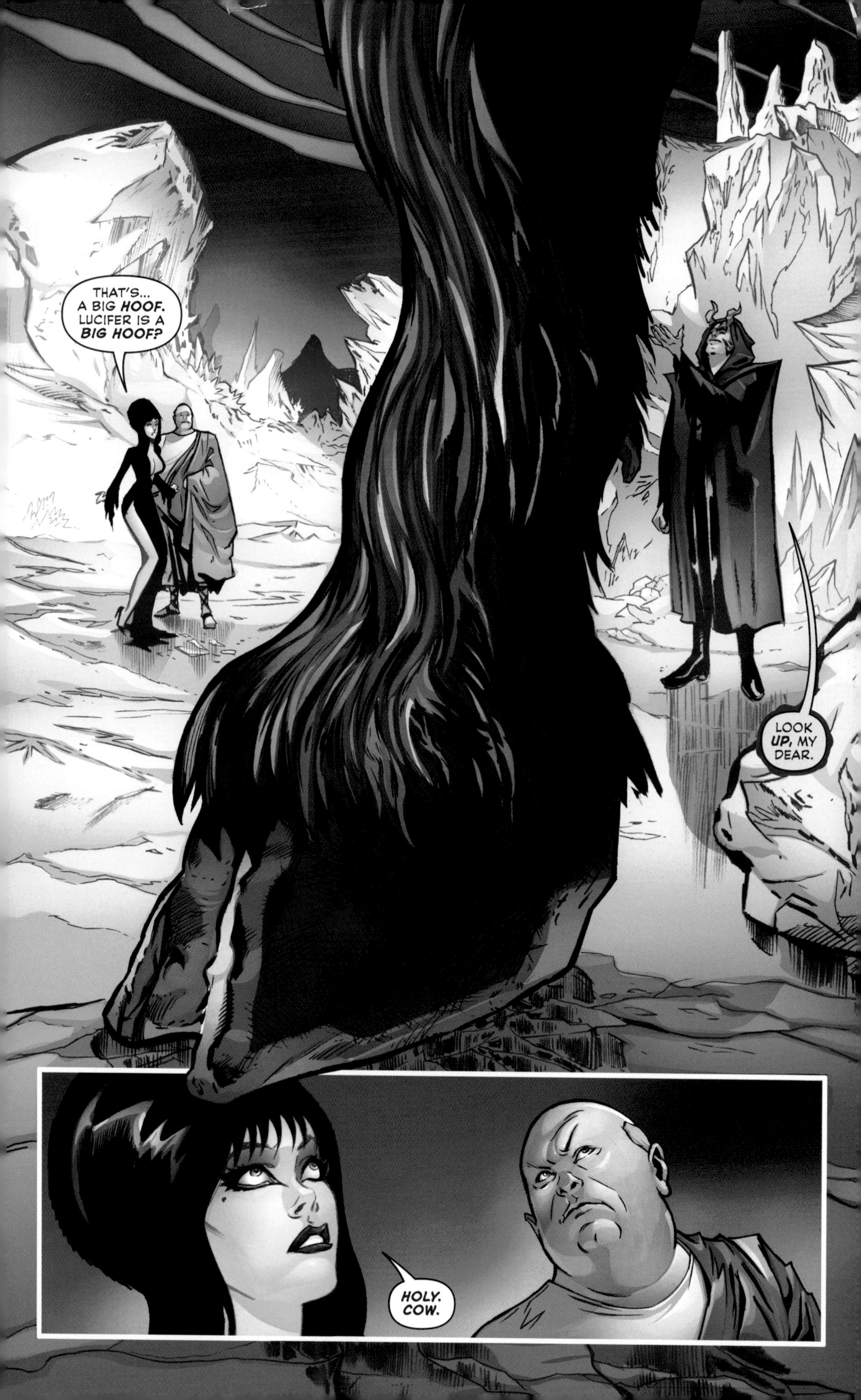
THAT'S... A BIG HOOF. LUCIFER IS A BIG HOOF?
LOOK UP, MY DEAR.
HOLY. COW.

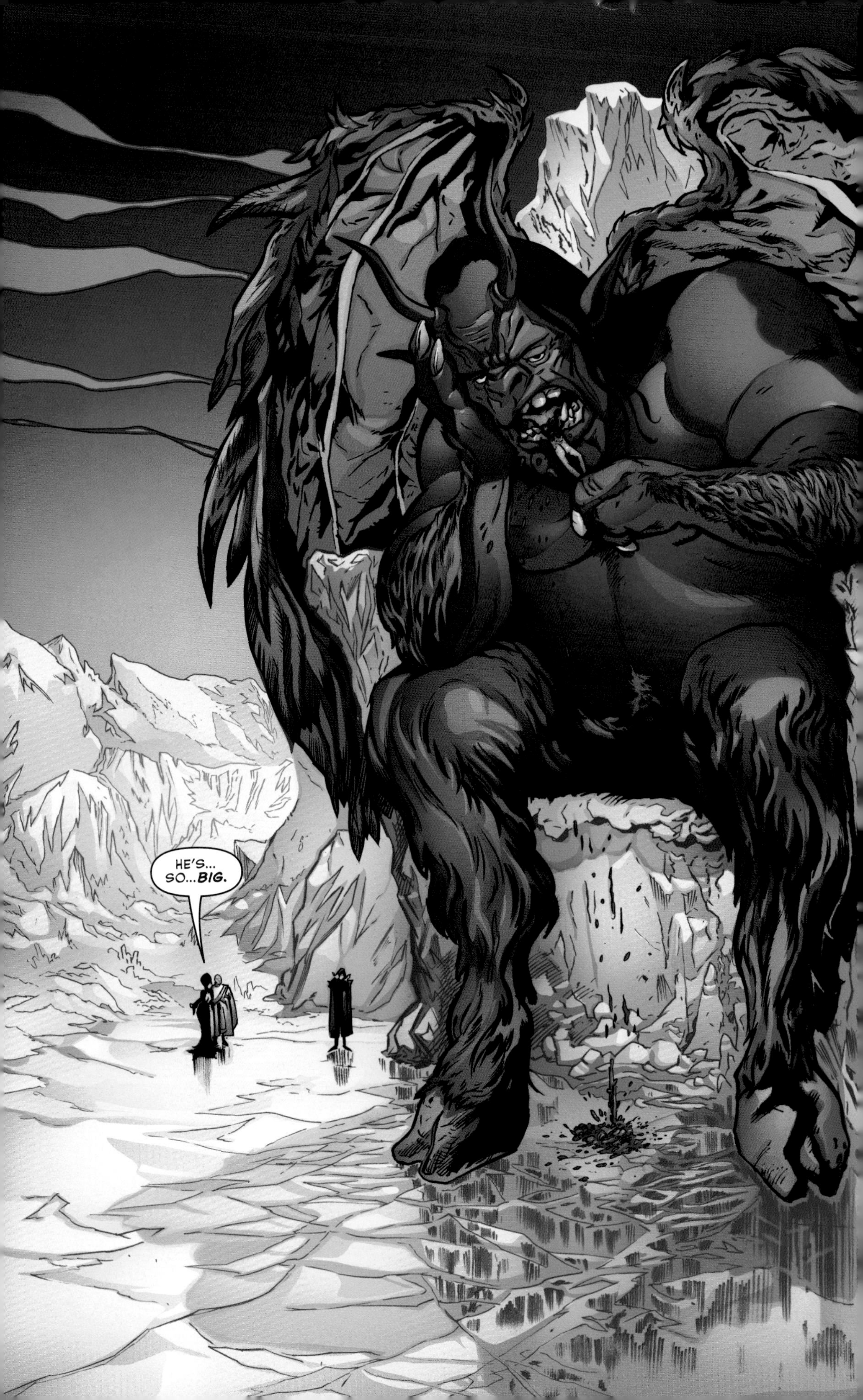
HE'S... SO...**BIG.**

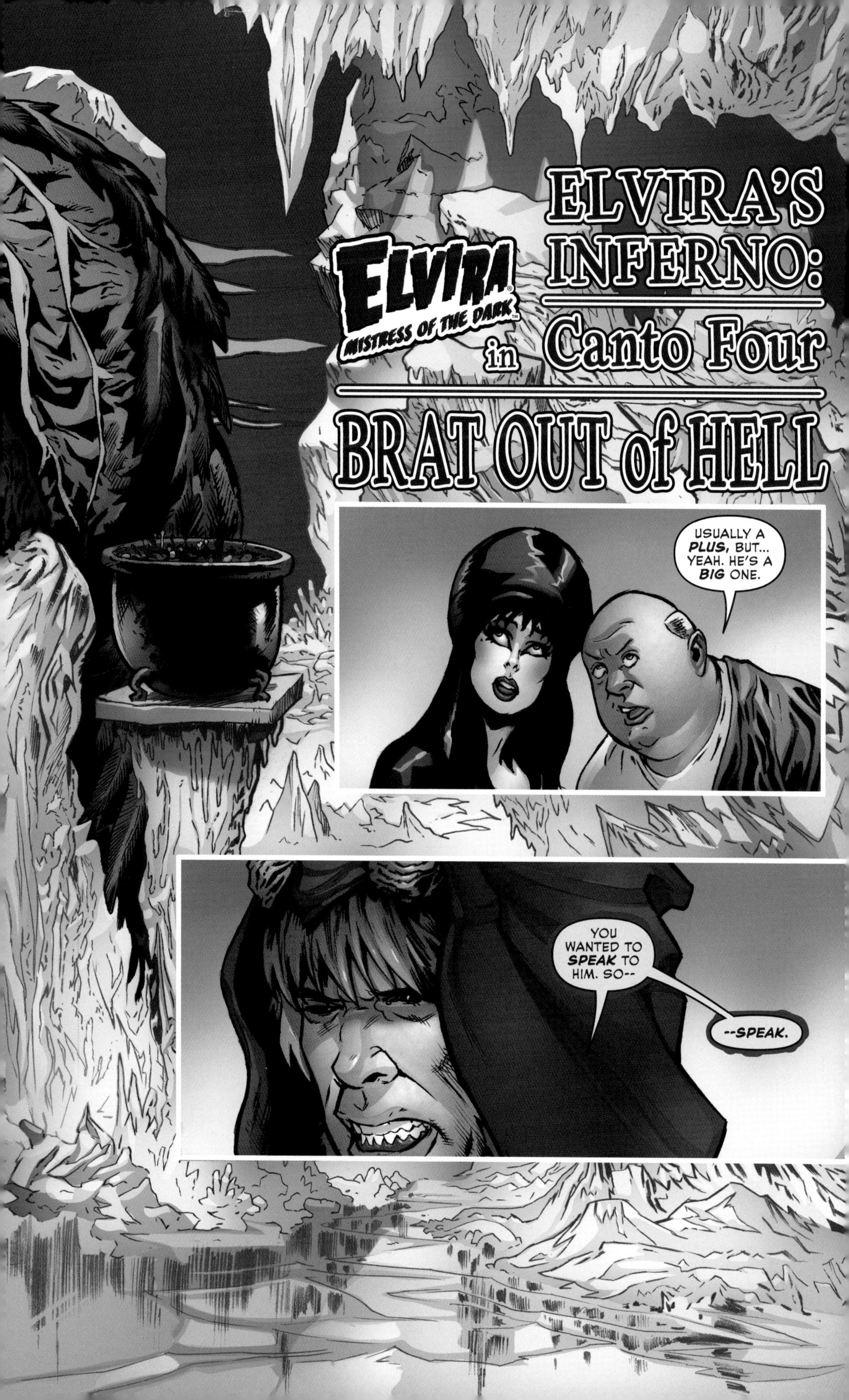
ELVIRA
MISTRESS OF THE DARK
in
ELVIRA'S INFERNO:
Canto Four
BRAT OUT of HELL
USUALLY A PLUS, BUT... YEAH. HE'S A BIG ONE.
YOU WANTED TO SPEAK TO HIM. SO--
--SPEAK.

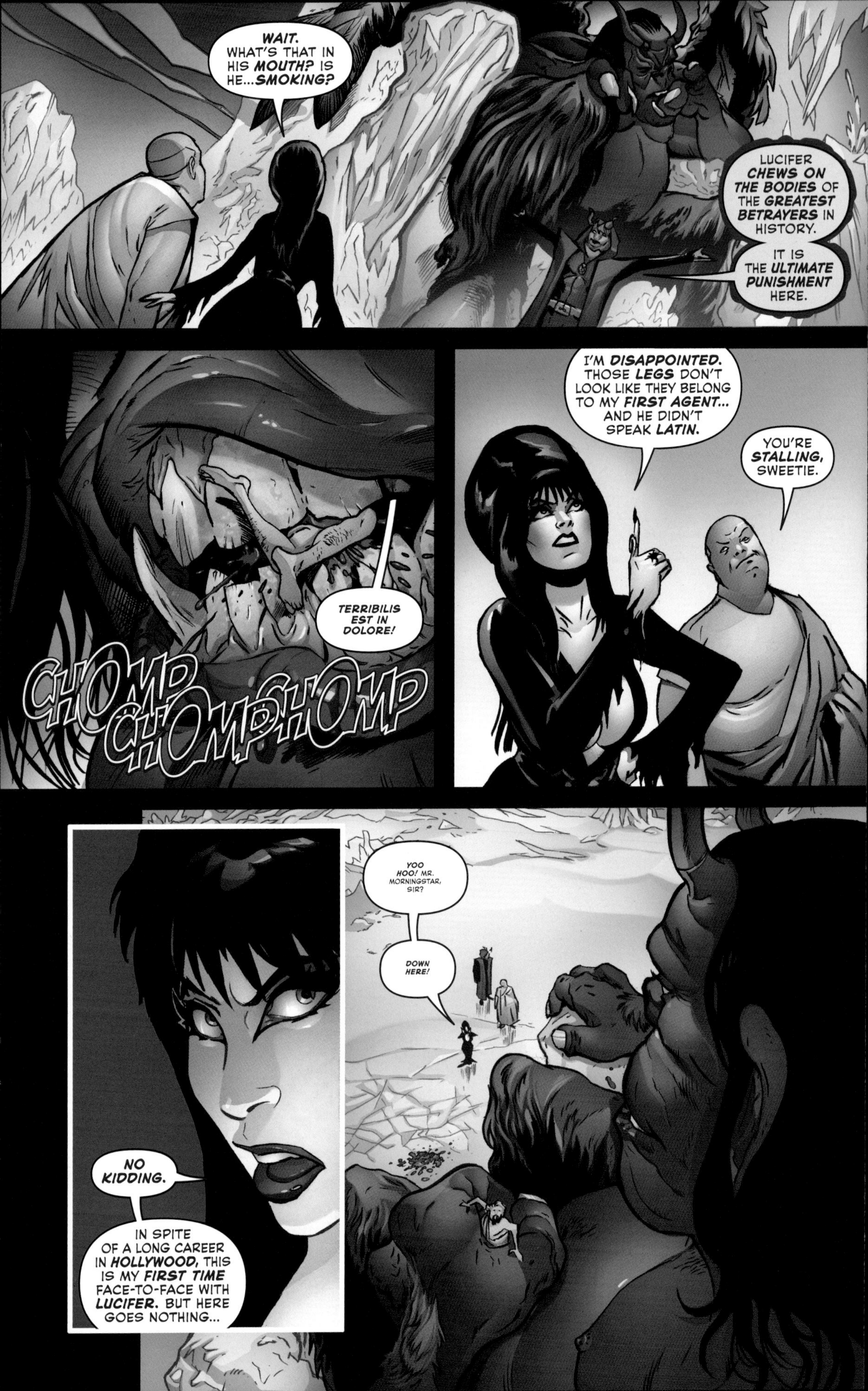
WAIT. WHAT'S THAT IN HIS MOUTH? IS HE...SMOKING?
LUCIFER CHEWS ON THE BODIES OF THE GREATEST BETRAYERS IN HISTORY.
IT IS THE ULTIMATE PUNISHMENT HERE.
TERRIBILIS EST IN DOLORE!
CHOMP CHOMP CHOMP CHOMP
I'M DISAPPOINTED. THOSE LEGS DON'T LOOK LIKE THEY BELONG TO MY FIRST AGENT... AND HE DIDN'T SPEAK LATIN.
YOU'RE STALLING, SWEETIE.
NO KIDDING.
IN SPITE OF A LONG CAREER IN HOLLYWOOD, THIS IS MY FIRST TIME FACE-TO-FACE WITH LUCIFER. BUT HERE GOES NOTHING...
YOO HOO! MR. MORNINGSTAR, SIR?
DOWN HERE!

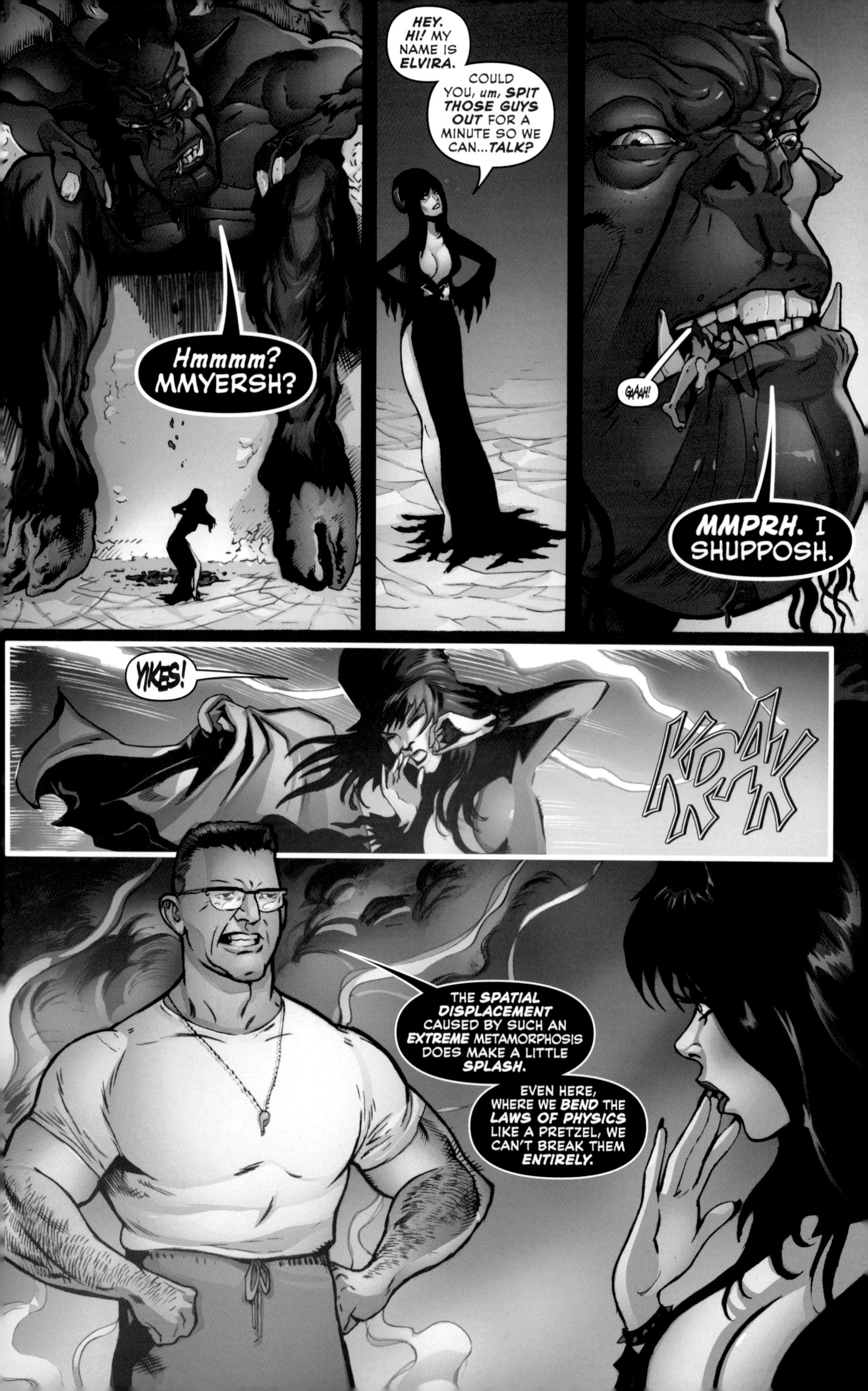
Hmmmm? MMYERSH?
HEY. HI! MY NAME IS ELVIRA.
COULD YOU, um, SPIT THOSE GUYS OUT FOR A MINUTE SO WE CAN...TALK?
GAAH!
MMPRH. I SHUPPOSH.
YIKES!
KRAK
THE SPATIAL DISPLACEMENT CAUSED BY SUCH AN EXTREME METAMORPHOSIS DOES MAKE A LITTLE SPLASH.
EVEN HERE, WHERE WE BEND THE LAWS OF PHYSICS LIKE A PRETZEL, WE CAN'T BREAK THEM ENTIRELY.

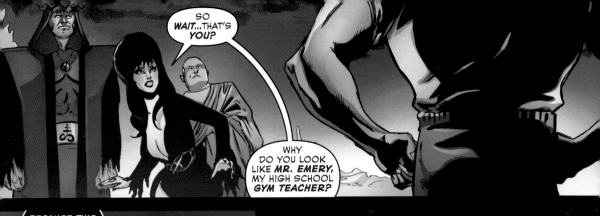

SO WAIT...THAT'S YOU?

WHY DO YOU LOOK LIKE MR. EMERY, MY HIGH SCHOOL GYM TEACHER?

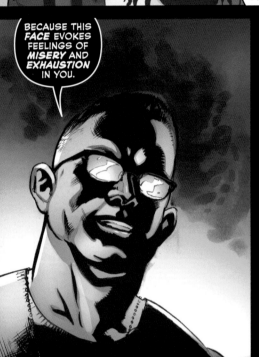

BECAUSE THIS FACE EVOKES FEELINGS OF MISERY AND EXHAUSTION IN YOU.

I HATED HIM SO MUCH.

I KNOW! I FEEL IT! LIKE I SAID. FUNNY.

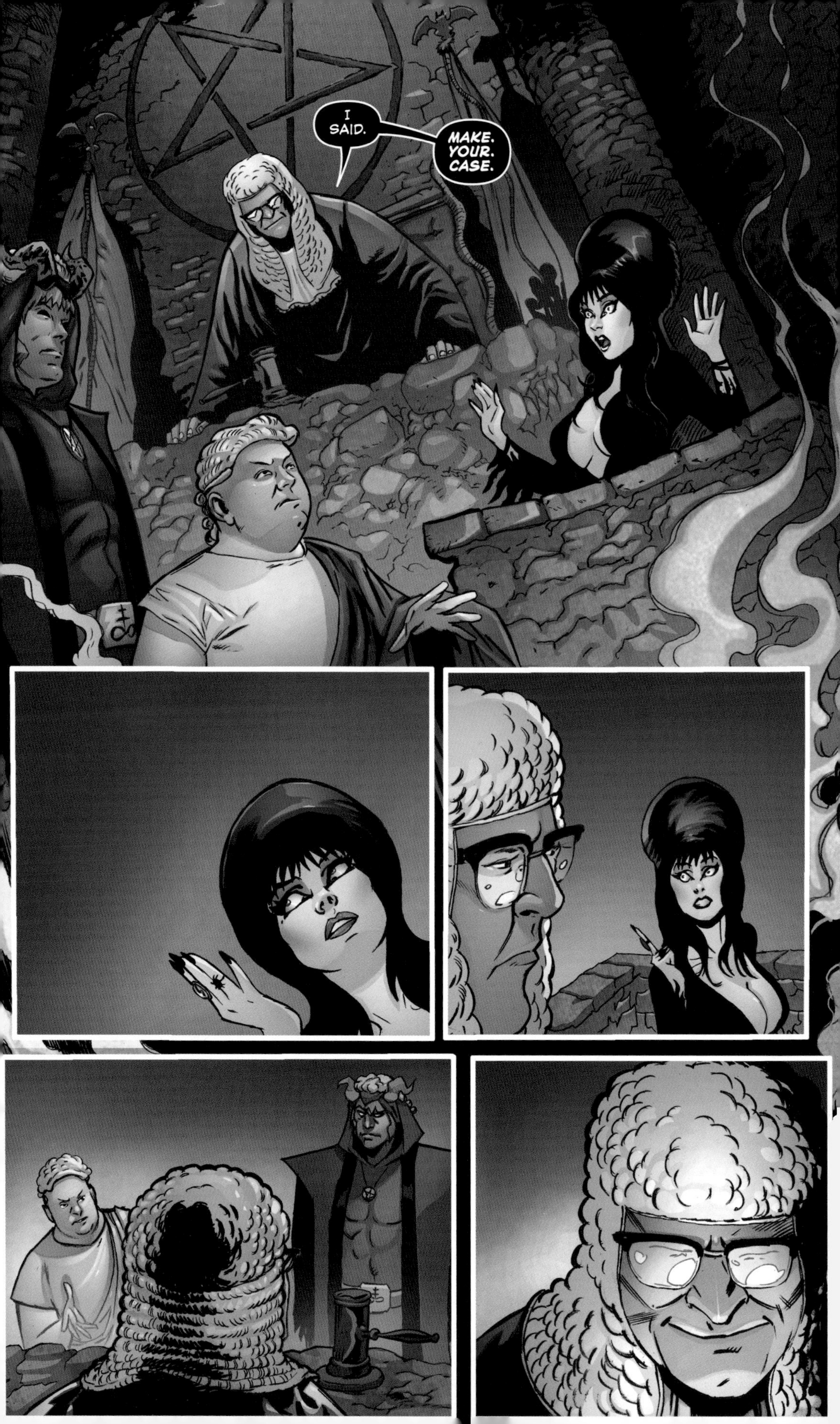
I SAID.
MAKE. YOUR. CASE.

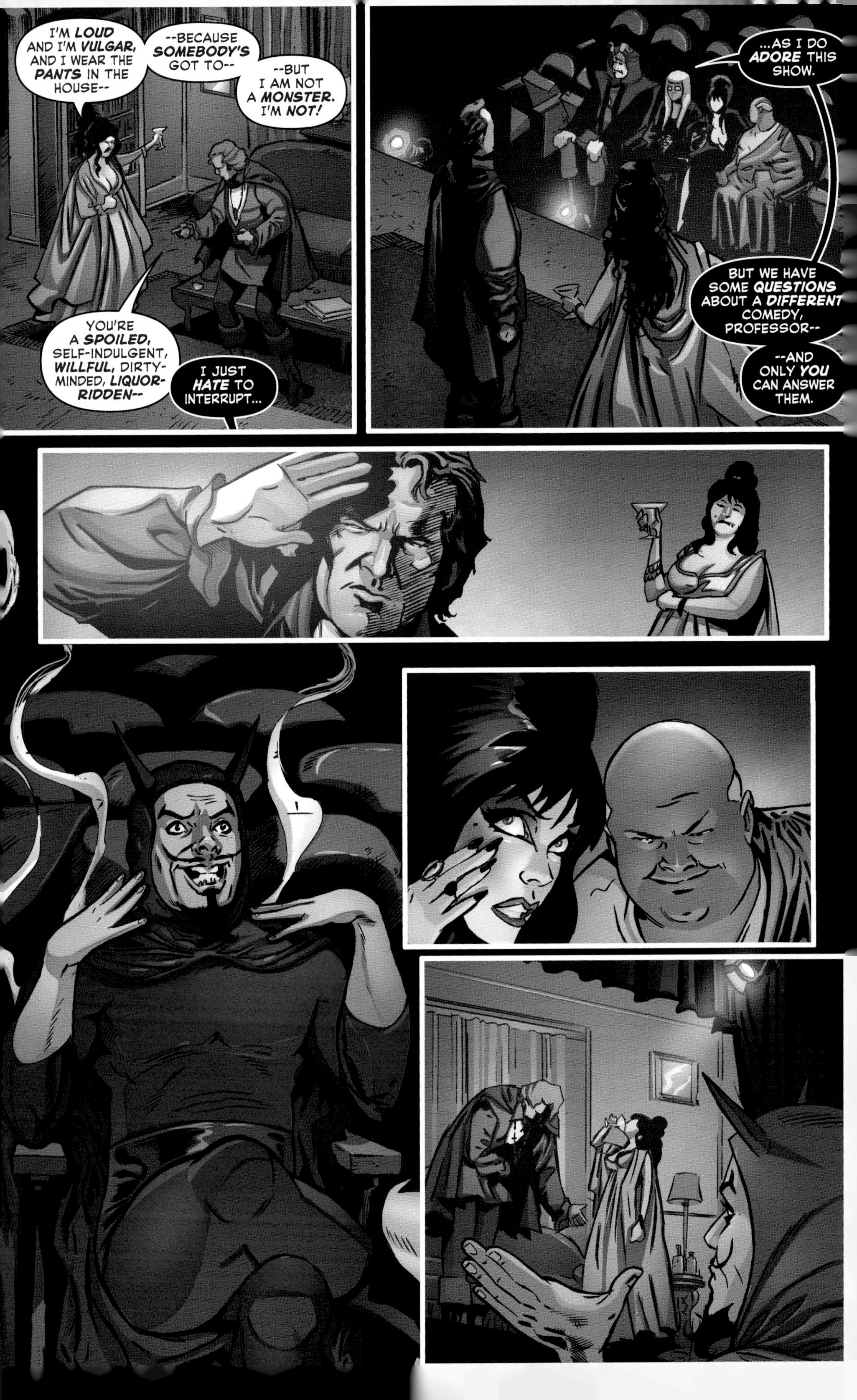

I'M LOUD AND I'M VULGAR, AND I WEAR THE PANTS IN THE HOUSE--
--BECAUSE SOMEBODY'S GOT TO--
--BUT I AM NOT A MONSTER. I'M NOT!
YOU'RE A SPOILED, SELF-INDULGENT, WILLFUL, DIRTY-MINDED, LIQUOR-RIDDEN--
I JUST HATE TO INTERRUPT...
...AS I DO ADORE THIS SHOW.
BUT WE HAVE SOME QUESTIONS ABOUT A DIFFERENT COMEDY, PROFESSOR--
--AND ONLY YOU CAN ANSWER THEM.

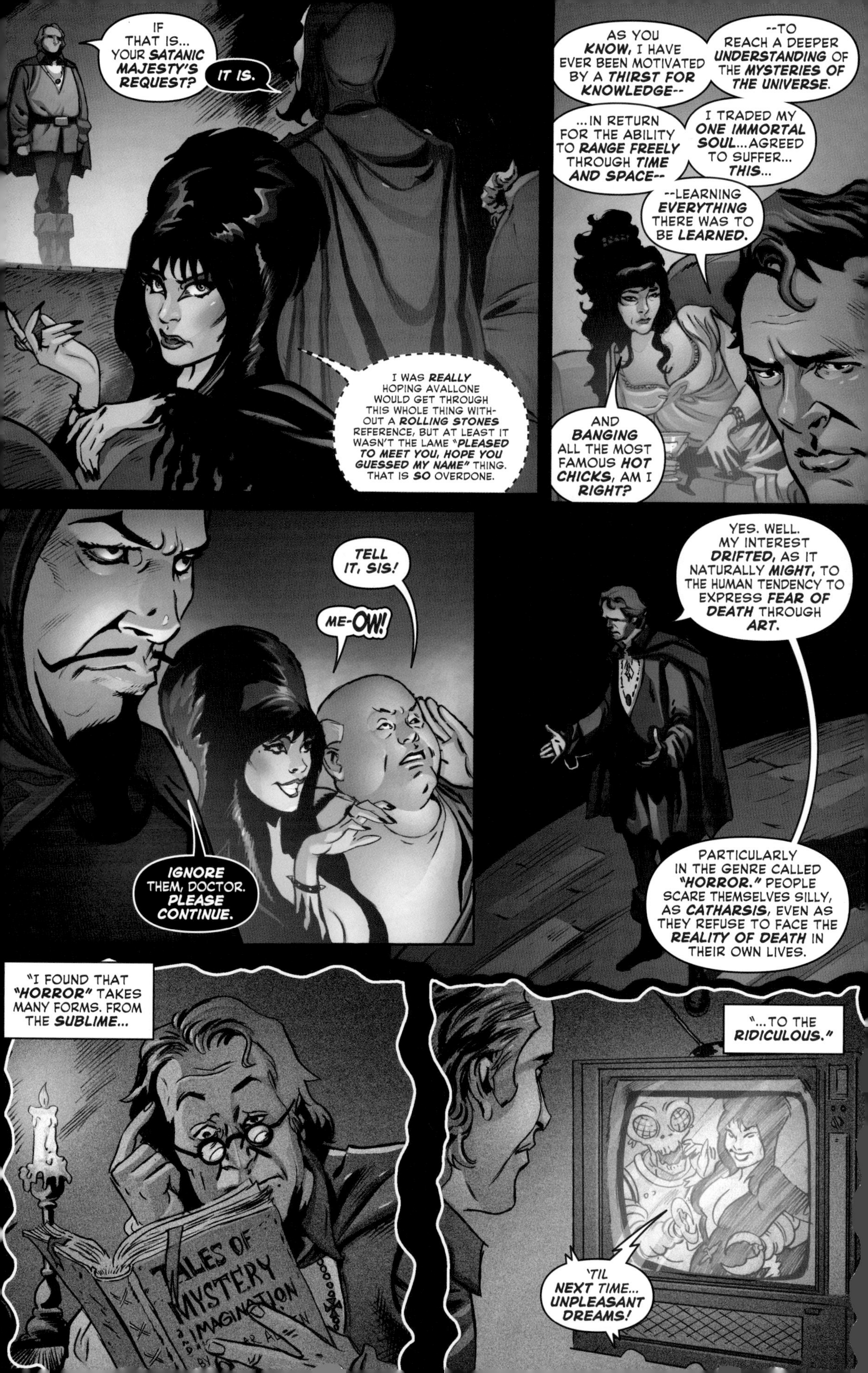
IF THAT IS... YOUR SATANIC MAJESTY'S REQUEST?
IT IS.
I WAS REALLY HOPING AVALLONE WOULD GET THROUGH THIS WHOLE THING WITH-OUT A ROLLING STONES REFERENCE, BUT AT LEAST IT WASN'T THE LAME "PLEASED TO MEET YOU, HOPE YOU GUESSED MY NAME" THING. THAT IS SO OVERDONE.
AS YOU KNOW, I HAVE EVER BEEN MOTIVATED BY A THIRST FOR KNOWLEDGE--
--TO REACH A DEEPER UNDERSTANDING OF THE MYSTERIES OF THE UNIVERSE.
I TRADED MY ONE IMMORTAL SOUL...AGREED TO SUFFER... THIS...
...IN RETURN FOR THE ABILITY TO RANGE FREELY THROUGH TIME AND SPACE--
--LEARNING EVERYTHING THERE WAS TO BE LEARNED.
AND BANGING ALL THE MOST FAMOUS HOT CHICKS, AM I RIGHT?
TELL IT, SIS!
ME-OW!
IGNORE THEM, DOCTOR. PLEASE CONTINUE.
YES. WELL. MY INTEREST DRIFTED, AS IT NATURALLY MIGHT, TO THE HUMAN TENDENCY TO EXPRESS FEAR OF DEATH THROUGH ART.
PARTICULARLY IN THE GENRE CALLED "HORROR." PEOPLE SCARE THEMSELVES SILLY, AS CATHARSIS, EVEN AS THEY REFUSE TO FACE THE REALITY OF DEATH IN THEIR OWN LIVES.
"I FOUND THAT "HORROR" TAKES MANY FORMS. FROM THE SUBLIME...
TALES OF MYSTERY IMAGINATION
"...TO THE RIDICULOUS."
'TIL NEXT TIME... UNPLEASANT DREAMS!

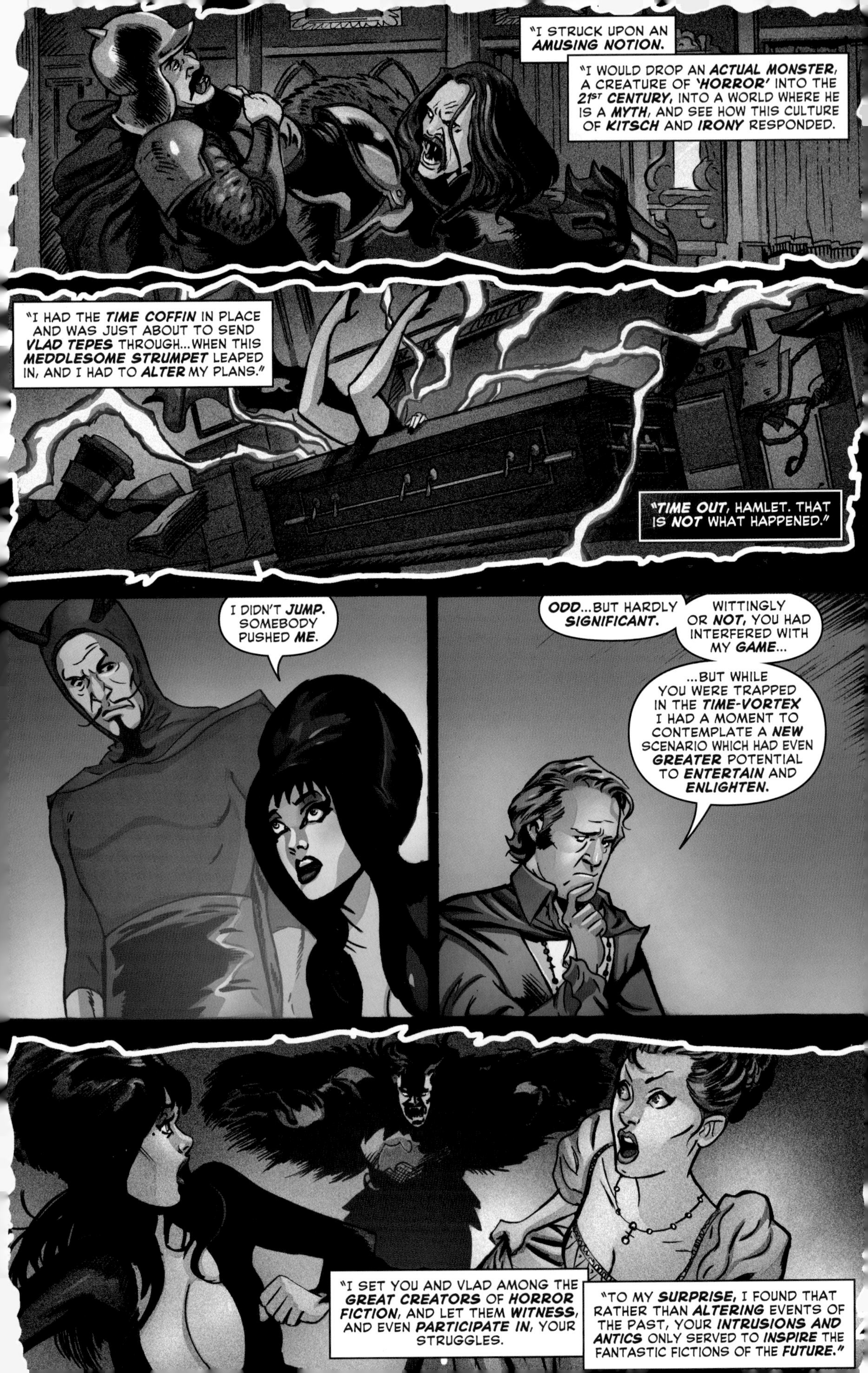

"I STRUCK UPON AN AMUSING NOTION.
"I WOULD DROP AN ACTUAL MONSTER, A CREATURE OF 'HORROR' INTO THE 21ST CENTURY, INTO A WORLD WHERE HE IS A MYTH, AND SEE HOW THIS CULTURE OF KITSCH AND IRONY RESPONDED.
"I HAD THE TIME COFFIN IN PLACE AND WAS JUST ABOUT TO SEND VLAD TEPES THROUGH...WHEN THIS MEDDLESOME STRUMPET LEAPED IN, AND I HAD TO ALTER MY PLANS."
"TIME OUT, HAMLET. THAT IS NOT WHAT HAPPENED."
I DIDN'T JUMP. SOMEBODY PUSHED ME.
ODD...BUT HARDLY SIGNIFICANT.
WITTINGLY OR NOT, YOU HAD INTERFERED WITH MY GAME...
...BUT WHILE YOU WERE TRAPPED IN THE TIME-VORTEX I HAD A MOMENT TO CONTEMPLATE A NEW SCENARIO WHICH HAD EVEN GREATER POTENTIAL TO ENTERTAIN AND ENLIGHTEN.
"I SET YOU AND VLAD AMONG THE GREAT CREATORS OF HORROR FICTION, AND LET THEM WITNESS, AND EVEN PARTICIPATE IN, YOUR STRUGGLES.
"TO MY SURPRISE, I FOUND THAT RATHER THAN ALTERING EVENTS OF THE PAST, YOUR INTRUSIONS AND ANTICS ONLY SERVED TO INSPIRE THE FANTASTIC FICTIONS OF THE FUTURE."

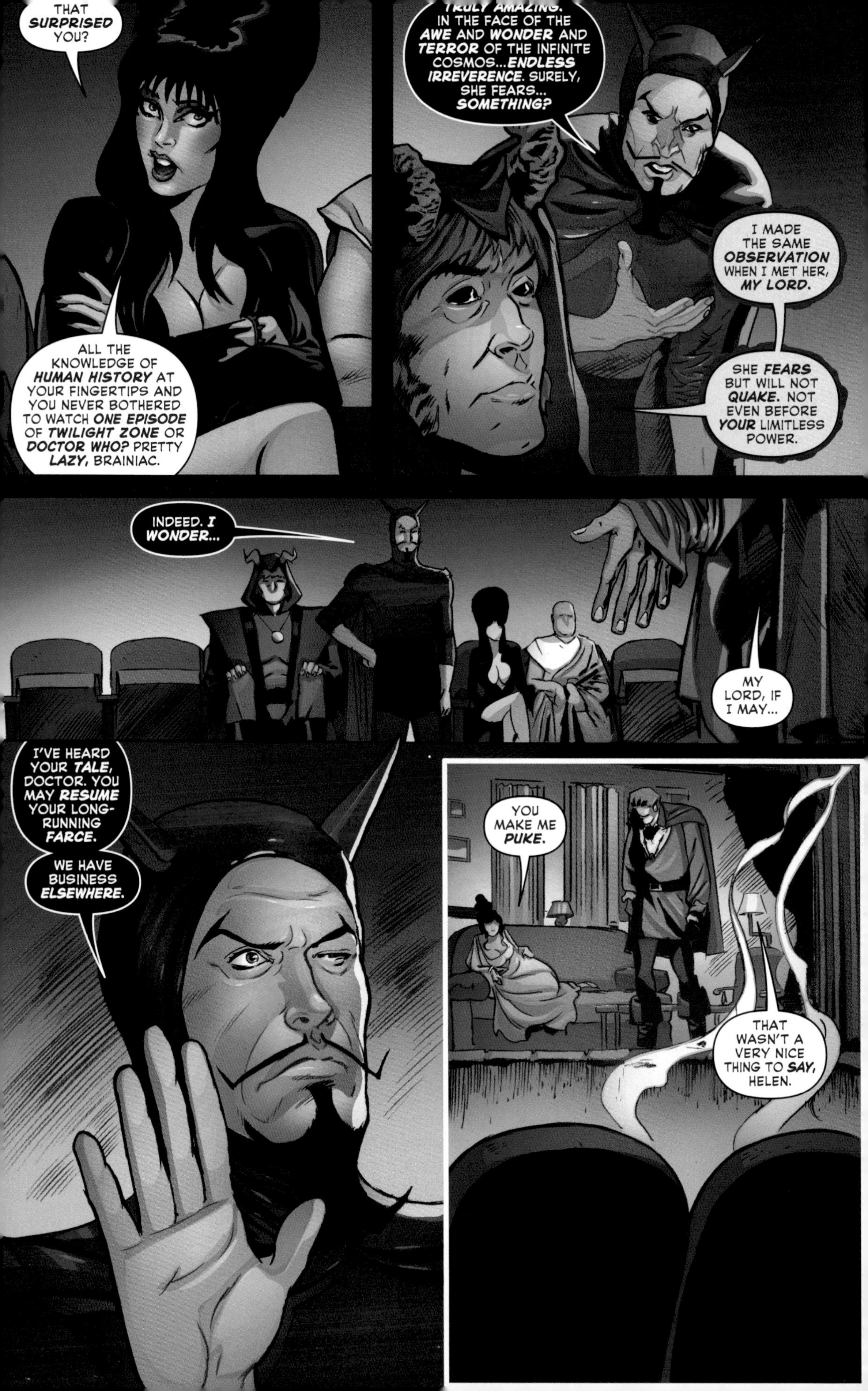
THAT SURPRISED YOU?
ALL THE KNOWLEDGE OF HUMAN HISTORY AT YOUR FINGERTIPS AND YOU NEVER BOTHERED TO WATCH ONE EPISODE OF TWILIGHT ZONE OR DOCTOR WHO? PRETTY LAZY, BRAINIAC.
TRULY AMAZING. IN THE FACE OF THE AWE AND WONDER AND TERROR OF THE INFINITE COSMOS...ENDLESS IRREVERENCE. SURELY, SHE FEARS... SOMETHING?
I MADE THE SAME OBSERVATION WHEN I MET HER, MY LORD.
SHE FEARS BUT WILL NOT QUAKE. NOT EVEN BEFORE YOUR LIMITLESS POWER.
INDEED. I WONDER...
MY LORD, IF I MAY...
I'VE HEARD YOUR TALE, DOCTOR. YOU MAY RESUME YOUR LONG-RUNNING FARCE.
WE HAVE BUSINESS ELSEWHERE.
YOU MAKE ME PUKE.
THAT WASN'T A VERY NICE THING TO SAY, HELEN.

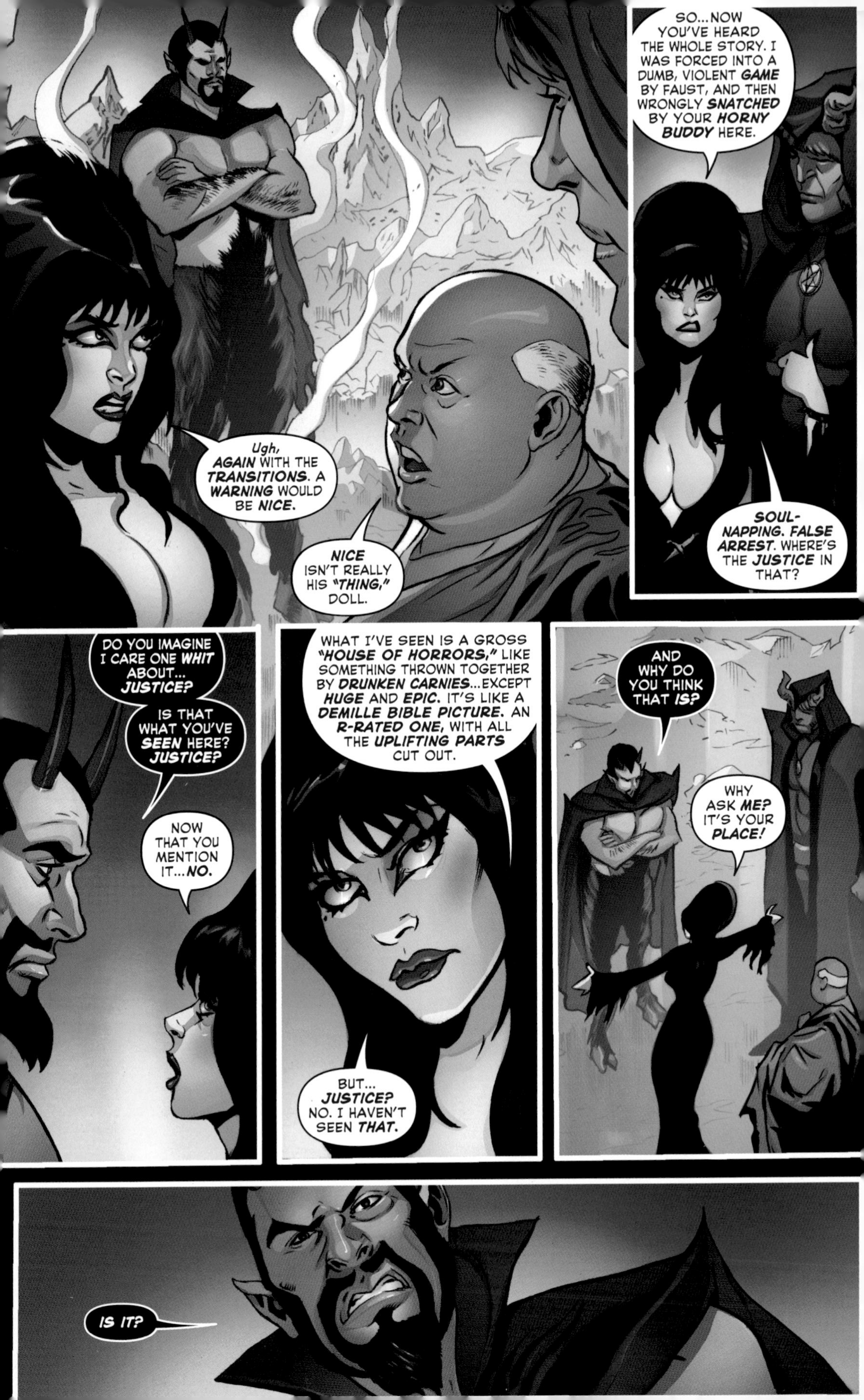
Ugh, AGAIN WITH THE TRANSITIONS. A WARNING WOULD BE NICE.
NICE ISN'T REALLY HIS "THING," DOLL.
SO...NOW YOU'VE HEARD THE WHOLE STORY. I WAS FORCED INTO A DUMB, VIOLENT GAME BY FAUST, AND THEN WRONGLY SNATCHED BY YOUR HORNY BUDDY HERE.
SOUL-NAPPING. FALSE ARREST. WHERE'S THE JUSTICE IN THAT?
DO YOU IMAGINE I CARE ONE WHIT ABOUT... JUSTICE?
IS THAT WHAT YOU'VE SEEN HERE? JUSTICE?
NOW THAT YOU MENTION IT...NO.
WHAT I'VE SEEN IS A GROSS "HOUSE OF HORRORS," LIKE SOMETHING THROWN TOGETHER BY DRUNKEN CARNIES...EXCEPT HUGE AND EPIC. IT'S LIKE A DEMILLE BIBLE PICTURE. AN R-RATED ONE, WITH ALL THE UPLIFTING PARTS CUT OUT.
BUT... JUSTICE? NO. I HAVEN'T SEEN THAT.
AND WHY DO YOU THINK THAT IS?
WHY ASK ME? IT'S YOUR PLACE!
IS IT?

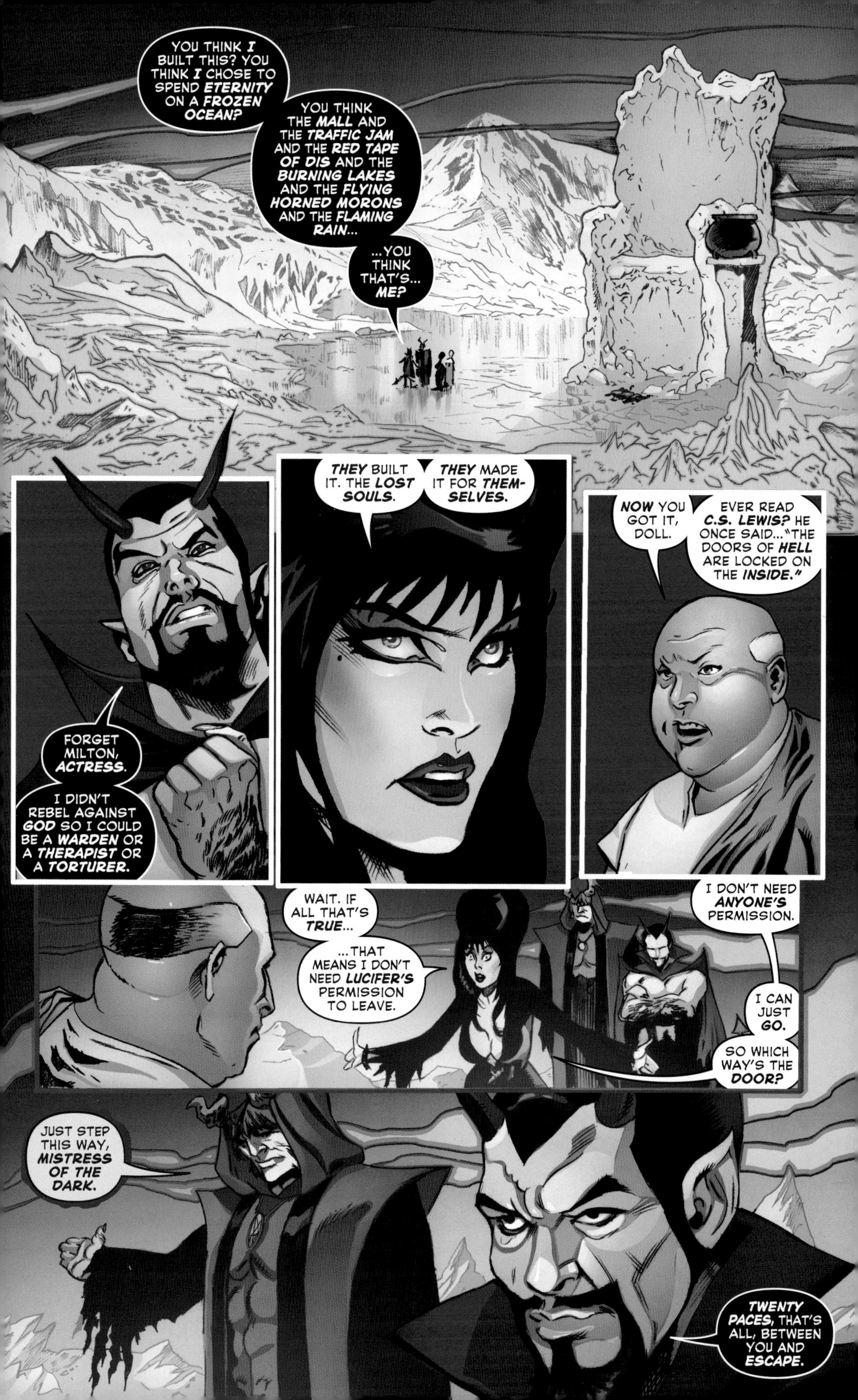
YOU THINK *I* BUILT THIS? YOU THINK *I* CHOSE TO SPEND *ETERNITY* ON A *FROZEN OCEAN?*
YOU THINK THE *MALL* AND THE *TRAFFIC JAM* AND THE *RED TAPE OF DIS* AND THE *BURNING LAKES* AND THE *FLYING HORNED MORONS* AND THE *FLAMING RAIN*...
...YOU THINK THAT'S... *ME?*
FORGET MILTON, *ACTRESS*.
I DIDN'T REBEL AGAINST *GOD* SO I COULD BE A *WARDEN* OR A *THERAPIST* OR A *TORTURER*.
THEY BUILT IT. THE *LOST SOULS*.
THEY MADE IT FOR *THEM-SELVES*.
NOW YOU GOT IT, DOLL.
EVER READ *C.S. LEWIS?* HE ONCE SAID..."THE DOORS OF *HELL* ARE LOCKED ON THE *INSIDE*."
WAIT. IF ALL THAT'S *TRUE*...
...THAT MEANS I DON'T NEED *LUCIFER'S* PERMISSION TO LEAVE.
I DON'T NEED *ANYONE'S* PERMISSION.
I CAN JUST *GO*.
SO WHICH WAY'S THE *DOOR?*
JUST STEP THIS WAY, *MISTRESS OF THE DARK*.
TWENTY PACES, THAT'S ALL, BETWEEN YOU AND *ESCAPE*.

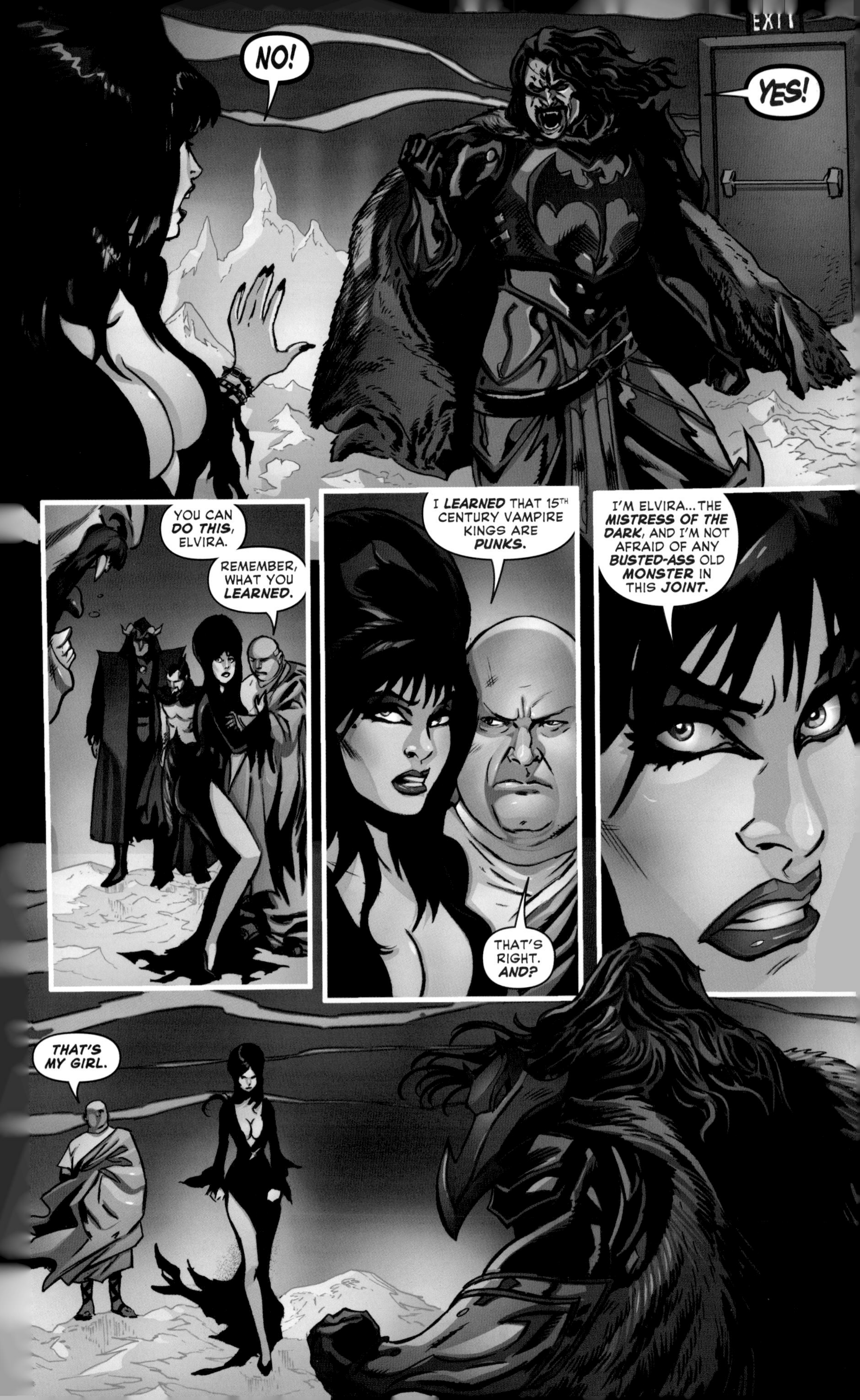

EXIT
NO!
YES!
YOU CAN DO THIS, ELVIRA.
REMEMBER, WHAT YOU LEARNED.
I LEARNED THAT 15TH CENTURY VAMPIRE KINGS ARE PUNKS.
THAT'S RIGHT. AND?
I'M ELVIRA...THE MISTRESS OF THE DARK, AND I'M NOT AFRAID OF ANY BUSTED-ASS OLD MONSTER IN THIS JOINT.
THAT'S MY GIRL.

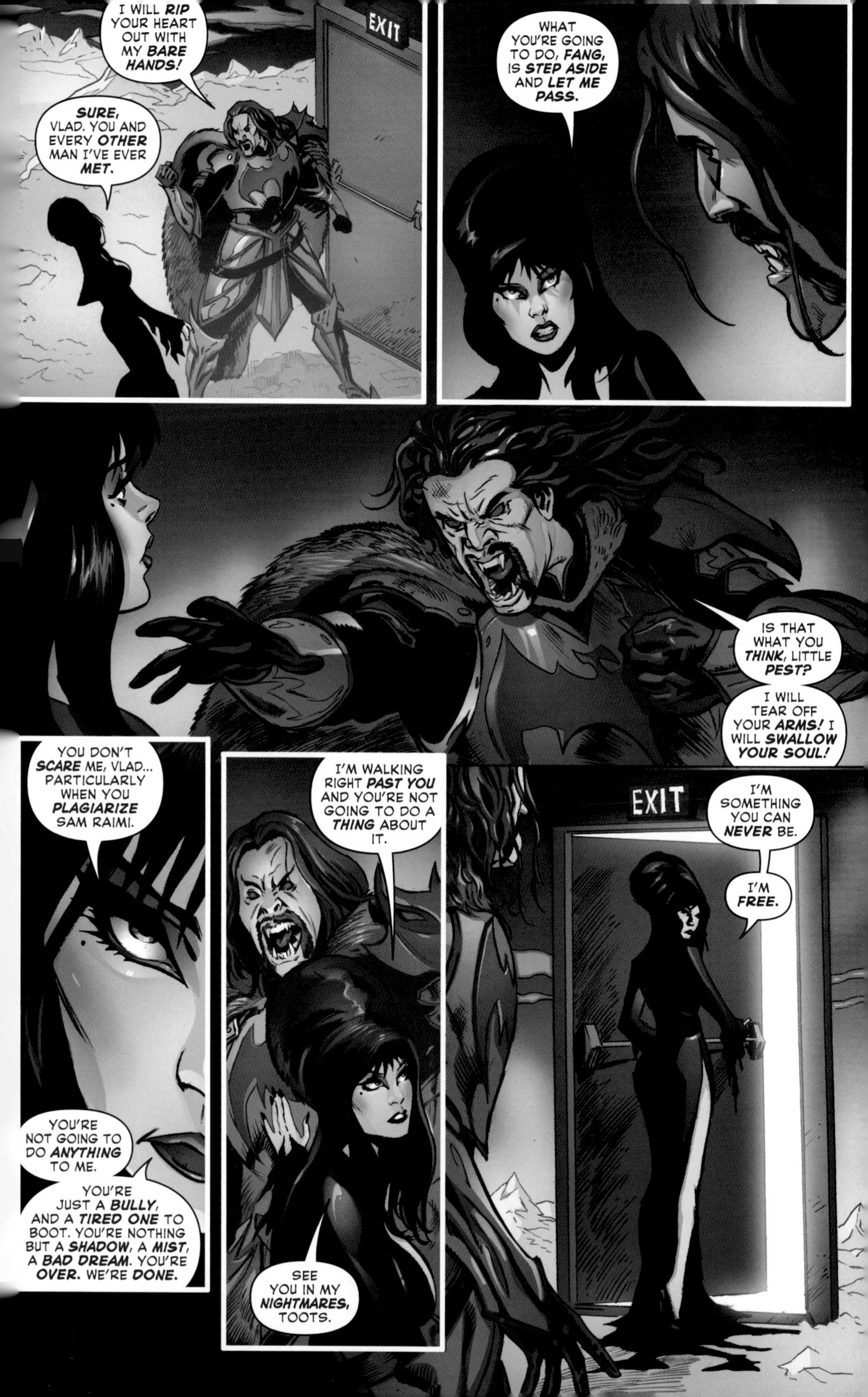

EXIT
I WILL RIP YOUR HEART OUT WITH MY BARE HANDS!
SURE, VLAD. YOU AND EVERY OTHER MAN I'VE EVER MET.
WHAT YOU'RE GOING TO DO, FANG, IS STEP ASIDE AND LET ME PASS.
IS THAT WHAT YOU THINK, LITTLE PEST?
I WILL TEAR OFF YOUR ARMS! I WILL SWALLOW YOUR SOUL!
YOU DON'T SCARE ME, VLAD... PARTICULARLY WHEN YOU PLAGIARIZE SAM RAIMI.
YOU'RE NOT GOING TO DO ANYTHING TO ME.
YOU'RE JUST A BULLY, AND A TIRED ONE TO BOOT. YOU'RE NOTHING BUT A SHADOW, A MIST, A BAD DREAM. YOU'RE OVER. WE'RE DONE.
I'M WALKING RIGHT PAST YOU AND YOU'RE NOT GOING TO DO A THING ABOUT IT.
SEE YOU IN MY NIGHTMARES, TOOTS.
EXIT
I'M SOMETHING YOU CAN NEVER BE.
I'M FREE.

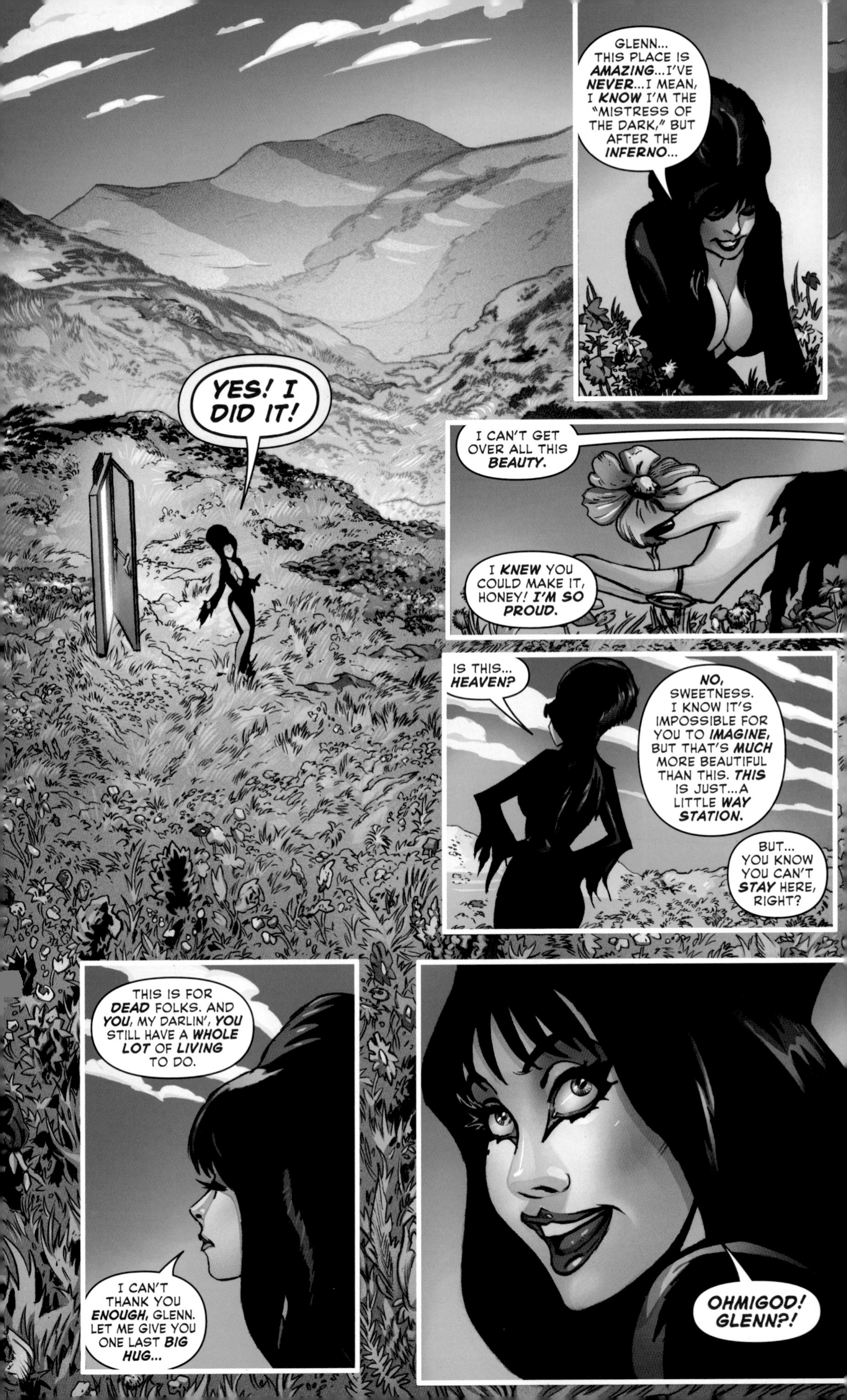
YES! I DID IT!
GLENN... THIS PLACE IS AMAZING...I'VE NEVER...I MEAN, I KNOW I'M THE "MISTRESS OF THE DARK," BUT AFTER THE INFERNO...
I CAN'T GET OVER ALL THIS BEAUTY.
I KNEW YOU COULD MAKE IT, HONEY! I'M SO PROUD.
IS THIS... HEAVEN?
NO, SWEETNESS. I KNOW IT'S IMPOSSIBLE FOR YOU TO IMAGINE, BUT THAT'S MUCH MORE BEAUTIFUL THAN THIS. THIS IS JUST...A LITTLE WAY STATION.
BUT... YOU KNOW YOU CAN'T STAY HERE, RIGHT?
THIS IS FOR DEAD FOLKS. AND YOU, MY DARLIN', YOU STILL HAVE A WHOLE LOT OF LIVING TO DO.
I CAN'T THANK YOU ENOUGH, GLENN. LET ME GIVE YOU ONE LAST BIG HUG...
OHMIGOD! GLENN?!

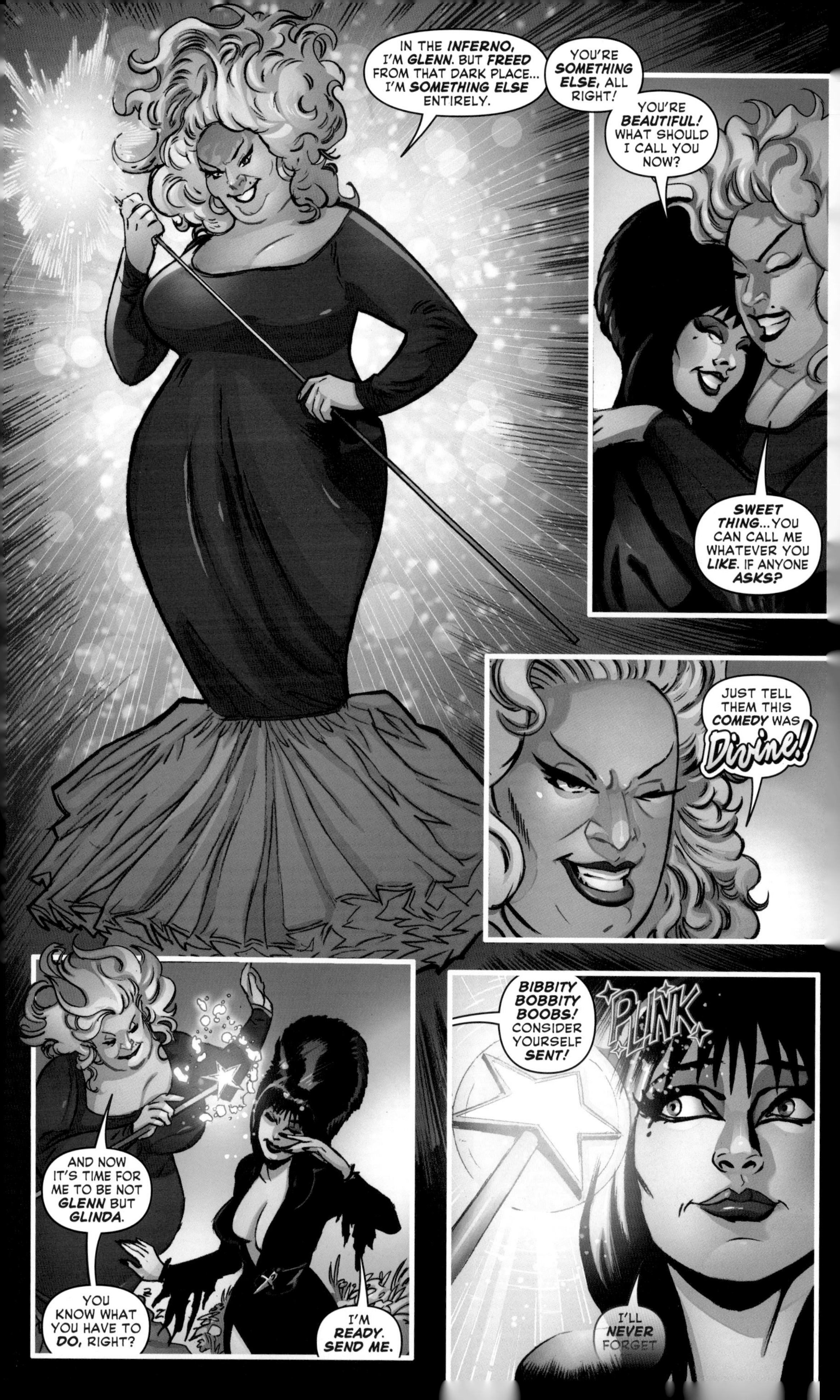
IN THE INFERNO, I'M GLENN. BUT FREED FROM THAT DARK PLACE... I'M SOMETHING ELSE ENTIRELY.
YOU'RE SOMETHING ELSE, ALL RIGHT!
YOU'RE BEAUTIFUL! WHAT SHOULD I CALL YOU NOW?
SWEET THING...YOU CAN CALL ME WHATEVER YOU LIKE. IF ANYONE ASKS?
JUST TELL THEM THIS COMEDY WAS Divine!
AND NOW IT'S TIME FOR ME TO BE NOT GLENN BUT GLINDA.
YOU KNOW WHAT YOU HAVE TO DO, RIGHT?
I'M READY. SEND ME.
BIBBITY BOBBITY BOOBS! CONSIDER YOURSELF SENT!
PLINK
I'LL NEVER FORGET

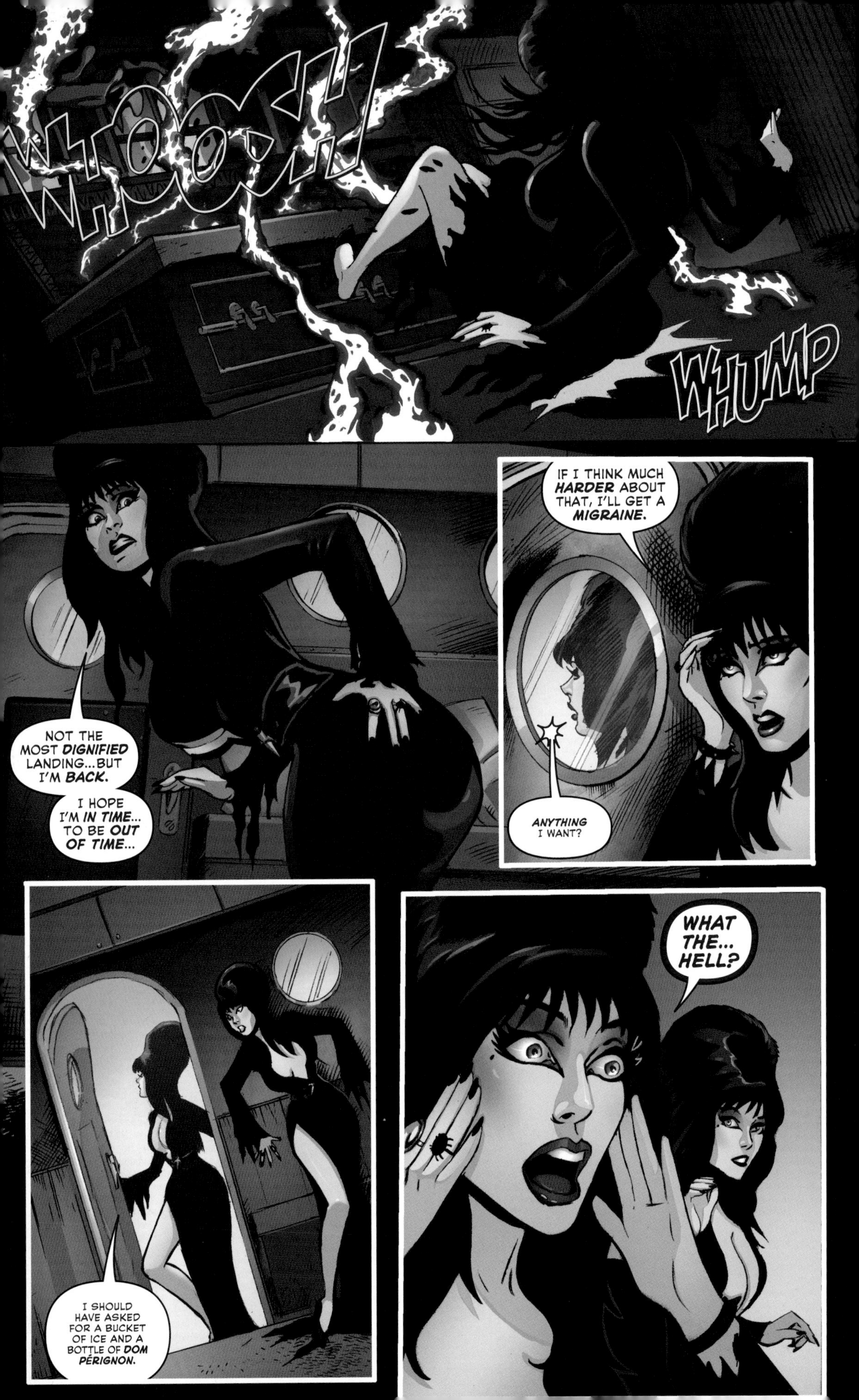
WHOOSH
WHUMP
NOT THE MOST DIGNIFIED LANDING...BUT I'M BACK.
I HOPE I'M IN TIME... TO BE OUT OF TIME...
IF I THINK MUCH HARDER ABOUT THAT, I'LL GET A MIGRAINE.
ANYTHING I WANT?
I SHOULD HAVE ASKED FOR A BUCKET OF ICE AND A BOTTLE OF DOM PÉRIGNON.
WHAT THE... HELL?

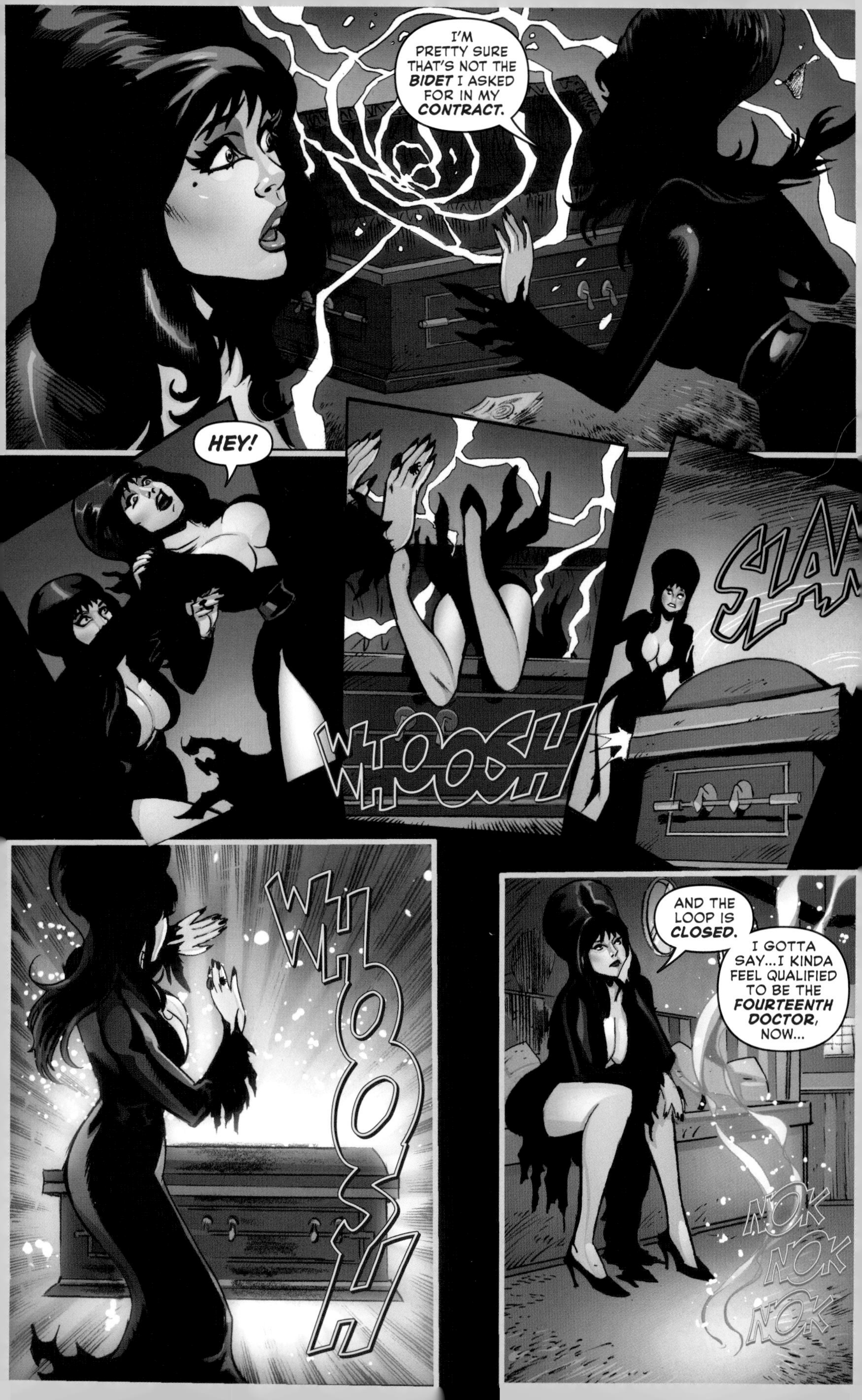
I'M PRETTY SURE THAT'S NOT THE ***BIDET*** I ASKED FOR IN MY ***CONTRACT.***
HEY!
WHOOSH
WHOOSH
AND THE LOOP IS ***CLOSED.***
I GOTTA SAY...I KINDA FEEL QUALIFIED TO BE THE ***FOURTEENTH DOCTOR,*** NOW...
NOK NOK NOK

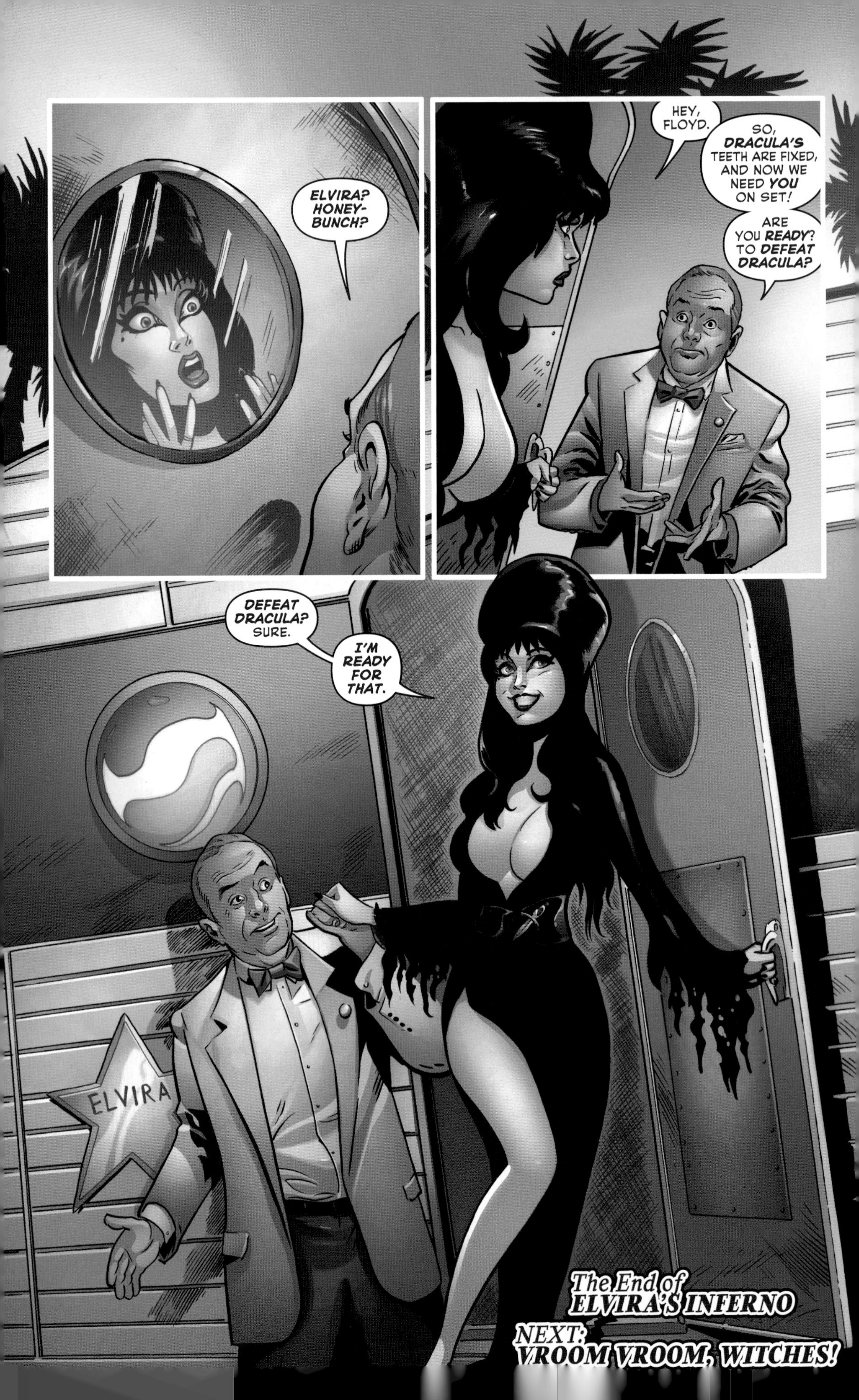
ELVIRA? HONEY-BUNCH?
HEY, FLOYD.
SO, DRACULA'S TEETH ARE FIXED, AND NOW WE NEED YOU ON SET!
ARE YOU READY? TO DEFEAT DRACULA?
DEFEAT DRACULA? SURE.
I'M READY FOR THAT.
ELVIRA
The End of ELVIRA'S INFERNO
NEXT: VROOM VROOM, WITCHES!

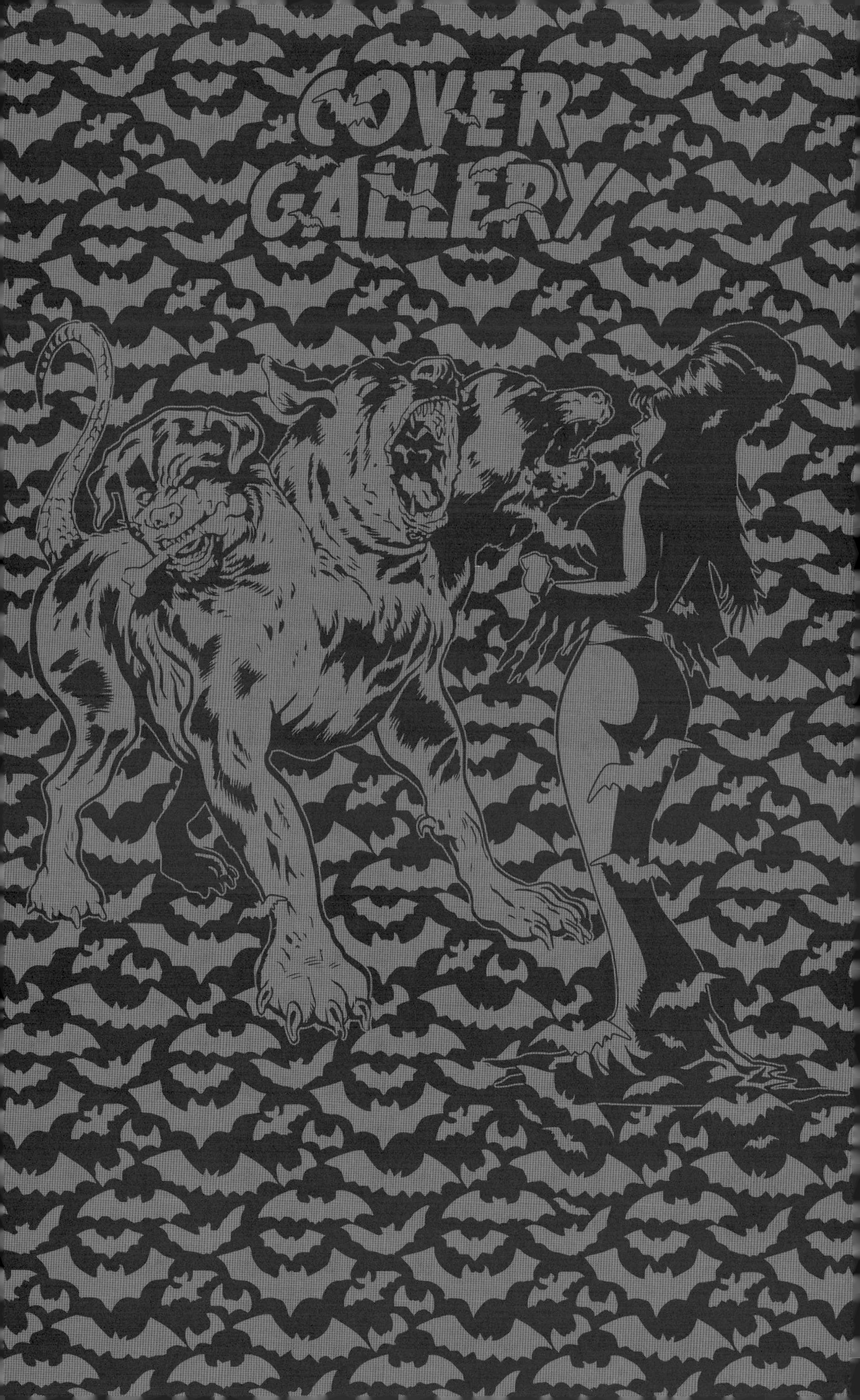
COVER GALLERY

5

COVER ART: CRAIG CERMAK

COLORS: BRITTANY PEZZILLO

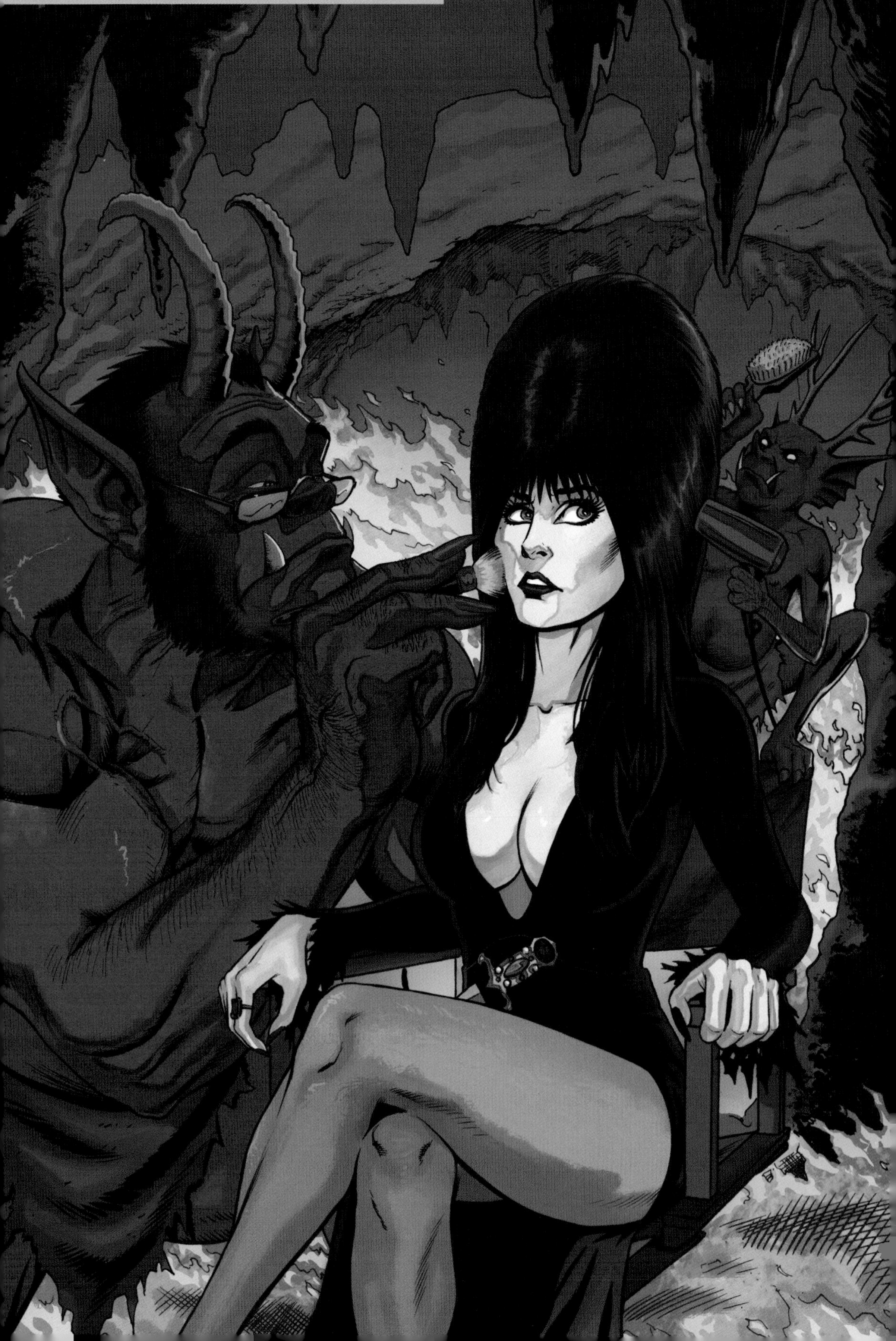

5 COVER ART: ROBERT HACK

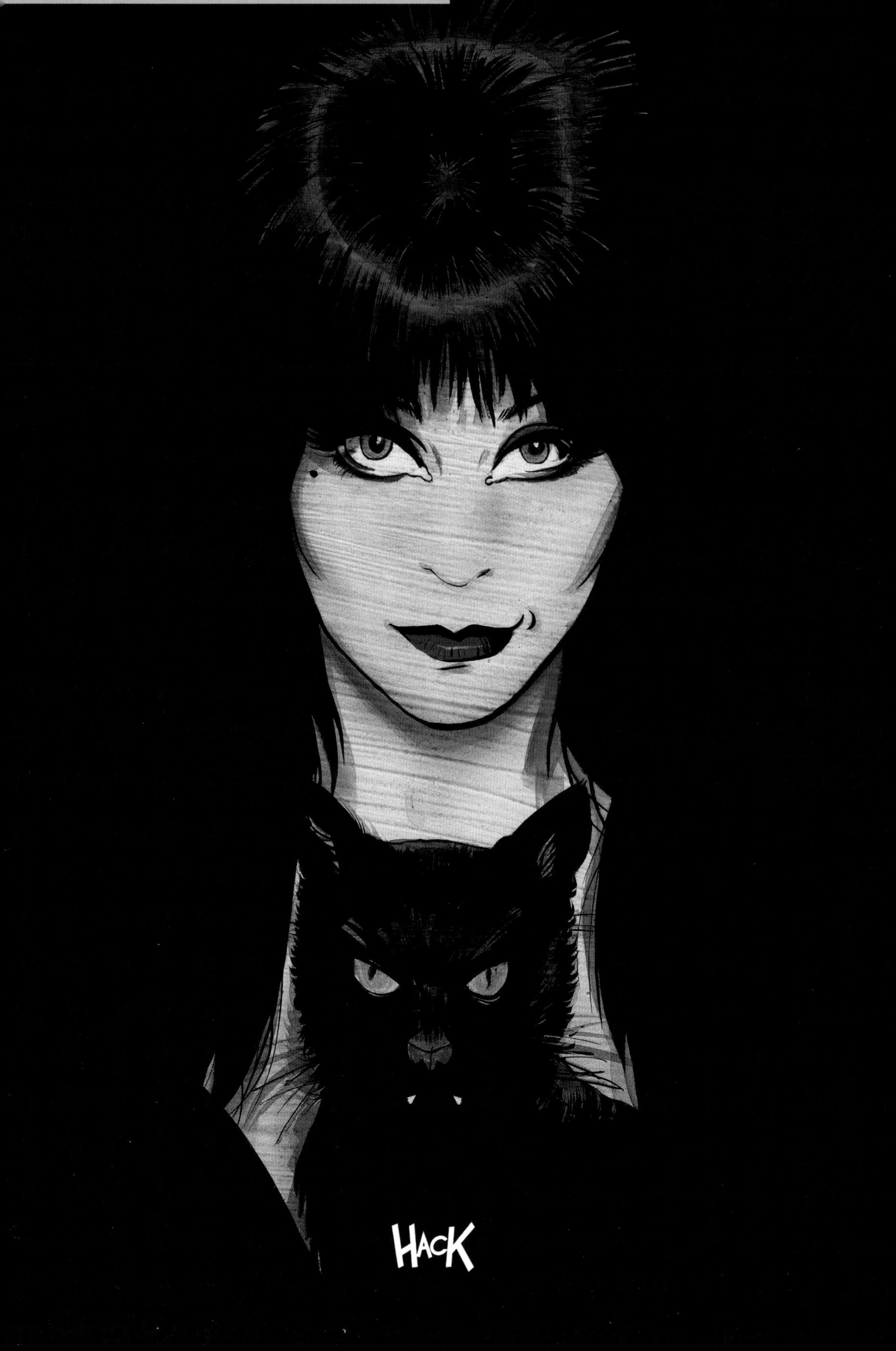
HACK

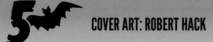

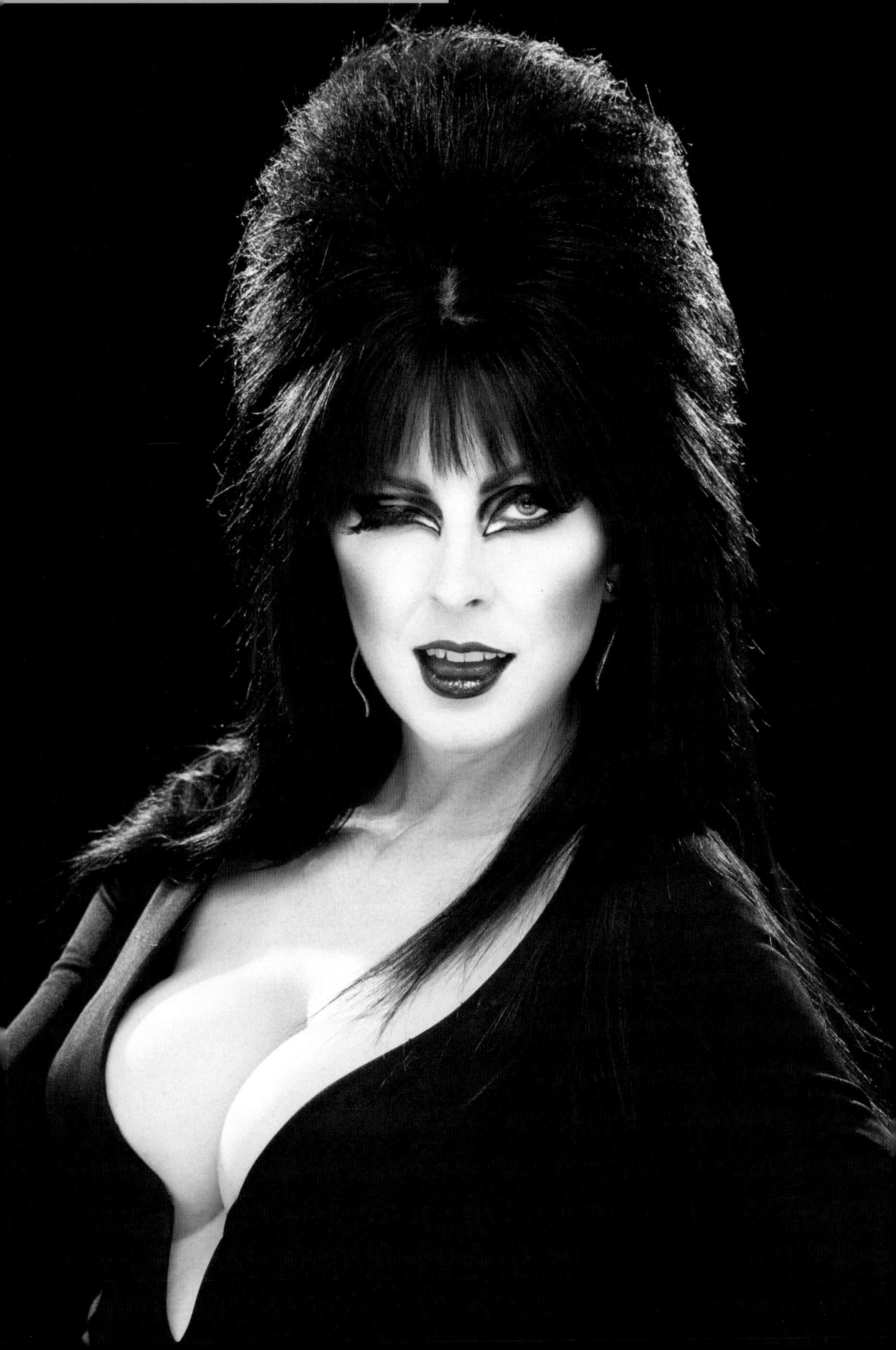

5

COVER ART: ROBERTO CASTRO
COLORS: SALVATORE AIALA

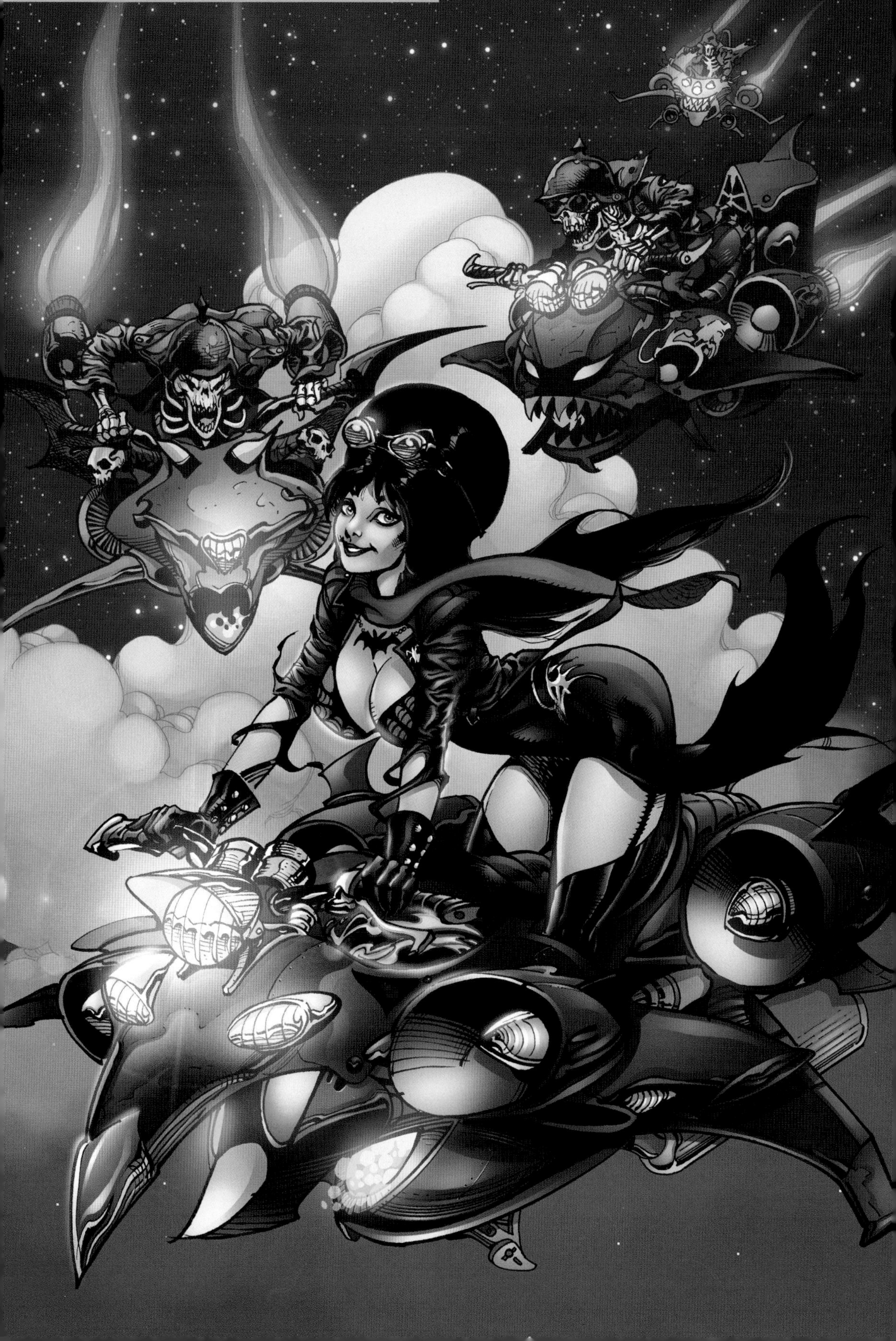

6

COVER ART: CRAIG CERMAK
COLORS: BRITTANY PEZZILLO

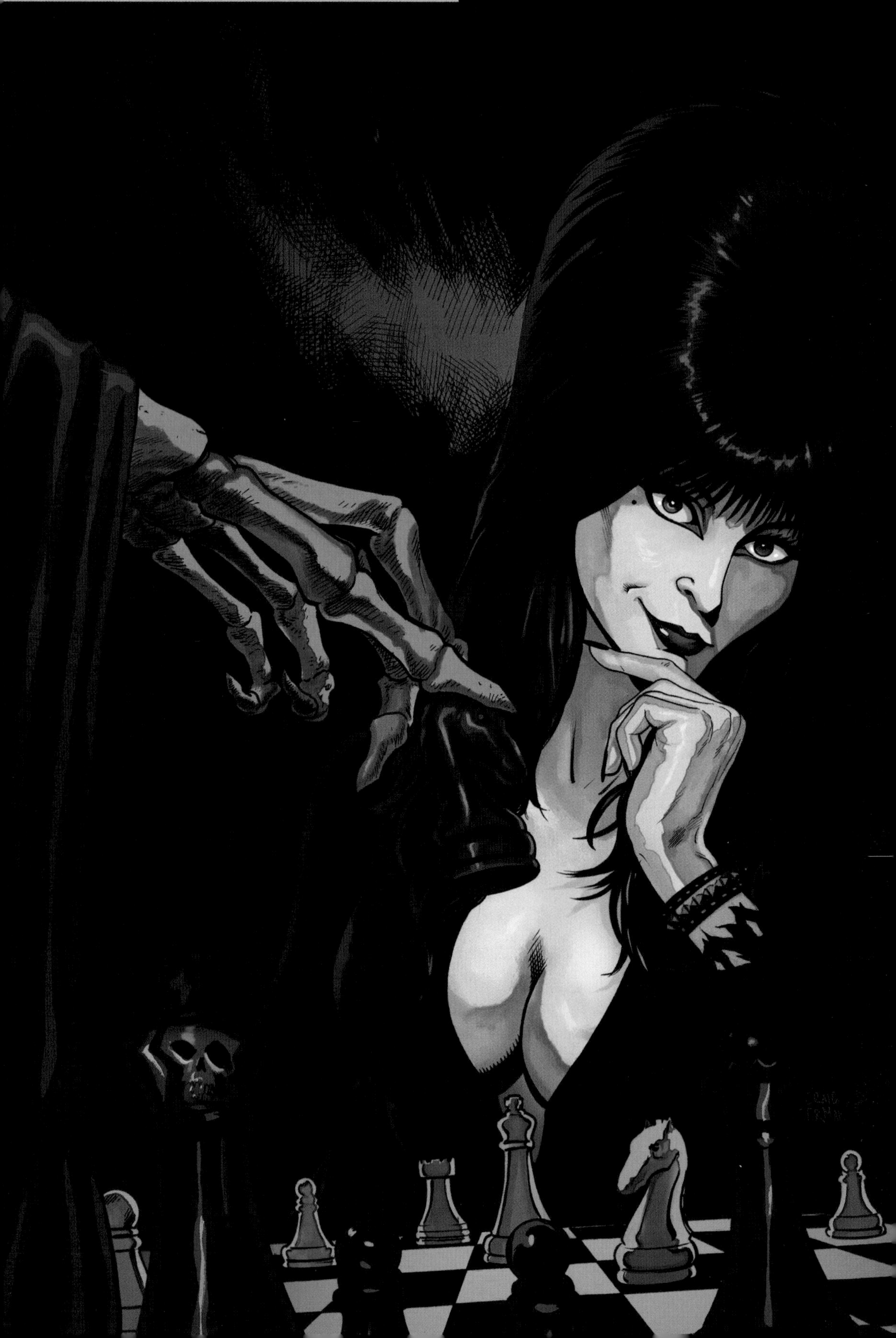

6

COVER ART: JOHN ROYLE

COLORS: MOHAN

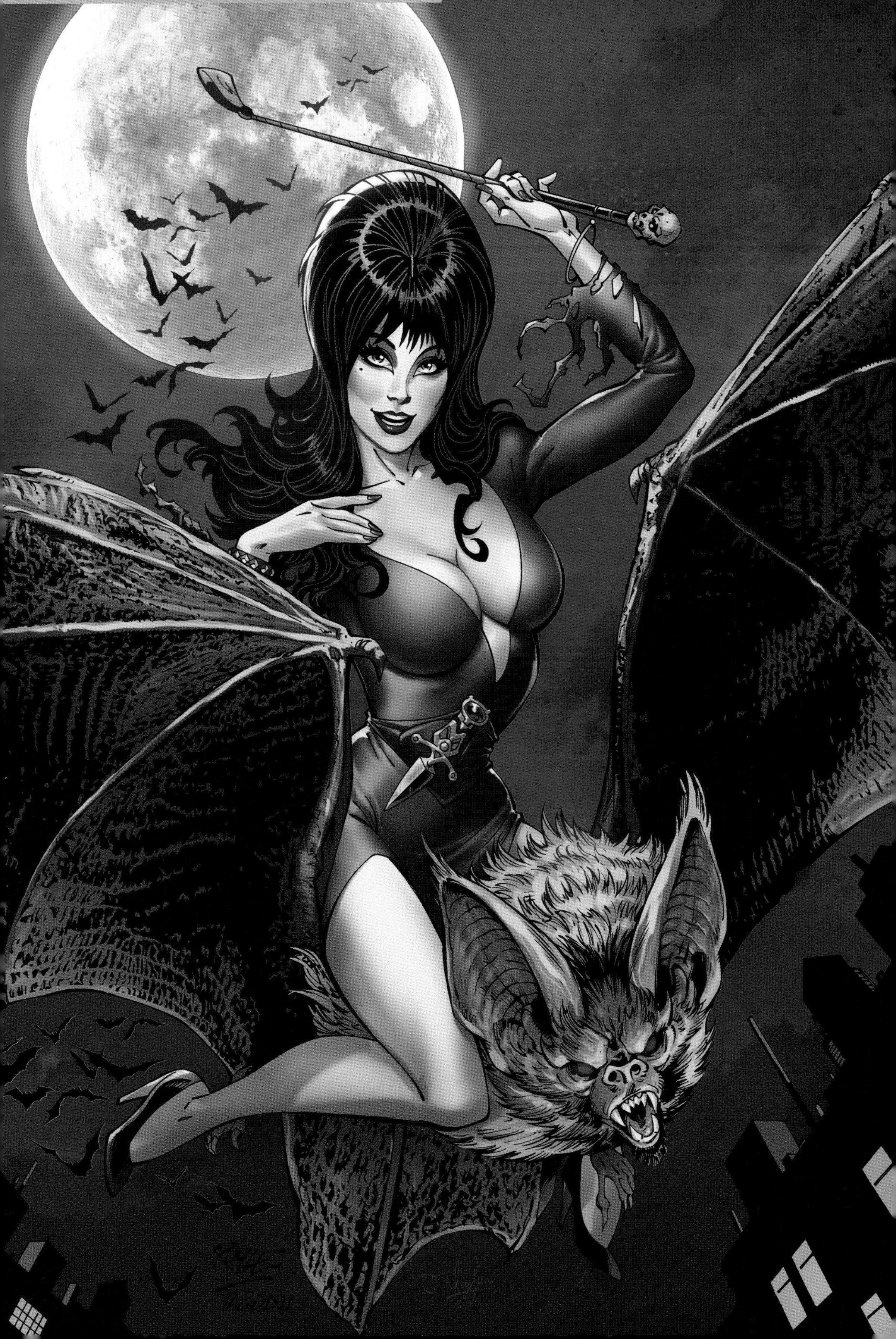

6 PHOTO COVER

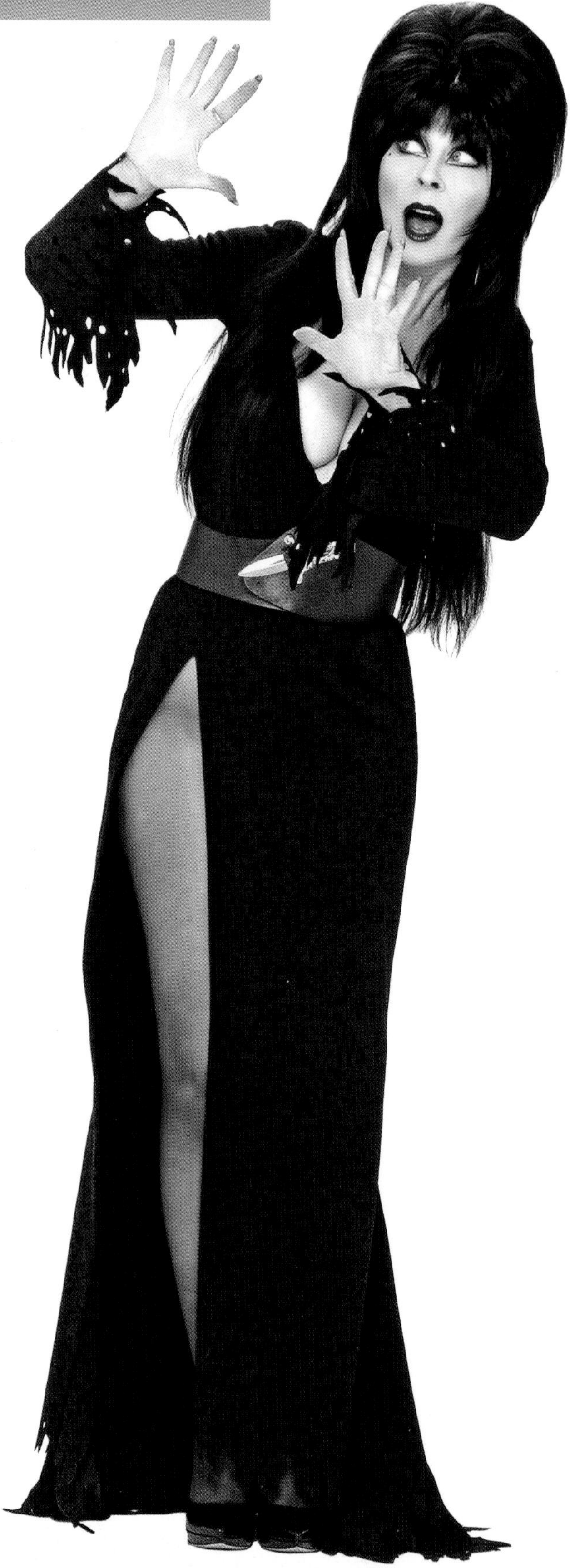

6

COVER ART: ROBERTO CASTRO
COLORS: SALVATORE AIALA

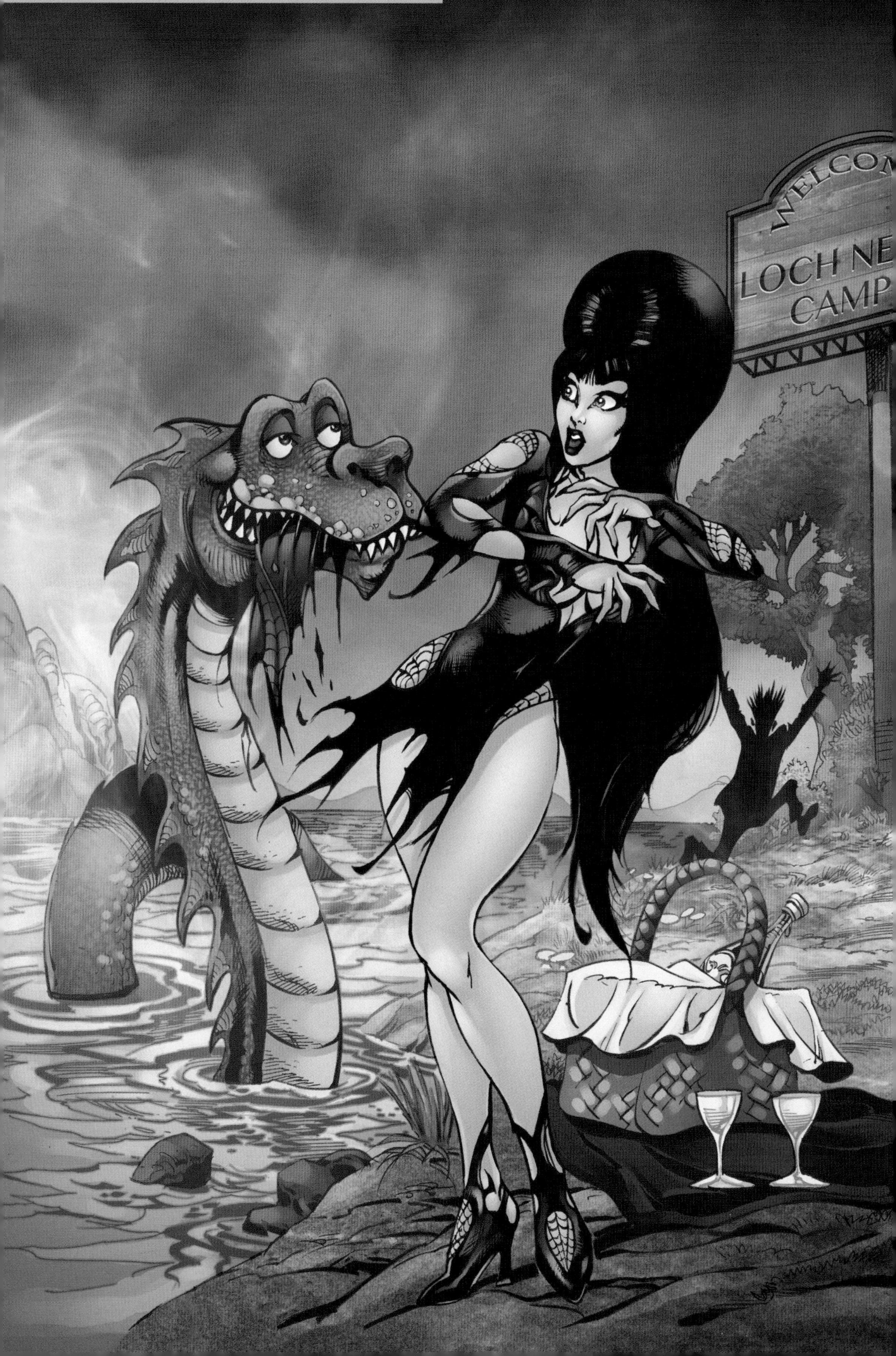
WELCOM
LOCH NE
CAMP

7

COVER ART: CRAIG CERMAK
COLORS: BRITTANY PEZZILLO

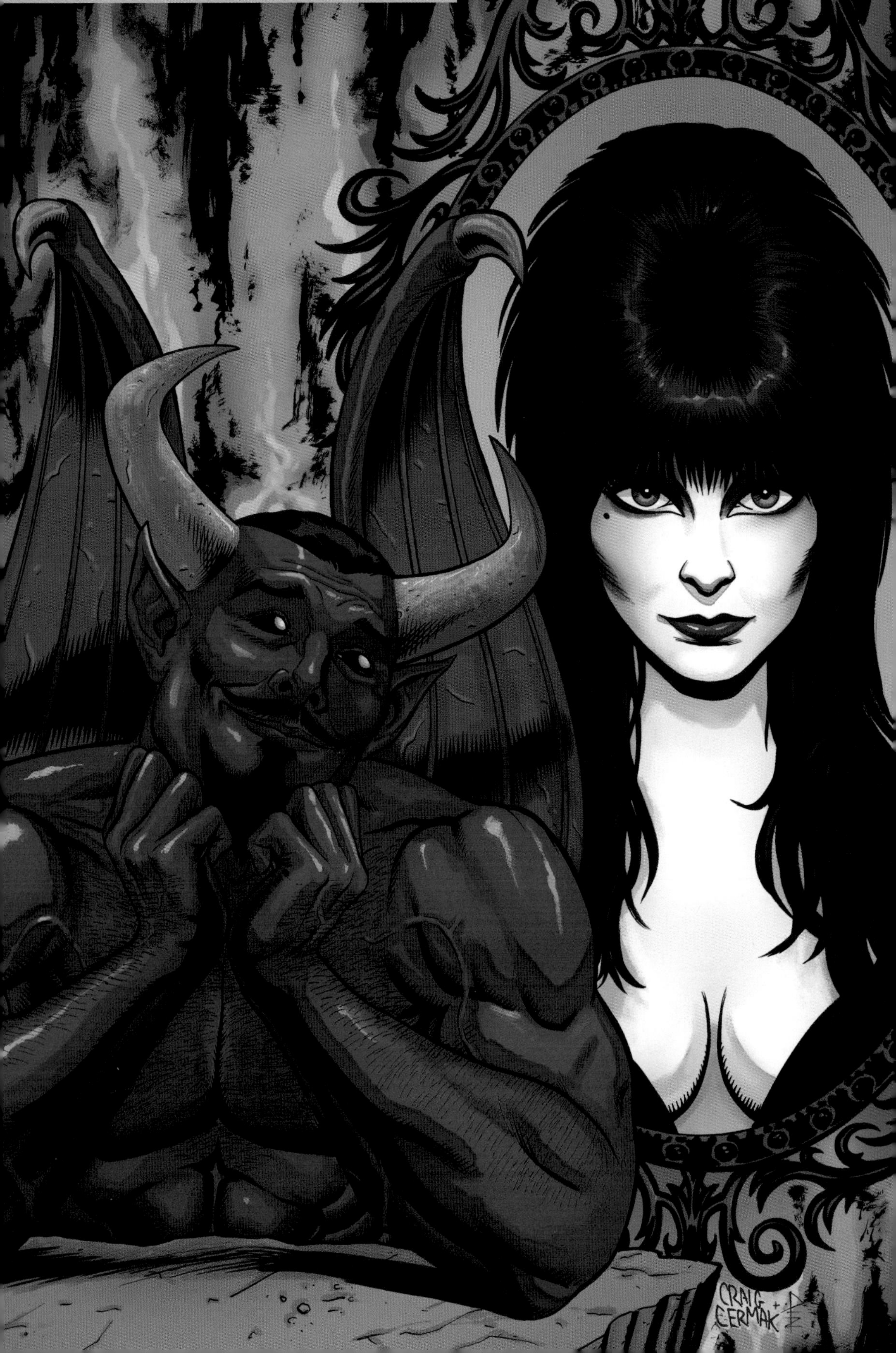
CRAIG + CERMAK

7

COVER ART: JOHN ROYLE
COLORS: MOHAN

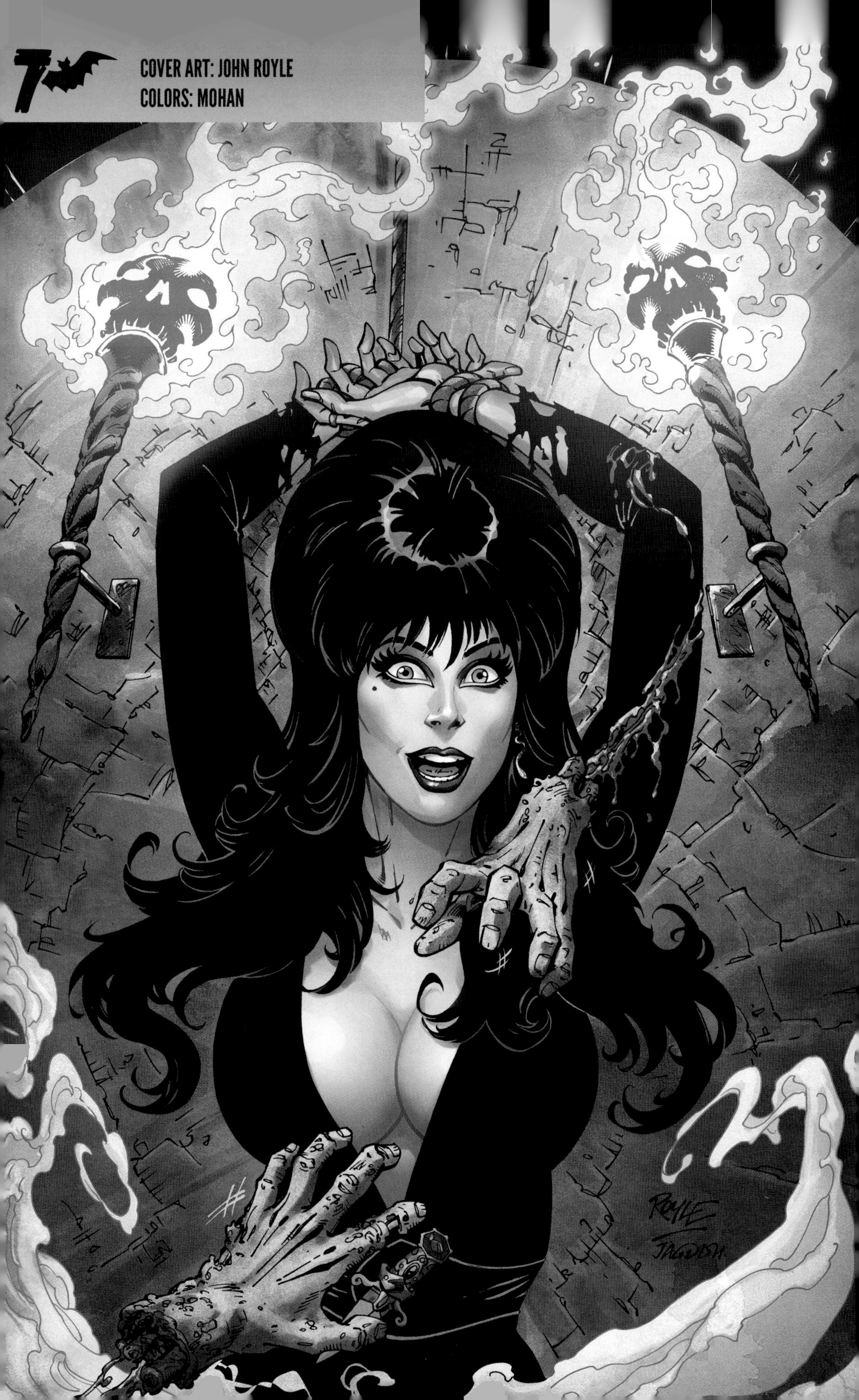
ROYLE

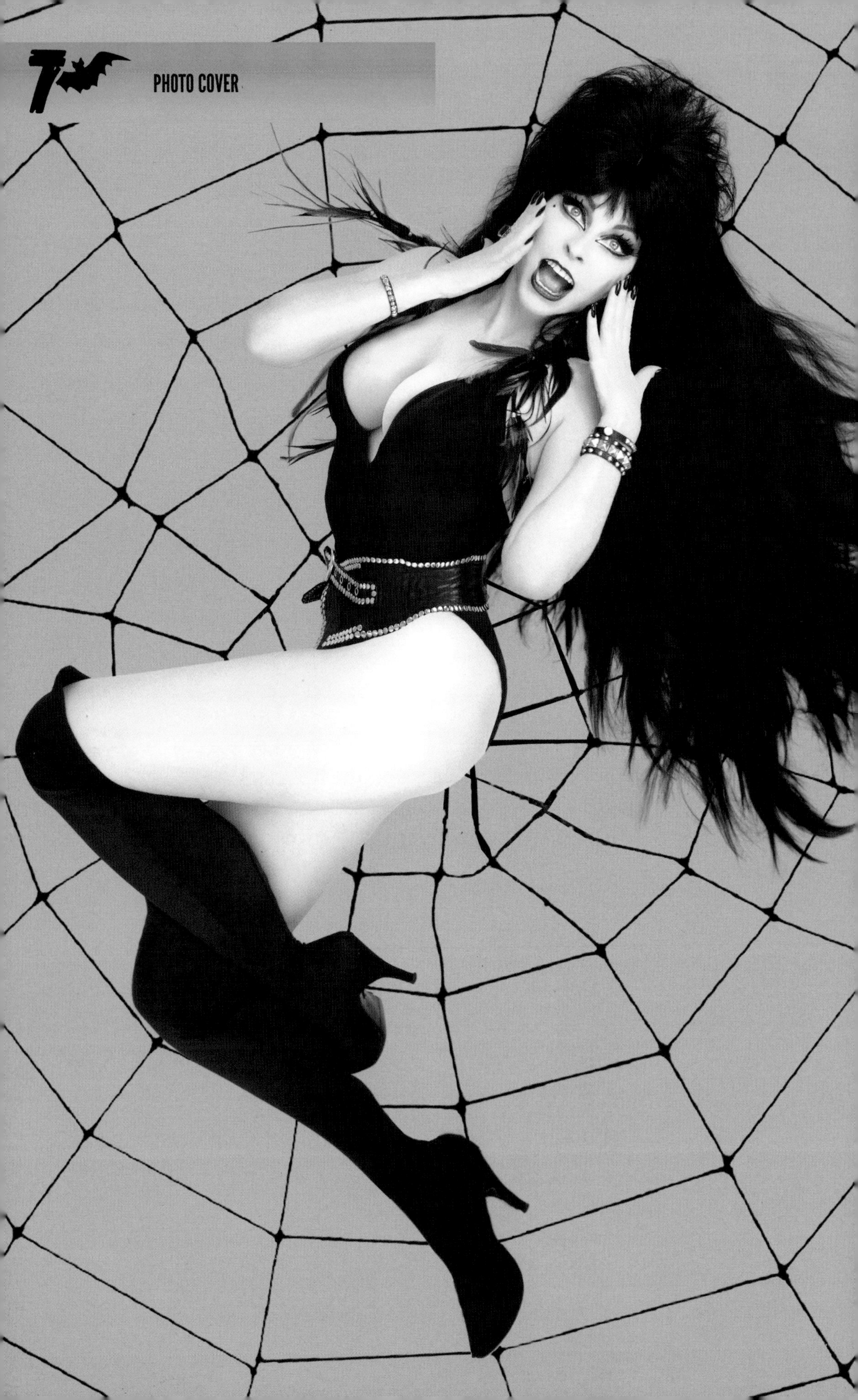

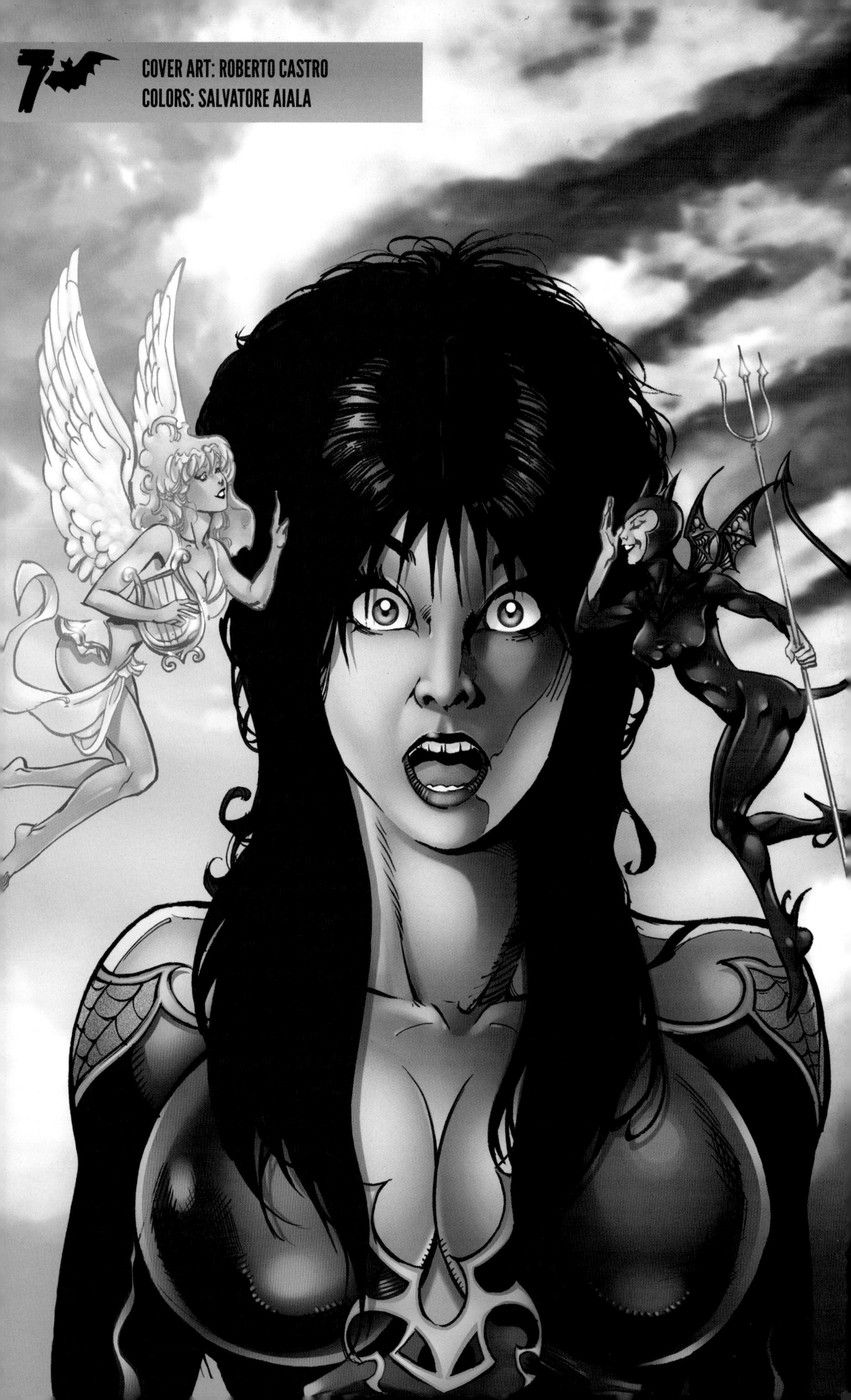

7

COVER ART: ROBERTO CASTRO
COLORS: SALVATORE AIALA

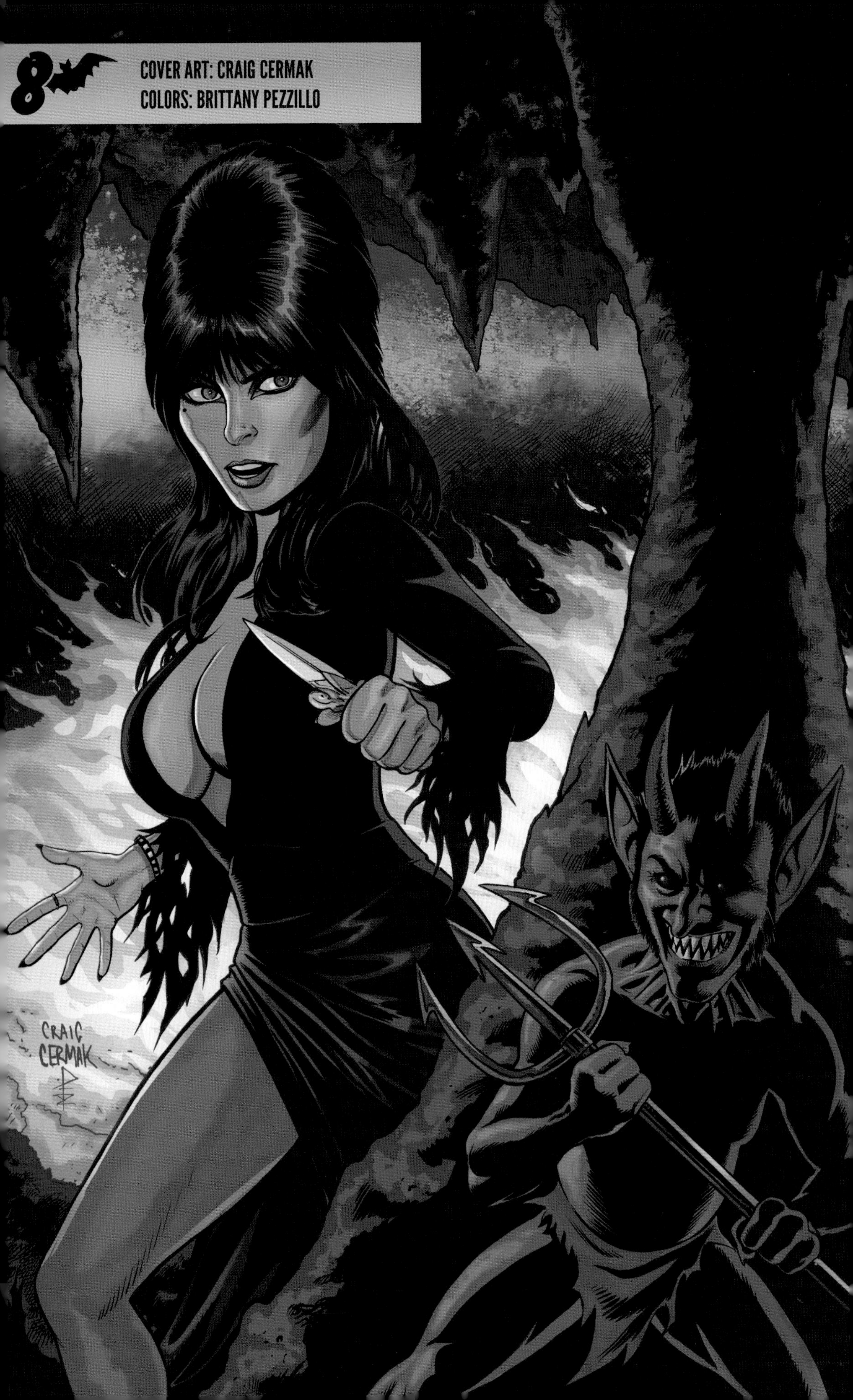
CRAIG CERMAK

8 COVER ART: CRAIG CERMAK
COLORS: BRITTANY PEZZILLO

8

COVER ART: JOHN ROYLE
COLORS: MOHAN

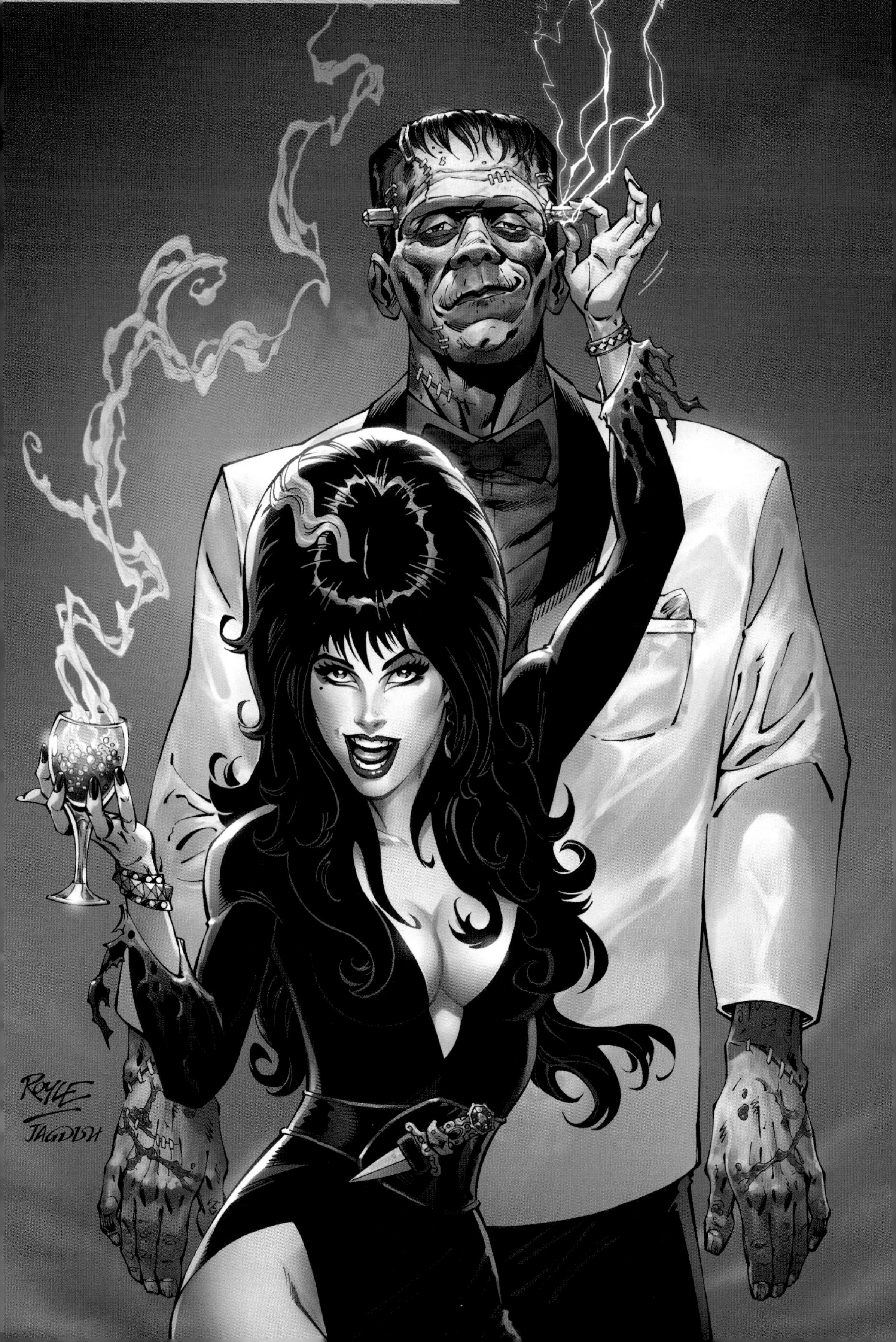
ROYLE
JAGDISH

8 PHOTO COVER

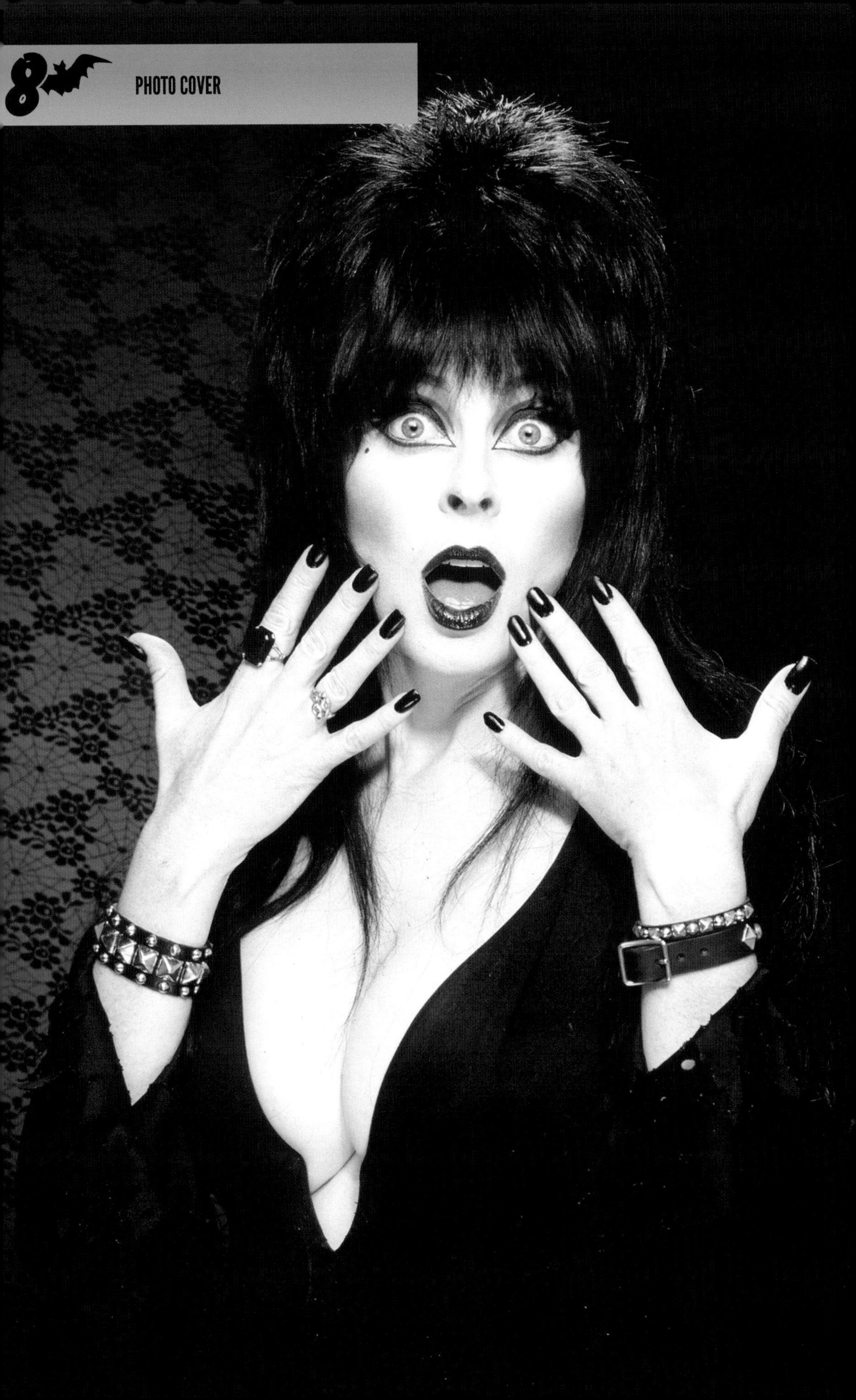

8

COVER ART: ROBERTO CASTRO
COLORS: SALVATORE AIALA

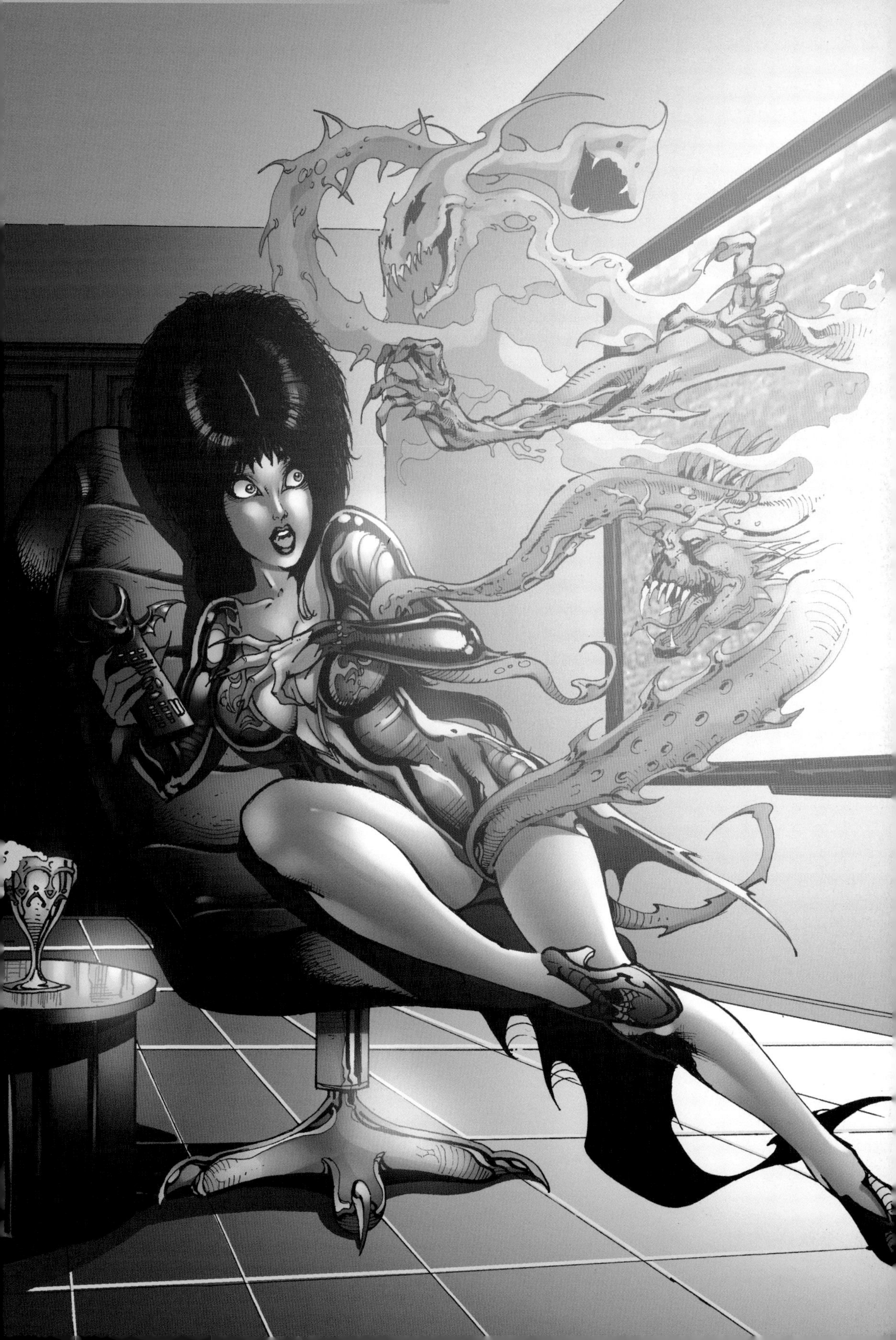

ELVIRA'S INFERNO: AFTERWORD

This wasn't in the original plan.

When I was asked to write *Elvira: Mistress of the Dark*, a four-issue miniseries was requested, which I dutifully outlined and pitched, and with the blessings of Elvira herself... Cassandra Peterson... I got to work.

The result was volume one of this series, *Elvira: Timescream*. I was having a blast writing it, and moving towards my well-planned climax in issue four... when I was told that the sales had been amazing and Dynamite would like another four-issue arc. Where to go next?

I had originally come up with an "Elvira in Hell" pitch before we started the first arc, but it felt too dark at the time, so I abandoned it. For one thing, Elvira had to die to get to Hell. (In the first draft, I believe she was hit by a semi full of sex toys. Like I said. Dark.) But remembering that I had set up Faust as the overall villain gave me a new way to get Elvira to Hell. Faust was heading there anyway. What if Elvira got dragged along?

These four issues are, for very obvious reasons, hugely influenced by Dante Alighieri's epic poem *The Divine Comedy*, which is broken into three sections (of which Inferno is the first.) In *Dante's Inferno*, Dante himself is transported to Hell, and his guide is the Roman poet Virgil. But who could be a fitting iconic tour guide for Elvira? True story: I decided that Glenn Milstead/Divine would be perfect before I even noticed the pun of The "Divine" Comedy. It was just that magical coincidence... or my subconscious working overtime. I was also inspired somewhat by Larry Niven and Jerry Pournelle's science fiction novel *Inferno*, which imagines a modern sci-fi writer dying and finding himself in Hell. Like Niven and Pournelle, I had a lot of fun updating Dante's medieval tortures to something more modern.

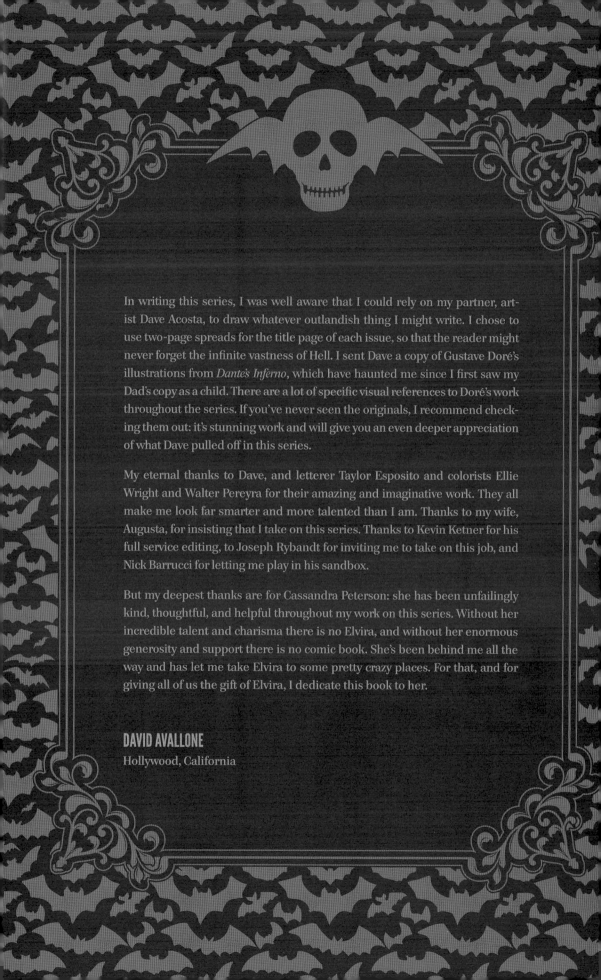

In writing this series, I was well aware that I could rely on my partner, artist Dave Acosta, to draw whatever outlandish thing I might write. I chose to use two-page spreads for the title page of each issue, so that the reader might never forget the infinite vastness of Hell. I sent Dave a copy of Gustave Doré's illustrations from *Dante's Inferno*, which have haunted me since I first saw my Dad's copy as a child. There are a lot of specific visual references to Doré's work throughout the series. If you've never seen the originals, I recommend checking them out: it's stunning work and will give you an even deeper appreciation of what Dave pulled off in this series.

My eternal thanks to Dave, and letterer Taylor Esposito and colorists Ellie Wright and Walter Pereyra for their amazing and imaginative work. They all make me look far smarter and more talented than I am. Thanks to my wife, Augusta, for insisting that I take on this series. Thanks to Kevin Ketner for his full service editing, to Joseph Rybandt for inviting me to take on this job, and Nick Barrucci for letting me play in his sandbox.

But my deepest thanks are for Cassandra Peterson: she has been unfailingly kind, thoughtful, and helpful throughout my work on this series. Without her incredible talent and charisma there is no Elvira, and without her enormous generosity and support there is no comic book. She's been behind me all the way and has let me take Elvira to some pretty crazy places. For that, and for giving all of us the gift of Elvira, I dedicate this book to her.

DAVID AVALLONE
Hollywood, California

ELVIRA IS BACK AND THIS TITLE WILL LEAVE US ALL

DYING FOR MORE.

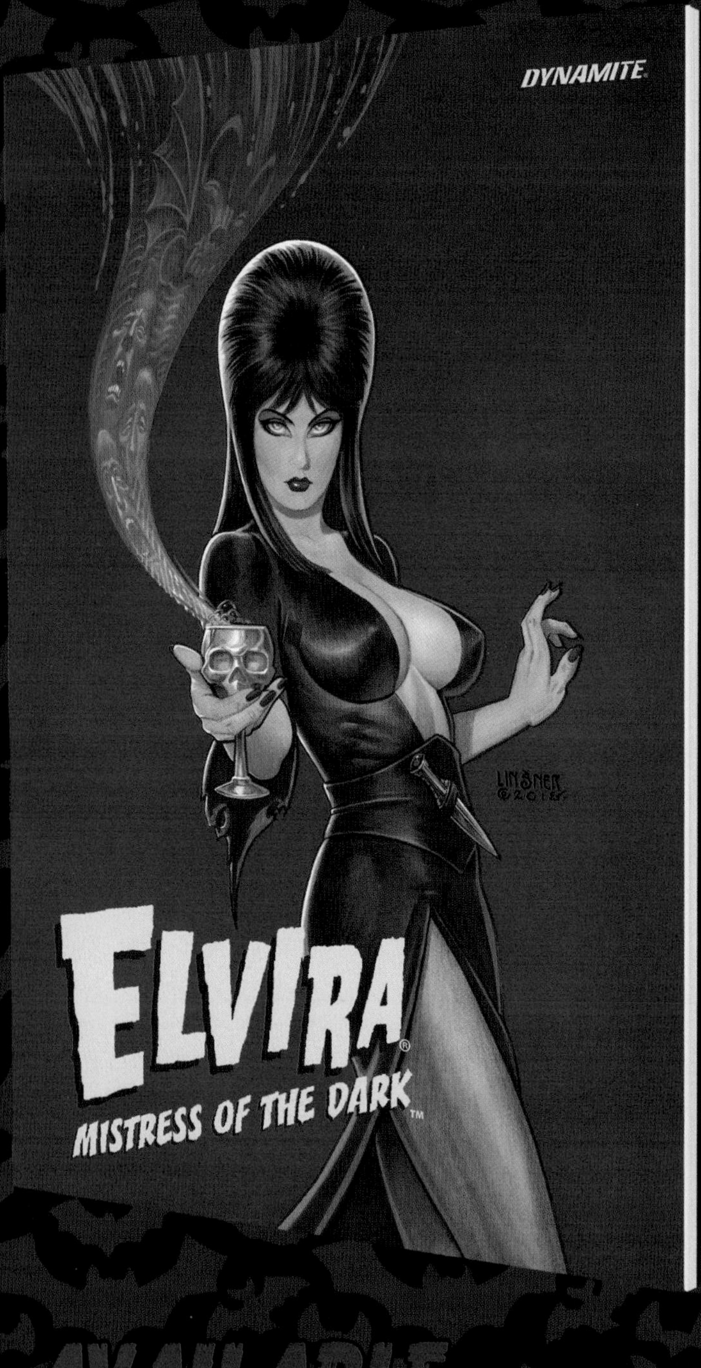
DYNAMITE
ELVIRA®
MISTRESS OF THE DARK™

The Mistress of the Dark has become unstuck in time! Elvira begins an epic journey through horror history, stalked by the most terrifying nightmare to ever walk the Earth. (No spoilers!)

Writer **David Avallone** (Bettie Page, Twilight Zone) and **Dave Acosta** (Doc Savage) bring you the thrills, chills and double-entendres you've all been waiting for!

"YOU KNOW WHAT TO EXPECT WHEN ELVIRA IS INVOLVED AND THIS COMIC DELIVERS ON THAT FUN IN SPADES."

– Horror Talk

"DO YOU LIKE ELVIRA? DO YOU LIKE THE CAMPY HUMOR, THE HARMLESS TITILLATION, AND THE 4TH WALL BREAKING? I DO AND THAT'S WHY I LOVE THIS COMIC."

– Comic Buzz

AVAILABLE NOW

DYNAMITE

www.dynamite.com

/dynamitecomics

@dynamitecomics

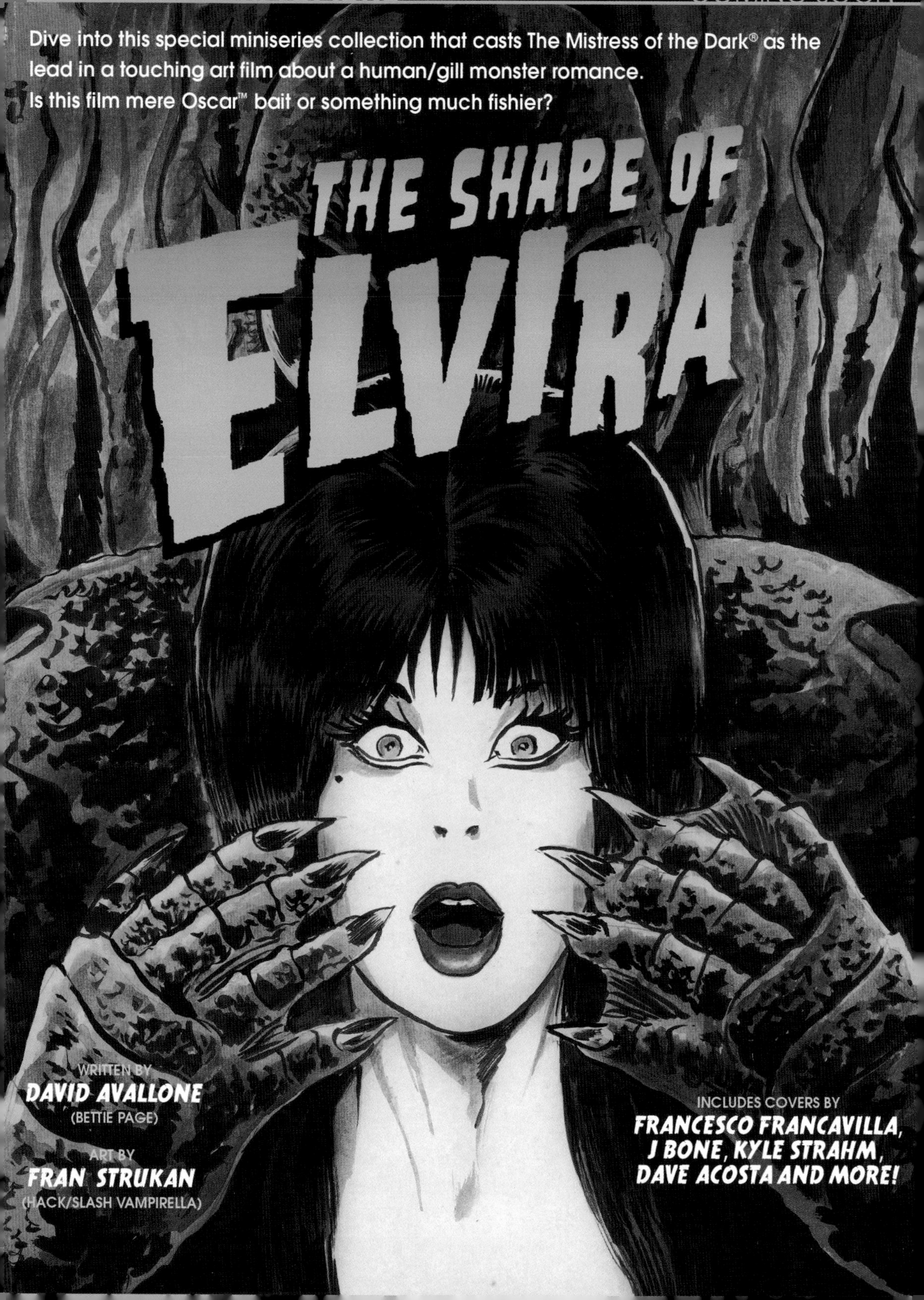
Dive into this special miniseries collection that casts The Mistress of the Dark® as the lead in a touching art film about a human/gill monster romance.
Is this film mere Oscar™ bait or something much fishier?
THE SHAPE OF
ELVIRA
WRITTEN BY
DAVID AVALLONE
(BETTIE PAGE)
ART BY
FRAN STRUKAN
(HACK/SLASH VAMPIRELLA)
INCLUDES COVERS BY
FRANCESCO FRANCAVILLA, J BONE, KYLE STRAHM, DAVE ACOSTA AND MORE!